Also by Alison Chapman

ICON CRITICAL GUIDE TO ELIZABETH GASKELL'S *MARY BARTON* AND *NORTH AND SOUTH* (*editor*)

The Afterlife of Christina Rossetti

Alison Chapman
Department of English
University of Dundee

Eyes that have been supernaturalized recognise, not literally only, but likewise in a figure, how darkness reveals more luminaries than does the day: to the eye pertains a single sun; to the night innumerable, incalculable, by man's perception inexhaustible stars.

— Christina Rossetti, *Face of the Deep*

First published in Great Britain 2000 by
MACMILLAN PRESS LTD
Houndmills, Basingstoke, Hampshire RG21 6XS and London
Companies and representatives throughout the world

A catalogue record for this book is available from the British Library.

ISBN 0–333–72183–7

First published in the United States of America 2000 by
ST. MARTIN'S PRESS, LLC,
Scholarly and Reference Division,
175 Fifth Avenue, New York, N.Y. 10010

ISBN 0–312–23461–9

Library of Congress Cataloging-in-Publication Data
Chapman, Alison, 1970–
The afterlife of Christina Rossetti / Alison Chapman.
p. cm.
Includes bibliographical references (p.) and index.
ISBN 0–312–23461–9 (cloth)
1. Rossetti, Christina Georgina, 1830–1894—Criticism and interpretation–
–History. 2. Women and literature—England—History—19th century. I. Title.

PR5238 .C47 2000
821'.8—dc21

00–026190

This book is printed on paper suitable for recycling and made from fully managed and sustained forest sources.

10 9 8 7 6 5 4 3 2 1
09 08 07 06 05 04 03 02 01 00

Printed and bound in Great Britain by
Antony Rowe Ltd, Chippenham, Wiltshire

In Memoriam
Judith and Christine

Contents

Acknowledgements

I gratefully acknowledge the financial support of the Snell Newlands research fund, which funded my postgraduate work on Christina Rossetti at the University of Glasgow. The Erasmus exchange scheme funded an idyllic three months at the Università degli studi di Firenze, which gave me the space and facilities for translating Rossetti's Italian poetry and exploring her Italian heritage. Thank you to Jean Ellis D'Allessandro for conversations about Christina Rossetti and Italy, and to Gillian Wright for sharing the Florentine adventure.

Chapters 3 and 4 first appeared in *Victorian Literature and Culture* and *Victorian Poetry* respectively, and are reprinted in a revised form with permission of the editors. An earlier version of Chapter 6 first appeared in *The Culture of Christina Rossetti*, edited by Mary Arseneau, Antony H. Harrison and Lorraine Janzen Kooistra, and is reprinted here in a revised form with the permission of Ohio University Press/Swallow Press, Athens, Ohio.

I would particularly like to thank my supervisor, Richard Cronin, who guided and encouraged me through the doctoral research on which this study is based and which owes a tremendous debt to his sympathetic feedback, indefatigable support and good humour. Antony H. Harrison generously gave me pre-publication access to his edition of Christina Rossetti's letters. Although my Christina Rossetti may not be the figure he recognises, I could not have produced this book without his meticulous scholarship and gracious assistance. Conversations with Jan Marsh have enlivened and illuminated my acquaintance with the Rossettis. Thanks are owed to Catherine Maxwell for her time, enthusiasm and friendship. Former colleagues at Sheffield Hallam University gave important early encouragement, in particular Judy Simons and Chris Hopkins and Lisa Hopkins. For collegiality and fun, thanks are due to Jo George, Andrew M. Roberts, Jane Stabler and Keith B. Williams.

To my aunt, Anne Fleming, and my parents, thank you for generous support of every kind through the long haul of this book. And final thanks to Charlie, although his miaows have too often distracted me from my desk.

List of Abbreviations

Crump	R.W. Crump (ed.), *The Complete Poems of Christina Rossetti*, 3 vols (Baton Rouge: Louisiana University Press, 1979–90)
CW: DGR	William Michael Rossetti (ed.), *The Collected Works of Dante Gabriel Rossetti*, 2 vols (London: Ellis and Scrutton, 1886)
DGR: FL	William Michael Rossetti (ed.), *Dante Gabriel Rossetti: His Family Letters*, 2 vols (London: Ellis and Elvey, 1895)
FL: CR	William Michael Rossetti (ed.), *The Family Letters of Christina Georgina Rossetti* (London: Brown, Langham, 1908)
Letters	Antony H. Harrison (ed.), *The Letters of Christina Rossetti* (Charlottesville: University Press of Virginia, 1997–)
PW: CR	William Michael Rossetti (ed.), *The Complete Poetical Works of Christina Georgina Rossetti* (London: Macmillan, 1904; repr. 1906)
SE	James Strachey (ed. and trans.), *Standard Edition of the Complete Psychological Works of Sigmund Freud*, 24 vols (London: Hogarth Press, 1953)
Surtees	Virginia Surtees (ed.), *The Paintings and Drawings of Dante Gabriel Rossetti (1828–1882): a Catalogue Raisonné*, 2 vols (Oxford: Clarendon Press, 1971)

List of Plates

Introduction: the Haunting of Christina Rossetti

> The secret of history is [. . .] causality, and the secret of causality is history. History therefore becomes a causality of causalities, which means the unending production of *effects* – but never the *effectivity* of a beginning.
>
> Jean-Luc Nancy[1]

> The hardest step is at the threshold.
>
> Christina Rossetti[2]

How to begin talking about Christina Rossetti in history? The best place to start, paradoxically, is with Christina Rossetti's death. Her close friend Lisa Wilson remembers her last visit to Rossetti's deathbed in a commemorative poem:

'Farewell, until tomorrow,' thou didst say
  And, clasping close my hand, didst still delay
My going, till the shadows round us lay
  Dark on thy face and mine.

'Until tomorrow.' In the eventide
  We parted; in the darkness I could hide
My tears – and so I left thee, satisfied.
  No tears, O friend, were thine.

'Until tomorrow.' When the morrow came
  We did not meet; thy flickering, fading flame
Of life went out; as on thy lips a name
  Was breathed, with one Divine.

'Until tomorrow.' And I spake to thee
  And thou wert silent; silent even to me
Kneeling beside thee. Silent even to me,
  No word, no smile, no sign. . . .[3]

Rossetti's death on 29 December 1894 prompted a wave of elegies and reminiscences and, although Wilson's is the among the most bereft, her response is symptomatic.[4] Her elegy transforms the poet into a suffering saint whose death is the culmination – apotheosis, even – of her exemplary life. But Wilson's reiteration of Rossetti's banal yet touching last words to her, 'until tomorrow', signifies both an appropriation of the voice of the poet who has now become a muse and signifies that poet as silent, unresponsive, and utterly absent. This double move is typical of the late nineteenth-century response to the dead Rossetti and her literary remains. Although Rossetti gives 'no word, no smile, no sign', her total silence makes way for critical appropriation and, most recently, after a long neglect, critical recovery.

While she has been rapidly emerging from the shadows of New Critical disregard for her work, which Tricia Lootens claims is a direct if ironic result of her Victorian canonisation,[5] in her afterlife as historical personage and woman poet Christina Rossetti continues to haunt her readers. This book offers Christina Rossetti's afterlife in a multiple and inter-related sense: partly as a reception history, partly as an account of the posthumous in her œuvre, partly as an analysis of the trope Christina Rossetti, and partly as a disembodied and fetishised commodity in the literary and critical marketplace. Although historical accounts of Rossetti's work, and that of other marginalised Victorian women writers, continue to insist on the recoverability of the poetry, no critic has paused to consider the efficacy of recovery. What does it mean to recover Victorian women's poetry? Is it really an unproblematic uncovering of lost, forgotten and silenced works, or is this somehow always a re-covering? How do we let the poetry speak once its imposed silence within the literary canon has been exposed? How do we relate the poetry to its context and how does our new understanding of the canon inflect our critical approaches as readers? These are questions that new historicism – that mode of reading that so dominates Victorian studies and that insists upon recovery as its political imperative – has yet to address. But the issue is a crucial one, for by setting up and then recovering lost poetry, and neglected poets, as silenced, contemporary new historicist readings aim to give back their voice, to make them speak. The question is in what way do we, the critical readers, give these texts their voice? Do we speak with them, in place of them, through them or on behalf of them?

As earnestly as Christina Rossetti is approached, she tenaciously vanishes from our critical narrative. Tomás Eloy Martínez, who attempts to track the bizarre afterlife of Eva Peron's embalmed corpse, finds that:

> once I began trying to narrate Evita I noted that, if I approached her, she withdrew from me. I knew what she wanted to tell and what the structure of my narrative was going to be. But once I turned the page, Evita disappeared from my sight, and I was left clutching nothing but air.[6]

Approaching another mythologised figure, Jacqueline Rose finds something similar: 'Sylvia Plath haunts our culture. She is – for many – a shadowy figure whose presence draws on and compels.'[7] Plath's poem 'The Lady and the Earthenware Head' dramatises the impossibility of banishing representations of Plath from critical readings; an impossibility which turns out, in Rose's analysis, to be just as frustrating as the speaker's attempt to destroy a clay model of her head: 'the effigy haunts the original' as well as culture (p. 2). Although this is true of any dead writer, 'it takes in an added significance in relation to Plath, because the editorial control and intervention have been so visible, but also because of the intensity with which writing on Plath seems to invest itself in the idea of her person' (pp. 2–3). For Rose, this cultural interest is doubly deadly, for Plath figures death and also femininity as death.

An attempt to access a dead author – their personality, psychology, contexts, presence – leads us frustratingly further away from the authorial and material origin of the writing. Marjorie Garber explores the ways in which Shakespeare has come to haunt our culture and argues that his presence is grossly overdetermined 'as text, as authority, as moral arbiter and theoretical template'.[8] The critical fascination for Shakespeare is a transference of desire: '"Shakespeare" is the transferential love-object of literary studies' (p. xiv). In relation to the debate over the authenticity of Shakespeare's authorship, Garber comments: 'the search for an author, like any other quest for parentage, reveals more about the searcher than about the sought, for what is demanded is a revisitation of the primal scene' (p. 27). For the critical reader, however, origins are perpetually deferred. In order to exemplify her point, Garber turns to Keats's fragment 'This Living Hand', which ends with a gesture that usurps the line between life and death, writing and reading:

This living hand, now warm and capable
Of earnest grasping, would, if it were cold
And in the icy silence of the tomb,
So haunt thy days and chill thy dreaming nights
That thou wouldst wish thy own heart dry of blood
So in my veins red life might stream again,
And thou be conscience-calmed – see here it is –
I hold it toward you.

Garber glosses these lines as a statement about the act of writing as 'a sleight of hand through which the dead hand of the past reaches over to *our* side of the border'. For her, this exemplifies 'the uncanny connection between Shakespeare's propensity to write ghosts and his continuing capacity to write *us*' (p. xv). Andrew Bennett similarly turns to Keats's fragment as exemplary of the Romantic crisis of readership, most simply put as the anxiety of the private made public, which led Keats to figure writing as well as reading as posthumous: 'reading [. . .] can only ever be other to itself, constituting *itself* as a kind of remainder or supplement of writing'. Keats's fragment imagines the reader's death as a condition of the author's revivification.[9]

Early in her career as a poet, on 18 January 1849, two days before St Agnes' Eve, Christina Rossetti wrote a posthumously published elegy for Keats:

A garden in a garden: a green spot
  Where all is green: most fitting slumber-place
  For the strong man grown weary of a race
Soon over. Unto him a goodly lot
Hath fallen in fertile ground; there thorns are not,
  But his own daisies: silence, full of grace,
  Surely hath shed a quiet on his face:
His earth is but sweet leaves that fall and rot.
What was his record of himself, ere he
  Went from us? *Here lies one whose name was writ*
  In water: while the chilly shadows flit
    Of sweet St Agnes' Eve; while basil springs,
    His name, in every humble heart that sings,
Shall be a fountain of love, verily.

(Crump 3: 168)

Rossetti recalls Keats's famous tombstone inscription. Although the inscription figures the poet's signature as transient and insubstantial, Rossetti's sonnet figures the dead poet's body and name as fertile and productive, even though it is nevertheless still absent and silent. He is depicted in a doubly fertile grave – 'A garden in a garden: a green spot / Where all is green.' In this self-enclosure, his name is reanimated into a fountain within the hearts of his readers. The springing basil is, of course, a macabre figure for life sustained by death, for it is a reference to Keats's *Isabella,* which would become a favourite topic of the Pre-Raphaelites, whose eponymous heroine grows basil in a pot which contains her murdered lover's head.[10] Rossetti's sonnet re-works the Keatsian signature into a fertile and productive oscillation between absence and presence, death and life.

Although Rose and Garber both argue that their authors are special cases, their comments about the haunting of Plath and Shakespeare demonstrate the durability of the mythologised dead writer in culture. This, of course, runs somewhat counter to the announcement of the author's demise, to which I will return in Chapter 1, which has come to mean, in literary studies, that an author is nothing more than a name appended to a text – in other words, a signature. For new historicism, this translates into a concern with multiple and fragmented centres of power and with the gamut of ideological forces which shape a text, rather than with an author's intentions, agency, or presence. Derrida suggests, however, that the signature is the sign of the 'living hand' which makes presence and absence simultaneous. The signer has been here, this is the mark of his presence, but it is a mark that stands in for his absence. For Derrida, the signature is both origin and representation, source and sign of absence:

> By definition, a written signature implies the actual or empirical nonpresence of the signer. But, it will be said, it also marks and retains his [sic] having-been-present in a past now, which will remain a future now, and therefore in a now in general, in the transcendental form of nowness. [...] In order to function, that is, in order to be legible, a signature must have a repeatable, iterable, imitable form; it must be able to detach itself from the present and singular intention of its production. It is its sameness which, in altering its identity and singularity, divides the seal.[11]

This does not mean, then, that the literary signature only signifies absence and death, for the signature is also the sign of originary, but now absent, source and plenitude.

Subjectivities in Rossetti's poetry repeat the vacillation between presence and absence, accessibility and inaccessibility, which offers a figure for reading the signature Christina Rossetti. The speaker of 'Winter: My Secret', in a playful and coy manner typical of Rossetti's poetry, both gives and withdraws the moment of personal revelation.

> I tell my secret? No, indeed, not I:
> Perhaps some day, who knows?
> But not today; it froze, and blows, and snows,
> And you're too curious: fie!
> You want to hear it? well:
> Only, my secret's mine, and I won't tell.
>
> (Crump 1: 47)

What is the secret? The sentimental tradition, seen in the nineteenth-century as the only properly feminine mode for women poets, insists that women's poetry is confessional and personal, for female creativity is posited as a direct experiential reflex. In other words, women's writing was seen to be inherently self-representational and its subject matter restricted to the domestic and private sphere; thus, in a metonymical chain, woman is experience is text. For poets, such as Elizabeth Barrett Browning, who write on social and political themes, this prescription for women's writing castigates their work as masculine and 'muscular'.[12] While Christina Rossetti was cautious to distinguish herself from Barrett Browning's poetics, reassuring her brother D.G. Rossetti that 'it is not in me, and therefore it will never come out of me, to turn to politics or philanthropy with Mrs Browning', her poetry sits very uneasily within the gender and genre ideology of her time.[13] In fact, her poetry's resistance to that ideology of female poetic creativity, from within the sentimental tradition, signifies a 'secret' that is precisely the rhetorical vacillation between disclosure and confession. The 'secret' can be interpreted as the very absence of the feminine subject that the sentimental tradition is predicated upon and, furthermore, the subject is captured in the process of fading from the text, or oscillating between presence and absence. The 'secret' is that there might be no subject to disclose: 'Suppose there is no secret after all, / But only just my fun.'

Rossetti's subversion of the Victorian sentimental tradition of women's poetry presents a number of methodological problems. If the subjectivity in her poetry is coyly both offered and withheld, and if her poetry documents this very process, then her œuvre, like the poem 'Winter: My Secret', may be said to be predicated on nothing: perhaps there is no secret to tell, and no subject to disclose. If this is so, then what happens to the new historicist project of recovery, which aims to give a voice to, and reconstruct a context for, silenced and forgotten texts? What context can be recovered when the poetry so insists upon its own act of self-deletion and, often, its lyrical ahistoricism? In the case of Rossetti, whose poetry defiantly resists the ideology of self-representation from within, such a project of recovery becomes a dangerously overdetermined act of ventriloquy on the part of the historicist critic, who interprets the text by reference to contextual data. Although granted that the task of recovery has an urgent and obvious political agenda, it may also unwittingly reproduce the very ideology that the poetry critiques, by insisting that the writing is wholly explicated through the writer's historical position. Thus, the nineteenth-century homologic formula for women's poetic creativity, the matrix text/experience/woman, becomes the new historicist text/context/author.

It is intriguing that such a methodological problem seems most acute in nineteenth-century studies, which so far lacks the urgency of Renaissance new historicism's self-questioning. New historicists working in the nineteenth century have not explicitly made the attempt, for example by Stephen Greenblatt, to follow Michel Foucault in insisting upon historical discourses as multiple, fragmented and inherently conflicted; although, as Chapter 2 explicates, even this approach in Rossetti studies is problematical. Consequently, history and text become equated, monolithically and univocally, in a naive reproduction of Victorian gender ideology.[14] Brook Thomas, commenting on Renaissance studies, points out that the attempt to reproduce history in academic discourse as non-monolithic might always be doomed to fail, and convincingly demonstrates how Foucault's own prose undermines his project in precisely this way. Thomas's tentative suggestion is to adopt multiple points of view in academic prose, in an attempt to resist a critical will to power that figures literary text and history as a chiasmus, crossing over the differences between them.[15] But this strategy seems artificial and impractical.

The problem of how to figure the relation between history and literature is particularly acute in the study of Victorian women's poetry, and, indeed, exposes the tensions between the agendas of feminism and the poststructuralist origins of new historicism. Feminism has a special affinity to the personal and to the historical construction of the personal. Ros Ballaster argues that the intention of new historicism to problematise the category of history and to attempt to erase the stable and empirical historical subject may be politically premature for feminists.[16] But the failure of new historicism in practise to abandon the grand narrative of history for local and unstable centres of power should open up a space for the reconsideration of the interface between text and context, but also the conception of the historical and literary subject as agent. Chapters 1 and 2 explore problems at the root of historical recovery in terms of the gaze and the voice respectively. Both chapters suggest alternative approaches to Christina Rossetti and her poetry, approaches which refuse to overdetermine and reify her otherness and which acknowledge her inaccessibility even as her phantom presence tenaciously inheres in critical readings. Crucial to these chapters, and to the study as a whole, is the premise elaborated in Chapter 1, that a lack of visibility is the paradoxical condition of reading the signature Christina Rossetti. Her entry for 20 February in her reading diary *Time Flies* gives an account of a visit to a waxwork exhibition, in which her usual shyness of people is transferred from the crowd to the wax effigies. She concludes:

> things seen are as that waxwork, things unseen as those real people. Yet over and over again we are influenced and constrained by the hollow momentary world we behold in presence, while utterly obtuse as regards the substantial eternal world no less present around us though disregarded. (p. 36)

Seeing what is not usually in focus is a theme to which Rossetti continually returns, as part of her Tractarian typological heritage; as she urges, again in *Time Flies*, 'less depends on the "seeing" than on the seer' (p. 42). This study turns on this figure of looking at the unseen, the vanishing, the out of focus, as a figure for reading 'Christina Rossetti'.

In terms of critical readings of Victorian women's poetry, the failure of new historicism should also allow us to conceive alternatives to redeploying nineteenth-century gender ideology. The problem is particularly acute for readings of Christina Rossetti, because her poetics typically inscribe a subjectivity that vacillates between presence and absence and a subjectivity that, furthermore, seems to have erased its own historical context (although there are exceptions to this).[17] Jerome McGann was the first historicist critic to read this self-erasure as a critique of Victorian amatory and social values, thus he inadvertently stabilises the poems' ambivalences and indeterminacy.[18] But it is the vacillation between presence and absence that provides an alternative mode of reading. Taking 'Winter: My Secret' as the paradigmatic Rossettian resistance to self-representation from within the sentimental tradition, the oscillation between confession and concealment is the sign of an hysterical text that refuses to accept its assigned gender and genre norms and that circulates around the illusion that there might be no fully present subject that speaks. In this sense, it is problematic to speak of Christina Rossetti as a woman poet with access to a representative and uniquely female modality of experience, although readings in this growth period of Rossetti studies are often predicated upon that assumption. The rhetorical move of oscillation is no mere doubling of subversion and collusion (a favourite new historicist interpretation), but a *process* of generating a radical if uncanny subjectivity that is produced by the text's position in relation to an extremely conflicted ideological field. While the term 'hysterical' has been deployed by nineteenth-century critics in a derogatory and pathological way to castigate women poets who transgress the gender norms of women's writing, hysteria can also be motivated as simultaneously both a symptom of femininity and a subversive strategy to unsettle gender norms. This is because, as Chapter 3 argues, it is a sign for the excessively, superlatively, feminine.

Christina Rossetti's most self-consciously autobiographical text offers a wry subversion of the ideology of female poetic creativity. The short story *Maude* was written in 1849–50 and published posthumously in 1897, edited by William Michael Rossetti. As Margaret Linley notes in a perceptive reading of the text, this posthumous edition is crucial to the cultural construction of Rossetti as a female icon, confirming the writer's afterlife as a marginalised commodity for a reading public hungry for Rossetti nostalgia.[19] *Maude* is the story of a 15-year-old middle-class girl who struggles to reconcile the vocation of a poet with Victorian codes of femininity. Torn between the need for public circulation of her verses – at social gatherings, for the scrap books of friends and acquaintances – and the terror of pride and self-display, Maude suffers from a spiritual crisis and then, more improbably, a sudden traffic accident that leaves her with a fatal wound. The moral seems to be, as Jan Marsh notes, that the conflict between Victorian girlhood and a poet's vocation can only be resolved in death.[20] Maude's affectations are, however, gently mocked by the narrator; in particular, Maude's concern that a sprig of bay slipped into a garland by her cousin Agnes will smack of pride, is followed by the narrator's pointed observation that Maude is reluctant to remove the bay. Rossetti's ironic narrator leaves us with a tale that is an allegory of the impossibility of female authorship within a narrative that explicitly questions the gendered ideology of female creativity and, as Linley notes, within the commodification that marginalises the text before and after the author's death (pp. 291–6).

The novella opens with Maude's mother, who asks her daughter, 'a penny for your thoughts', while Maude, 'surrounded by a chaos of stationery, was slipping out of sight some scrawled paper' (p. 20). Maude pointedly refuses to divulge her thoughts while, with a sleight of hand, suggests that they are not for public, or economic, consumption. This is a curious autobiography that denies the reader, as well as Maude's mother, access to personal information while suggesting that its textual representation is displaced from our gaze. But in this instance the narrator, ironically, *does* give us the private writing that she concealed from her mother. Maude copies the concealed sonnet into her writing-book when next alone:

> Yes, I too could face death and never shrink:
> But it is harder to bear hated life;
> To strive with hands and knees weary of strife;
> To drag the heavy chain whose every link
> Galls to the bone; to stand upon the brink
> Of the deep grave, nor drowse, though it be rife
> With sleep; to hold with steady hand the knife
> Nor strike home: this is courage as I think.
> Surely to suffer is more than to do:
> To do is quickly done; to suffer is
> Longer and fuller of heart-sicknesses:
> Each day's experience testifies of this:
> Good deeds are many, but good lives are few;
> Thousands taste the full cup; who drains the lees? –

'Having done which', the narrator continues, 'she yawned, leaned back on her chair, and wondered how she should fill up the time till dinner' (p. 20). Following from this ironic disavowal of the poetry as inherently autobiographical, there comes a passage in which the narrator refuses to confirm why Maude's verses are so morbid:

> [I]t was the amazement of every one what could make her poetry so broken-hearted, as was mostly the case. Some pronounced that she wrote very foolishly about things she could not possibly understand;

> some wondered if she really had any secret source of uneasiness; while some simply set her down as affected. Perhaps there was a degree of truth in all these opinions. But I have said enough: the following pages will enable my readers to form their own estimate of Maude's character. (p. 21)

Along with the text's coy refusal to assign Maude's poetry directly to her experience, to expose her 'secret', the narrative itself problematises its generic status as autobiography. The problems of a woman writer, in particular how to reconcile the public vocation with the cultural codes of femininity, including the account of an adolescent breakdown, uncannily mirror the life of Christina Rossetti. But the story cannot be securely identified as autobiographical, for, as Angela Leighton comments, it 'is as emotionally secretive as any of the poet's best verse', and it playfully and coyly presents us with inconsistencies and contradictions.[21] Further, despite its overtly autobiographical theme, the narrative displays an ironical difference between the narrator and the character of Maude. In a paradoxical rhetorical move that – we might say hysterically – denies what it affirms, the autobiographical text insists upon the necessity of erasing the personal.

Chapter 3 unravels this issue in relation to the biographical representation of Rossetti, which is structured in terms of hysterical narrative which conceals as it reveals and ends up disembodying the trope Christina Rossetti. Indeed, part of the problem of reading *Maude* as autobiography stems from the impossibility of recovering Christina Rossetti as an historical personage, for Rossetti herself seems to have colluded with the erasure of her historically specific identity. Christina Rossetti has come down to us as a legend of the feminine ideal, a Pre-Raphaelite muse and model, and later 'Santa Christina', piously suffering from the disfiguring (and, tragically, aptly named) Graves' disease. But it was a legend that she did little to discourage. Chapters 4 and 5 explore her duplicitous complicity in the process of her entry into the literary marketplace. Ironically, the attempt to preserve her privacy by withholding from publication anything that might be read as a comment upon her personal life, and her anxious destruction of family correspondence, served to bolster her image as the superlatively feminine, an image produced by the sentimental tradition that interpreted women's poetry as autobiographical. Deleting the personal, or refusing to publish autobiographical writing, did the very reverse of protecting her identity from the voyeuristic gaze of her readership. Writing shortly after Rossetti's death, Arthur Benson defines her poetry as innately autobiographical, but also predicts the intense biographical interest in her life as a function of critical readings of her poetry:

> [Her] writings, exquisite as they are, are but the outworks and bastions of the inner life. One could almost wish that Christina Rossetti were farther removed by time and space, and had passed beyond the region of letters, biographies, and personal memoirs, which before long will possibly begin 'to tear her heart before the crowd'.[22]

As Chapter 3 elucidates, the biographical personage is predicated on the very removal that Benson suggests would protect her: the removal from history.

As a hybrid, incomplete, and eclectic text, the writing in Maude's locked manuscript book performs a more tentative and provisional subjectivity than can be accounted for in new historicist readings. Isobel Armstrong notes that the female sentimental and expressive tradition of the nineteenth century that Rossetti was associated with flirts dangerously with hysteria as its pathological symptom.[23] As Rossetti's text refuses to be named an autobiography and yet teasingly presents itself as such, the text itself could be said to display a generic or textual hysteria at the same time as the heroine, Maude, may be said to be suffering from the same clinical complaint in her adolescent crisis. The generic vacillation is thus coterminous with a performance of the impossibility of nineteenth-century femininity from within the codes of women's poetic creativity.

The generic uncertainty is evinced by the short story's integration of the narrator's prose and Maude's poetry. By interspersing Maude's private thoughts with the detached and often wry comments of the omniscient narrator, the reader is left uncertain of the story's status as cautionary, ironic, autobiography, or moral tale. The generic hybridity is also a feature of Maude's writing practice:

> Her writing-book was neither Common-Place Book, Album, Scrap-Book, nor Diary; it was a compound of all of these; and contained original compositions not intended for the public eye, pet extracts, extraordinary little sketches and occasional tracts of journal. (p. 20)

This hybrid and eclectic writing is not intended for a public readership, and when Maude knows she is dying she leaves instructions for obviously personal writing to be destroyed. The scraps of paper found in Maude's room are, to her cousin Agnes, surprisingly various and fragmentary, and some are found to be written in a secret code. Significantly, Agnes cannot judge which writing is clearly personal and which is not, so she destroys most of it to ensure the elimination of the personal (and the materiality of the writing), as Maude had instructed:

> Many of these were mere fragments, many half-effaced pencil scrawls, some written on the torn backs of letters, and some full of incomprehensible abbreviations. Agnes was astonished by the variety of Maude's compositions. Piece after piece she committed to the flames, fearful lest any should be preserved not intended for general perusal: but it cost her a pang to do so. (pp. 49–50)

Although Agnes does not open and read the contents of the locked book that she finds, we know from the beginning of the story that it contains a mixture of diary entries, extracts, and Maude's poetry – all not intended for public consumption. Agnes's act of placing the manuscript in Maude's coffin uncannily prefigures D.G. Rossetti's similar melodramatic gesture in 1862, when he sealed his poetry manuscript in his wife Lizzie Siddal's coffin, full of remorse and guilt for her death (although, before long, this is regretted and the coffin exhumed). By burning the manuscripts that seem to be personal, and by burying the locked book with Maude, Agnes performs literally what the narrative does rhetorically: an erasure of the personal. But, as the narrator has made clear, Maude's writing is not necessarily to be equated with Maude herself. Thus Agnes's gesture performs the deletion of the personal secret, or the subject, from the text of the story *Maude*; but this deletion still keeps the subject provisionally and tentatively in play. The personal is under erasure and this reaffirms the hysteric voice of the text, which circulates around the unrepresentable, absence, and loss.

During the last conversation between Maude and Agnes before her death, Maude is asked if she would change places with any of her female friends who have chosen between rather limited options available: marriage (Mary) or an Anglican sisterhood (Magdalen). Maude replies:

> 'Not with Mary, certainly. Neither should I have the courage to change with you; I never should bear pain so well: nor yet with Sister Magdalen; for I want her fervour of devotion. So at present I fear you must even put up with me as I am. Will that do?' There was a pause. A fresh wind had sprung up and the sun was setting. (pp. 47–8)

Poignantly, knowing how near death Maude is, Agnes does not reply. But Maude's seeming intransigence belies the radical insecurity of her own identity as a woman writer. The pathological hysteria that she suffers from, together with the hysterical discourse of her writing, performs Maude's own temporary and tentative social identity.

Julia Kristeva terms this tentative positionality within social norms as a subjectivity in process/on trial, by which she means a non-oppressive identity that can be taken up by women writers to avoid the annihilation of difference perpetuated by the androcentric logic of the same. It is a mediation between different subject positions that acknowledges the alterity within and that does not attempt to stabilise the process.[24] The subject-in-process thus exposes the vulnerability of gender norms and produces a temporary identity that functions in the space between the rather limited choices on offer to Maude as either wife or Anglican Sister. This temporary identity, furthermore, is a site of transgression which corresponds with that of the Victorian woman writer who illicitly crosses over the boundaries between the private and public spheres.

Kristeva's conception of subjectivity is for her a way out of the double bind of the complete deconstruction of subjectivity, and the therapeutic necessity of maintaining the illusion of identity, a 'difficult balancing act' between 'the delirium of complete negation' and 'the totalitarianism of absolute identity'.[25] Kelly Oliver's extended discussion of the enabling features of the subject-in-process points out that it is a way of acknowledging alterity, negation, and difference within the subject which negotiates the double bind of identity and does away with the notion of a unified subject. For the critic working with Victorian women's poetry, the subject-in-process enables the shifts and negotiations between different levels of power and desire to be articulated without reverting to a naive collapse of text and context. The subject-in-process keeps in play differences and allows neglected voices to be recuperated without forgetting their uncanny otherness, and without overdetermining their agency within regimes of representation. In this regard, the figure of the mother is invoked theoretically throughout this study as a way of recuperating the uncanny double of plenitude and loss in our access to 'Christina Rossetti'.[26] Chapter 1 suggests a model for reading loss and recuperation, which is elaborated in Chapter 3 in order to explore the multiple configurations of femininity and death in biographical accounts of Christina Rossetti. Chapter 6 offers the maternal figure in terms of lost and longed-for homelands in Rossetti's poetry, weaving together the afterlife with the trope of exile and displacement. The haunting of Rossetti's most discussed poem, 'Goblin Market', is the focus of the final chapter which offers a meta-reading of the text in the literary and critical marketplace, and suggests a figure of reading based upon abjection, the adult subject's response to the legacy of maternal origins. Focusing throughout on the figure of Christina Rossetti as well as her poetry and other writings, this study attempts to forge a link between uncanny literary subjectivities and a new mode of critical reading that refuses to recuperate the personal and the author's personage as a stable monolithic presence.

The subject-in-process *par excellence* is evinced by the hysterical oscillations of the Victorian female poet. Christina Rossetti's resistance to inscribing the personal dramatises both the impossibility of Victorian femininity and the impossibility of the woman poet caught within the tradition of the sentimental tradition and the conflicted ideology of the literary marketplace. But it also suggests the *possibilities* of an alternative mode of subjectivity. Withholding the personal secret – and, indeed, deleting subjectivity itself – in Rossetti's writings is not merely a form of protest against the gender ideology that insists women's writing is autobiographical, nor is it merely an implicit critique of Victorian amatory and social values. It is, rather, the very provisional and tentative gesturing towards a new process of subjectivity that suggests an alternative *within* which maintains and mediates between differences and that, as this study argues, offers us new figures of reading women's poetry. Perhaps this is Christina Rossetti's secret.

1
'A Bizarre Medium': the Return of the Dead and New Historicism

The lost referent

'Tudor House and its grounds became a sort of wonderland; and once the author of "Wonderland" photographed us in the garden.'[1] Thus Christina Rossetti affectionately remembers the exotic pets, and other eccentric inhabitants, of her brother's bohemian residence at Tudor Walk in Chelsea. The 'Wonderland' of Dante Gabriel Rossetti's home was documented during four days in the Autumn of 1863 by Charles Dodgson, two years before the publication of *Alice's Adventures in Wonderland*. A photograph of the Rossetti family group survives that, rather than a Carrollian wonderland, discloses a carefully posed and rather mundane domestic scene (Plate 1). William Michael and Dante Gabriel frame Christina and her mother, who are positioned at the bottom of stairs, which lead to the garden. Christina here takes her favourite 'lowest place', while her mother is seated on a chair beside her.[2] Unlike another plate taken that afternoon, with Maria replacing her brother William Michael, the figures are crisp and clear. The details of their mid-Victorian dress, the shabby stairs, the fallen autumnal leaves, all present themselves as an access to the moment (or several moments) of the photographic exposure.

And yet loss haunts this photograph. Rather like the barred window on the extreme left side of the plate, this is no transparent window to the past, to that afternoon in which Charles Dodgson first made the acquaintance of the author of 'Goblin Market', which inspired his *Alice in Wonderland*.[3] Although William Michael Rossetti, in another context, describes photography as 'the irrefutable evidence of the sun',[4] this particular photographic session demonstrates the inability of photography to capture its subjects. Christina Rossetti explains, in her description of that afternoon, that the intention was 'to appear in the full family group of five; but whilst various others succeeded, that particular negative was spoilt by a shower, and I possess a solitary print taken from it in which we appear as if splashed by ink'.[5] The photograph of the family group on the stairs is, then, marked by the absence of Rossetti's sister Maria. But even the photograph of the family group is marred by black splashes and it is, unsurprisingly, a plate that has never been reproduced. The black splashes signify our lost access to the subjects captured by the photograph. Indeed, what Rossetti terms 'the full family group of five' is in any case haunted by the absence of their father Gabriele, who died in 1854. The wholeness, completion, and accessibility of the photographic image are illusory.[6]

Recent studies of nineteenth-century culture have been fascinated by the invention and popularity of photography. In a review essay which assesses three such recent studies, Jennifer Green-Lewis explains the grip that the photographic image has on us: 'since the goal of much materialist criticism and new historicism seems to be conversation with the dead, it is hardly surprising that Victorian photography has lately assumed a new authority as medium'.[7] Her comment is doubly significant. Firstly, it assumes that the recent approach to Victorian studies is to engage with some monument to or from the past, to speak with the dead. Crucially, however, photography can be both a referent as well as access (if troubled) to its subject, a vessel through which the dead speak. Secondly, she suggests that it is the authority of photography as just such a monument which accounts for its current academic popularity. Is, then, the goal of such criticism to interact with an authoritative medium from/to the past? I want to offer photography as an analogy to the process by which approaches to Christina Rossetti, invariably informed by new historicism, are predicated upon the illusion of an authentic original subject or referent. The slippery word 'medium' to some extent summarises my project. How far is the text, whether photographic or literary or biographical, an agent, and how far do we, as spectators or readers, have an agency in the interpretative process? Viewing Dodsgon's photograph of the Rossetti family group suggests that this concern with agency hinges upon the referent as both absent and present. To be more specific, the new historicist approach fetishistically covers up the absence of Christina Rossetti which was always at the heart of its methodology.

In her exploration of nineteenth-century photography, Lindsay Smith sets up Dodgson's photographs of Xie Kitchen against the aesthetics of Julia Margaret Cameron. Their differing techniques – Dodgson's 'child-friend' sharply focused and backed up against the wall of a domestic room, Cameron's figures captured up close and out of focus – are taken as diametrically opposed approaches to the gendered issue of focus in nineteenth-century photography. Smith argues that a photographic subject in focus confirms to the ideology of perceptual mastery, or the sovereignty of the viewer's gaze. Dodgson's in-focus photographs inscribe the scopic and, in sexual terms, the fetish:

> The oddly repetitive depth of field in Carroll, culminating in a captive displayed literally up against a wall, represents a space assumed necessary to mobilise that geometrical binary relation, which is also the space of male fantasy.[8]

This male fantasy mobilises the fetish by both mastering the field of vision and arresting the look either upon the focused subject or one of its details (for example a shawl). Smith comments:

> Focus as a photographic state may thus in a sense be fetishised with its antithesis 'out of focus' thereby becoming commensurate with a fear of castration (or with the 'unwelcome fact of the woman's castration') symbolised, we might say, in the loss of patriarchal power in the home. We can further rewrite this formation as the fetishism that *is* focus in the sense that focus in photographic representation newly mobilises the fetish. (p. 256)

Focus is fetishisation. As Dodgson's opposite, Cameron's soft or out of focus photography dismantles the mastery of the gaze and confronts the fact of woman's lack or castration. She denies the fetish: 'since a condition of "in" focus becomes fetishised (as a displacement of loss) then her denial of focus conversely prevents the look from being blocked or displaced' (p. 257). In other words, paradoxically, to focus is to deny or displace what one sees (the terror of woman's castration or lack), while to be out of focus enables one to see.

Although Smith's argument is compelling, to position Cameron and Dodgson as diametrically opposed is problematic. In a discussion of Xie's portraits, she explains the significance of a missing square of carpet as 'the *presence* of an absent piece', which 'serves as a tawdry inscription of the ideology of perceptual mastery' (p. 253, my emphasis). But the missing piece of carpet surely discloses the *absence* that the fetish covers over. In fact, Smith's concept of the fetish oddly (even fetishistically) disavows the absence of the phallus (by focusing the gaze upon an arrested point) *and* avows the absence of the phallus (by the very need to cover it up). This is a continuous oscillation, for, although the fetish depends upon the mastery of the focused gaze, it also predicates that mastery upon a terrifying lack. Thus, the mastery is always/already illusory.[9] As Freud comments: 'a fetish of this sort, doubly derived from contrary ideas, is of course especially durable'.[10]

The lyrical and very personal meditation on photography by Roland Barthes in *Camera Lucida* insists upon confronting the painful feelings of presence and absence that photographs inspire. Indeed, although he does not spell this out, his conceptualisation of the photographic referent as continually oscillating between presence and absence sets up the photograph as the fetish *par excellence*. The photographic image, with the objectification of the passive woman opposed to the male spectator, has been shown by contemporary film theory to lend itself easily to the fetish. For Barthes, however, the relationship between presence and absence that determines the structure of the fetish has a sting in its tail.

The 'rather terrible thing' in each photograph is 'the return of the dead'.[11] The photographic referent 'has been here, and yet immediately separated; it has been absolutely, irrefutably present, and yet already deferred' (p. 77). '[I]t is the living image of a dead thing' (p. 79), thus '[p]hotography has something to do with resurrection' (p. 82). The verisimilitude of photography is produced by the stickiness or persistence of the referent: it 'adheres'. The photograph thus carries with it its source, its origin: 'the photograph is literally an emanation of the referent' (p. 80). As *Camera Lucida* moves into the elegiac mode of its second part, it becomes clear that the photographic referent all along is Barthes's recently dead mother, whose photographs he is searching through. Barthes might thus be forgiven for indulging in the comforting illusion of the referent's presence. But he always, simultaneously, acknowledges that the moment has passed, that the experience of presence and plenitude is attained at the commensurate cost of the referent's death, whether metaphorical (the moment captured by the photograph has died) or literal (the subject has died).

The doubled figures of avowal and disavowal that connote the photographic referent do not, however, produce an unproblematic fetishisation. Firstly, along with the self-conscious activity of Barthes as the viewer of photographs, *Camera Lucida* repeatedly insists upon the agency of the photograph: 'it animates me and I animate it' (p. 20). For Carol Mavor, the complex movement between presence and absence constitutes this animation or, in her words, performance: 'what is no longer there performs upon us and we perform upon it. It bereaves us and we bereave it' (p. 4). What Mavor enacts in her study, Jane Gallop confronts and tries (perhaps impossibly) to pin down: a complex interaction with and openness to alterity, to an other. Gallop explores the notion, taken from *Camera Lucida*, of the *punctum*. The *punctum* is, for Barthes, the photograph's penetration of the viewer. It is an arrest of the visible, a punctuation, '[it] rises from the scene, shoots out of it like an arrow, and pierces me' (p. 26). It is a 'wound', a 'prick' (p. 26), a 'sting, speck, cut, little hole. [...] A photograph's *punctum* is that accident which pricks me (but also bruises me, is poignant to me)' (p. 27). Unlike what Barthes terms the *studium*, or the cultural meaning of a photograph, the *punctum* is not an act of consciousness: 'it is not I who seek it out' (p. 26). The attributes of the *punctum* correspond to the fetish: for Barthes, in his own private experience of various photographs (for he makes it clear that his experience may not be ours), the *punctum* inheres most often in bodily details or items of clothing. And, like the fetish, Barthes's description of being struck or wounded by the *punctum* suggests that it is somehow the photographic referent's phallus that wounds him, that leaves him with a hole. Gallop reads this agency of the photographic referent as other in terms of an erotic relationship with the viewer. It is her way of describing photography's 'quite special relation to the real':

> The erotic paradox is this strange combination of dependence and independence. In order to be erotic, the object must depend on the viewer, on the aroused one, on our fantasies, our imagination, our constructs, our framing, and yet, the object must also remain independent, still real, still other. Eroticism itself is a relation to something that is very much part of our imagination, our projection, our desires. Our eroticism is what is most narcissistic or most imperialist in our relation to the world, and yet, there is also some relation between our desires and something that is really out there, that is independent of our fantasies.[12]

Barthes's *punctum* is construed as an erotic moment, and for Gallop the photographic referent gestures to a 'real other [...] something that leads us outside the frame' (*Camera Lucida* p. 156). Indeed, Barthes observes in an erotic photograph by Mapplethorpe that 'the *punctum*, then, is a kind of subtle *beyond*' (p. 59). This 'real other', the *a prioria* of the photographic referent, is not simply the fantasy of an authentic origin.

Gallop points to one of Barthes' most sensuous and suggestive images of his relationship with the photographed object:

> The photograph is literally the emanation of the referent. From a real body, which was there, proceed radiations which ultimately touch me, who am here [...] light, though impalpable, is here a carnal medium, a skin I share with anyone who has been photographed.
>
> (*Camera Lucida* pp. 80–1)[13]

Gallop comments: 'the image of sharing a skin is extraordinary. If you say something touches you, there is a subject and an object of that verb, which has an active and a passive meaning. But if you are sharing a skin, there us another relation' (p. 157). Sharing a skin implies an intimacy between referent and viewer which Gallop interprets as sexual, as erotic. But her citation from *Camera Lucida* elides what is for me a more extraordinary image, which I give here in its context, that takes us back to the fetish: 'a sort of umbilical cord links the body of the photographed thing to my gaze: light, though impalpable, is here a carnal medium, a skin I share with anyone who has been photographed' (*Camera Lucida* p. 81). The shared skin is qualified as an umbilical cord. It is odd, given Gallop's interest in femininity, and the deliberately provocative book cover which depicts a baby's head emerging from between its mother's legs, that she should ignore this maternal inflection. Her emphasis is firmly, and rather blindly, upon the erotic relation as (hetero)sexual.[14] Barthes's mother is also Gallop's *punctum*, her loss of visibility, an arrest of sight.

It is clear from the image of the umbilical cord, however, that the *punctum* for Barthes represents not just a fetish-substitution of the lost maternal phallus but an Imaginary moment in which the phallus is restored. Liliane Weissberg notes:

> the *punctum* may change into an antifetish, as Barthes rejects any ersatz for the experience of desire, the goal and utopia of an imaginary union, and the realm of the imaginary itself. In reverting to the mother-son relationship, Barthes revises the oedipal story into a temporal space that can be wounded and restored.[15]

Elsewhere in *Camera Lucida*, the relationship between the photograph and the mother for Barthes is made clear. Charles Gifford's photograph 'The Alhambra' (1854) depicts a place which he longs to inhabit. Such a longing, he says, 'is fantasmatic, deriving from a kind of second sight which seems to bear me forward to a utopian time, or to carry me back to somewhere in myself' (p. 40). It is a 'double movement' which reminds him of Freud's description of the maternal body: 'there is no other place of which one can say with so much certainty that one has already been there'. This is what for him is canny (or knowable) and homely: '*heimlich*, awakening in me the Mother (and never the disturbing Mother)' (p. 40). The mother does not disturb because here she, reassuringly, in an Imaginary moment, possesses the phallus. In Part Two of *Camera Lucida*, when the analysis becomes more explicitly personal, Barthes describes the pain at viewing photographs of his dead mother, in order to 'find' her: 'photography thereby compelled me to perform a painful labor' (p. 66). The act of searching for a recognisable image of his mother, which matches his memory of her, is not only an act of performance in Carol Mavors' sense but is also an act of birth by which he engenders his mother. This is his 'painful labor'. Remembering how he nursed her during her fatal illness, Barthes discloses' ultimately I experienced her, strong as she had been, my inner law, as my feminine child. Which was my way of resolving Death. [. . .] I, who had not procreated, I had, in her very illness, engendered my mother' (p. 72). Although Barthes desolately declares that, now she is dead, he 'could do no more than await my total, undialectical death' (p. 72), it is clear that he nevertheless reproduces her in his contemplation of the absent photograph. Diana Knight, who argues that such engendering makes metaphorically fertile Barthes' homosexuality, says of this passage:

> In a strange moment in his handling of the narrative chronology, Barthes suggests that she has merged with the child of her first photo, even though she has not yet died and he has not yet discovered that photo. Although he has not literally procreated, he has nevertheless engendered his mother as his female child.[16]

The Winter Garden Photograph of his mother as a child which, for Barthes, captures his mother in a way that is familiar to him, is famously not reproduced in *Camera Lucida*. This absence serves to dramatise for us, Barthes' readers, his experience of the *punctum* when viewing the photograph, for the *punctum* is nothing less than a blind spot, a private authenticity that cannot be represented to others.[17] But as, to adopt Weissberg's suggestive phrase, 'a curious interruption of visibility' (p. 113), the *punctum* simultaneously bonds the fantasmatic authentic presence of the referent with an avowal of its absence. And, although the cord is severed, as all umbilical cords must be, the scar still tugs at us at the same time as the anti-fetish denies the loss: 'I wanted to explore [photography] not as a question (a theme) but as a wound.'[18]

Imaginary restorations

This study explores how Christina Rossetti wounds us, how despite her obvious referentiality – as photographic, pictorial, biographical, historical and literary subject – she nevertheless slips out of the frame. While new historicist analyses of her work depend upon a fantasmatic authorial presence that can be recuperated, Christina Rossetti, that trope which so impossibly and completely conflates feminine author with feminine text, eludes our gaze. Chapter 3 suggests that this tropic signature is the creation of a posthumous biographical subject by contemporary reviewers who position her as always/already deceased; but it is also, as Chapter 7 elucidates, an infectious discourse that invades modern literary studies. This study calls instead for an alternative approach that acknowledges the terrible and perhaps impossible intertwining of presence and absence, that the poetry carries its source with it, but a source that is absent and empty. It is precisely, however, her lack of visibility, her act of vanishing, which allows us to see her without fetishising her presence. In *Camera Lucida*, Barthes comes to understand the simultaneous presence and absence of the referent as a 'mad image' (p. 115):

> Now, in the Photograph, what I posit is not only the absence of the object; it is also, by one and the same movement, on equal terms, the fact that this object has indeed existed and that it has been there where I see it. Here is where the madness is, for until this day no representation could assure me of the past of a thing except by intermediaries; but with the Photograph, my certainty is immediate: no one in the world can undeceive me. The Photograph then becomes a bizarre *medium*, a new form of hallucination. (p. 115)

Responses to *Camera Lucida* point to a naivety in Barthes's belief that the camera never lies, that the sun gives the photographic image irrefutable evidence, that the photograph offers verisimilitude, the capture of a moment of presence. Jane Gallop, for example, argues: 'for Barthes the photograph is magical because what gets registered on the film actually comes from the real object. [. . .] Barthes's sense of photography is both very mystical and very naïve' (p. 156). Significantly, however, Barthes acknowledges that seeing the referent as both absent and present is a 'madness', a 'hallucination'. Although *Camera Lucida* insists that it is only the photograph that is such a 'bizarre medium', the act of writing for Barthes also reanimates his subject – his mother – at the same time as he mourns her absence.

Barthes's conceptualisation of the photographic referent operates in a similar way to the construction of Christina Rossetti as a historical subject – indeed, this is a process whose beginning is coterminous with the development of photography in the mid nineteenth century. Christina Rossetti is a signature, a historical and biographical personage, a trope that haunts a recovery of her writing. The act of being photographed, for Barthes:

> represents that very subtle moment when, to tell the truth, I am neither subject nor object but a subject who feels he is becoming an object: I then experience a micro-version of death (of parenthesis): I am truly becoming a spectre. (p. 14)

Christina Rossetti is also experienced as a subjectivity in parenthesis, a deanimated author who haunts critical readings of her work. Throughout this study, but especially in Chapter 2, the nineteenth-century conflation of text with poet is seen to inflect and infect new historicist recoveries of poetry and contexts. Such recoveries which aim to recuperate the literary subject, or referent, or author, are predicated on a fantasy of origin which always already eludes us. Jerome McGann's analysis of what he takes to be one of the most representative of Rossetti's poems, 'May', demonstrates the absence of referentiality which new historicist readings, such as his own, aim to make present:[19]

> I cannot tell you how it was;
> But this I know: it came to pass
> Upon a bright and breezy day
> When May was young; ah pleasant May!
> As yet the poppies were not born
> Between the blades of tender corn;
> The last eggs had not hatched as yet,
> Nor any bird foregone its mate.
>
> I cannot tell you what it was;
> But this I know: it did but pass.
> It passed away with sunny May,

With all sweet things it passed away,
And left me old, and cold, and grey.

(Crump 1: 51)

As McGann points out, 'it' is never identified and is as conditional and as contingent as the title of the poem.[20] Although the referent passes unidentified through the poem, teasing, as 'Winter: My Secret' does with its coy withdrawal of meaning, readings which insist on a definition, a context, a precise 'key' to the text, end up stabilising and mastering the referent's fragile vanishing act. The whole poem concerns 'the actions of an unspecified something ("it")'. McGann relates the poem to the biblical phrase 'it came to pass', but this is a context or source that does not help explicate the poem. Neither does the '*vanitas vanitatum*' theme which McGann identifies here and throughout Rossetti's poetry. He proceeds to observe that the pronoun 'it' 'pushes the work into a terrifying level of generality [...] something unknown and inexplicable both to speaker and reader'. In fact, '"it" finally comes to stand as a sign of total conceptual and experiential possibility'. McGann attempts to explain the poem in terms of the Christian (an explication of worldly illusion and vanity) and then the secular (transience of human love). The way in which the pronoun 'it' confounds the critic, however, can be read on a meta-textual level, for the subject of the poem has been present and yet eludes us. Indeed, although McGann ties the poem to rather wide religious and secular contexts, his interpretation does not account for the poem's ambiguity and withdrawal of meaning, nor its curiously haunting effect on the reader. Christina Rossetti, in a letter to Dante Gabriel dated 4 August 1881, refers ironically to this poem: 'considering that I was "old and cold and grey" so many years ago, it is (as you suggest) no wonder that nowadays I am "so shrunk and sere"'.[21] She identifies herself self-deprecatingly with the speaker of 'May' as someone depleted and diminished. The poem operates as a meta-textual figure for reading both Rossetti's poetics and also the trope Christina Rossetti: something that was present, has now passed, but which continues both to be conditional and to tug, umbilically, at the reader.

The conception of poetic presence in contemporary analyses – whether it be the presence of a syntactical referent, a subjectivity, or author – is dogged by an insistence on the stability of the presence, the guarantee of origin, the omniscience of the author, bugbears which criticism rejects. Deconstruction tells us, however, that whatever a reading rejects comes back to haunt it. As strenuously as new historicism denies the ultimate agency of the author, authorial origins creep into contextual recoveries.

Séan Burke provocatively argues that the agency and presence of the author never completely disappeared. Burke notes that the trumpet-call of the death of the author was based on an overstated notion of the author as absolute origin of the text, a god worthy of being slayed. *The Death and Return of the Author* unravels the critical discourse of Barthes, Foucault and Derrida to suggest that the concept of authorial presence has never been absent, even when the author is declared dead: in fact, 'the principle of the author most powerfully reasserts itself when it is thought absent'.[22] Burke urges that the concept of the author in a text be rethought through a model of 'situated subjectivity'. He points out that, despite its methodology, new historicism depends upon a notion of authorial presence, although it is a presence under erasure. In addition, new historicism, Burke argues, needs to confront and revise its notion of the author as a transcendental signified, for ironically 'criticism fails to overtly recognise that the author is that one category which clearly overlaps – one might even say conjoins – text and context' (p. 204). Indeed, as the following chapter proceeds to explore, new historicist approaches to Christina Rossetti are predicated both a fantasy of origin and presence, and the notion that the subject can be recuperated, despite adhering to the Foucaldian decentred subject. Intriguingly, however, it is from one of the theorists under attack in *The Death and Return of the Author* that a revised model of authorship emerges: Roland Barthes. Burke deftly illustrates the return of a concept of the authorial presence in Barthes even after the authorial demise, although it is a spectral author that is resurrected. But, as we have seen from *Camera Lucida*, Barthes's notion of the photographic subject can be translated to the literary subject, where mourning for the dead mother uncannily engenders her and allows a conflation of loss and restoration. One could say that Barthes also engenders himself as an uncanny authorial presence when he reproduces the maternal in his elegy.

If the act of focusing confirms perceptual mastery and covers over, as well as admits to, the loss at the origin of our subjectivity, a loss of focus would paradoxically allow the absence to be made visible and allow Christina Rossetti to slip through the frame while maintaining her umbilical relation to the text and to us as its reader. Such a paradigm for reading would indeed be a wonderland, in which the other is never fully absent, and in which the act of reading would involve a journey into the other. This is what Kristeva has in mind when she calls for a 'herethics' of the other: not a refusal to see presence, nor a yearning for the restoration of an Imaginary wholeness, but an acknowledgement of the spectrality of the other in which the pain of loss and the desire for presence is commensurate.

In 'Stabat Mater', Kristeva foreshadows *Camera Lucida*. Her lyrical prose in bold type disrupts the analysis of western discourses of virginity and motherhood. This experimental prose, written on 1976 after the birth of her son, writes the other within the subject using the metaphors associated with photography: '**FLASH**', '**Photos of what is not yet visible and that language necessarily skims over from afar, allusively**', '**Flash on the unnameable**'.[23] She describes the afterbirth as a '**graft, which wounds but increases me**' (p. 168). Elsewhere, Kristeva explains that the use of the two different kinds of typeface was intended to give the impression of a scar or wound. For her, the theoretician is 'posited precisely on the place of this scar' because, Kelly Oliver explains, of 'the painful transference between the theorist and her object'. Further, the prose in bold type expresses the repressed in discourses of maternity and also in theory; 'for Kristeva the repressed is an encounter with the maternal semiotic. The repressed is an encounter/identification with the mother. This repression leaves a scar'.[24] As Oliver notes, the scar is the mark of castration, the loss of the phallic mother and of Imaginary plenitude. Anna Smith makes a similar point about the implications of 'Stabat Mater': 'the text reads language and childbirth as originating from the site of a primary wound'.[25] For Smith, 'Stabat Mater' is about the act of reading and writing as journeying into otherness, particularly for the critical reader. Kristeva's metaphor of maternity and childbirth is the condition *par excellence* of otherness within, the condition which all adult subjects experience whether or not they have experienced childbirth. The confusion between subject and object, furthermore, is 'because when we attempt to speak of the existence of an other, we are led to speak of our own subjectivities'. This is 'a transference of personal affect to the site of what we desire to know' (p. 140). As Kristeva engenders the other in pregnancy, so she enfolds the other in her prose. She terms this 'herethics': heretical, here-ethics, her-ethics. It is an 'outlaw' ethics founded on the alterity within, and ethics which questions the agency of the ethical subject.[26] It compels the critical readers to confront their own transference in the act of reading and, in Kristeva's terms, makes 'the thought of death bearable: herethics is undeath, love'.[27] Her ethics, modelled on the relationship between mother and child during pregnancy, reconfigures our access to the referent without either reifying its presence or insisting on its absence. This would be reading in other ways, other wise.

2
Speaking with the Dead: Recovering Lost Voices

> Voice! That, too, is launching forth and effusion without return. Exclamation, cry, breathlessness, yell, cough, vomit, music. Voice leaves. Voice loses. She leaves. She loses. And that is how she writes, as one throws a voice – forward, into the void.
>
> Hélène Cixous[1]

> [T]he voice is inseparable from the person to whom it belongs. The voice which charms one generation is inaccessible to the next. Words cannot describe it, notes cannot register it; it remains as a tradition, it lingers only as a regret; or, if by marvellous modern appliances stored up and re-uttered, we listen not to any imitative sound, but to a reproduction of the original voice.
>
> Christina Rossetti[2]

Ventriloquies

The voice is perhaps both feminism's and new historicism's most potent trope.[3] As a metonymy, the voice works as not only an attribute of the text but also the author and, in some cases, the author's body as source of the voice. The process of historical recovery, with which new historicist and some feminist readings are engaged, aims to give a voice to the silenced texts, associating marginalisation, objectification and oppression with silence, and power, presence and the body with the voice. In this project of recovery, the voice itself is rarely in question. But how do we make the silenced speak, what is the power relationship between the critic and the text, and what are the methodological implications of voicing the silenced? This chapter addresses voicing the silent as a problematic recovery predicated on a fantasy of origin, and then turns to consider what this means for feminist new historicist readings of Victorian women's poetry.[4]

'I began with the desire to speak with the dead.' Thus Stephen Greenblatt, perhaps the most famous proponent of new historicism, opens his *Shakespearean Negotiations: the Circulation of Social Energy in Renaissance England* with what has become a notorious statement.[5] Greenblatt's confessional and rather lyrical account of his relationship as a critic with the texts he engages in communication offers the notion of text as silenced voice alongside a meditation of the text's otherness. The opening of *Shakespearean Negotiations* continues:

> Even when I came to understand that in my most intense moments of straining to listen all I could hear was my own voice, even then I did not abandon my desire. It was true that I could hear only my own voice, but my own voice was the voice of the dead, for the dead had contrived to leave textual traces of themselves, and those traces make themselves heard in the voices of the living. Many of the traces have little resonance, though every one, even the most trivial or tedious, contains some fragment of lost life; others seem uncannily full of the will to be heard. (p. 1)

The communion with the voices of the dead through their 'textual traces' is striking for the complex and rather confusing circulation of agency between Greenblatt as literary critic, and the voice of the dead as literary trace. In the middle sentence, he begins with the admission that it is only his own voice that he hears, but this slips into the voice of the dead, further transforming to become a trace with an agency of its own and a will to be heard. This explication of the project of speaking with the dead raises more questions that it answers, for the process of recovery first imagines the dead voice as a source of presence, a fantasmatic origin, and then depicts the relationship between critic and dead voice as projection in which the dead voice or textual trace speaks through the critic. This is a very one-sided conversation.

Greenblatt concludes an earlier study, *Renaissance Self-Fashioning*, with an anecdote that again intertwines death, voice and the other.[6] Greenblatt tells of a plane journey in the United States, when, intending to pass the time reading a book, he sits next to a passenger who looks as if he would not be likely to engage him in conversation. But, in fact, the man soon starts talking and tells Greenblatt the reason for his journey. He is on his way to visit his son in hospital who is seriously ill and has lost the ability to speak and the will to live. The passenger then discloses his worry that he won't be able to understand his son and, to Greenblatt's abject horror, the passenger insists that he mouth soundlessly the words 'I want to die. I want to die', so that he can recognise them if his son tries to speak. At this point, it occurs to Greenblatt that the man may be a psychotic who intends to blow up the plane if the words are mouthed and, anxious not to utter a death wish, Greenblatt refuses and passes the rest of the journey in an awkward silence.

This epilogue or postscript is explained as the dramatisation of Greenblatt's thesis: that words are crucially significant for self-fashioning, and that we all have an urgent need to believe in the illusion that we shape our own identities. Greenblatt interprets his reluctance to mouth the words 'I want to die' as his resistance to someone else providing him with a script and shaping his own sense of self. The project of this book is to explode such a myth of self-determination while also demonstrating its urgency and necessity. But the monograph's afterword serves another inadvertent function, for the other, as represented by the passenger, has a script of his own that the critic refuses to mouth, suggesting Greenblatt's fear that the other may exceed the critic's will to mastery, a fear that undermines the project of empathy with the past. Furthermore, the script of the passenger/other is projected by the father into the mouth of the speechless, dangerously ill son, positing, in Greenblatt's anecdote, the mute other as a fantasy of origin, the imagined source of meaning. This anecdotal postscript figures death as always/already new historicism's postscript to itself, the other that is militantly resistant to the critic's will to power. By figuring the historical and literary text as a dead voice that is made, through new historicist recovery, to speak, new historicism is signified as spectrality, as a dying art.[7]

New historicism, as exemplified by Greenblatt, is thus dependent upon the ultimately untenable notion that the voice is a stable and monolithic other, and its investment in the dead voice as plenitude ironically produces a ghostly effect which is the very reverse of a stable and pure origin. Nick Cox reads Derrida's account of the spectral in *Specters of Marx* alongside the introductory remarks to *Shakespearean Negotiations* in order to explicate Greenblatt's logocentrism which posits an originary, yet dead, voice. Cox argues that the new historicist fantasy of a voice denoting origin and presence is undermined by Greenblatt's act of recovery, for the exorcism of the dead voice always fails. The dead cannot be banished to their proper place: the dead voices are, in Greenblatt's methodology, manifested in 'textual traces' which become vessels of communication that cannot safely be considered dead. The past is, despite the exorcism, still posited as other. Consequently, Greenblatt's 'textual traces', the voices of the dead, are spectral traces, and 'the fear of the spectral trace is the fear that haunts all new historicism'.[8] The attempt to make the dead voices speak through the living, to turn textual/spectral traces into a communicative act with the critic, cannot fully or completely effect the transformation of dead into alive, of silence to voice, of other into self, of past to present, and of old to new.[9]

If the voice of the dead is new historicism's postscript, the resistance of the other to critical mastery does have a beneficial critical effect, in that it resists the creation of monolithic historical narratives and overdetermined agents. These have often been cited as evidence of the critical failure of new historicism to sustain its Foucaldian good intentions of the representation of history as local and unstable centres of power; Brook Thomas, for example, bemoans new historicism's failure to cope with pluralistic versions of history (pp. 45–6). But the failure to make the past new, to make the dead voice fully present and a speaking subject, produces a remainder that exceeds the critical mastery. This remainder may be figured as the uncanny, for oscillation, hesitation, plurality of significations and uncertainty, is what new historicism has failed to cover up and which, ironically, haunts us as its ghost.

An alternative to the project which thus strives to make the dead speak is to investigate the uncanny spectral dead voice of the other as a phenomenon that is not necessarily commensurate with presence and origin. In fact, recent theoretical explorations of the voice expose the limitations of the accepted Derridean account of the development of western metaphysics, which posits the voice as origin and as presence. Phonocentrism is not necessarily coterminous with logocentrism. Mladen Dolar reads Derrida's narrative of the primacy of the voice against the Lacanian narrative of the pre-œdipal phase. The mother's voice constitutes the first interaction with the other, which leads to retroactive fantasies of pre-œdipal unity with the mother prior to the entry to the symbolic order and the introduction of a lack. The archaic experience of fusion between the pre-subject and the mother is recalled retrospectively as a fantasy of unity, when the subject experiences the loss and otherness that are inevitably part of entry into symbolic structures. Dolar suggests, following the Lacanian account, that loss and fusion are always inherently intertwined in the subject's experience of the voice:

> for psychoanalysis, the auto-affective voice of self-presence and self-mastery was constantly opposed by its reverse side, the intractable

> voice of the Other, the voice that one could not control. But both have to be thought together: one could say that at the very core of narcissism, there lies an alien kernel that the narcissistic satisfaction may well attempt to disguise, but which continually threatens to undermine it from the inside.[10]

This other voice threatens rather than safeguards presence but exists alongside the voice as the guarantee of self-presence.

If the archaic and symbolic history of the voice of the other thus encodes both presence and absence, the voice of the other is spectrality *per se*. Slavoj Žižek suggests that this occurs when the subject enters the symbolic order, at which point there is a breach between body and voice:

> What we have to renounce is thus the common-sense notion of a primordial, fully constituted reality in which sight and sound harmoniously complement each other: the moment we enter the symbolic order, an unbridgeable gap separates forever a human body from 'its' voice. The voice acquires a spectral autonomy, it never quite belongs to the body we see, so that even when we see a living person talking, there is always some degree of ventriloquism at work: it is as if the speaker's own voice hollows him out and in a sense speaks 'by himself', through him.[11]

Thus, according to Žižek, not only is (even one's own) voice the voice of an other, but, because of the split between voice and body, the voice is always involved in an act of ventriloquy. Furthermore, the voice has a peculiar agency divorced from the subject who speaks. Žižek explores this phenomenon in terms of the relationship between voice and image. As the voice undermines self-presence, it also points to a gap in the image because of the disjunction between the body and its voice:

> Is, however, the voice not at the same time that which undermines most radically the subject's self-presence and self-transparence? I hear myself speaking, yet what I hear is never fully myself but a parasite, a foreign body in my very heart. [...] Voice is that which, in the signifier, resists meaning, it stands for the opaque inertia that cannot be recuperated by meaning. [...] [V]oice is neither dead nor alive: its primordial phenomenological status is rather that of the living dead, of a spectral apparition that somehow survives its own death, that is, the eclipse of meaning. (p. 103)

The voice produces the hiatus between itself and the body: '[voice] points toward a gap in the field of the visible, toward the dimension of what eludes our gaze. In other words, their relationship is mediated by an impossibility: *ultimately, we hear things because we cannot see everything*' (p. 93). But, as in the psychic work of fantasy which covers what it exposes and reveals what it conceals, the voice both cuts out a hole in the image and strives to fill out the image's whole. Voice is both absence and presence.[12]

Žižek pursues his analysis of the spectrality of the voice by considering Lacan's account of symbolisation. According to Lacan, symbolisation is always incomplete and, although reality is always already symbolised, there is inevitably a remainder, an excess of representation. The real can never be completely covered and Žižek concludes that '*this real (the part of reality that remains unsymbolised) returns in the guise of spectral apparitions*' (p. 112; original italics). In other words, the spectral signifies the failure of symbolisation, although it isn't exactly equivalent to reality:

> reality is never directly 'itself', it presents itself only *via* its incomplete, failed symbolisation, and spectral apparitions emerge in this very gap that forever separates reality from the real, and on account of which reality has the character of a (symbolic) fiction: the spectre gives body to that which escapes (the symbolically structured) reality. (p. 113)

If the voice is, like Plato's *pharmakon*, both the cure and poison, the rim and the hole, the cause and mask of the failure of the image to be whole, then the voice is also the vehicle for the spectrality that figures the excess or remainder of symbolisation. The spectral voice conceals not reality but that which cannot be represented, the repression of which is the ground of reality (p. 113).

Moving back to Stephen Greenblatt, what are we to make of a new historicism whose premise is the desire to speak with the dead? The 'dead voice' is an ironical symptom of the desire to deny the inherent spectrality of the voice *per se*, and of the attempt to repress the voice as a radical alterity which decomposes the boundary between the living and the dead. As Nick Cox points out, to figure the 'textual traces' as dead voices attempts to stabilise the other, to fix the voice as always already dead, is an impossible attempt to produce a secure alterity by distancing the dead voices as a pre-requisite to their recovery in order to close off the possibility of being haunted by spectres. But there is another methodological irony. If according to Žižek, voices are the spectral excess of representation, new historicism concerns itself with that which escapes symbolical reality, with the failure of symbolisation. How does this square with the claim to recover the textual traces which are a product of ideological matrices, of Foucaldian power struggles? By listening to what it figures as the voices of the dead, new historicism is engaged with the other to its implicit and explicit manifesto, with the other to representation.

Although the methodology of new historicism's project of speaking with the dead thus seems inherently fractured and contradictory, I wish to motivate what my analysis is left with: spectral voices. Indeed, a confrontation with what new historicism seems most to fear, spectral traces that elude critical mastery, is already just beginning to be part of a movement to question and revise the methodology. Jeremy Hawthorn's *Cunning Passages* begins with the suggestion that texts themselves might have an agency of their own, that we are read by literature:

> Are literary works the prostitutes of cultural life, dehumanised by the fantasies which successive readers and cultures project on to them – or are they possessed of some independent identity, some power to resist such readerly appropriation, something that makes a reader's desire to talk with their authors or characters more than the textual equivalent of harlotry?[13]

Rather than attempt to repress or exorcise their otherness, Hawthorn directly admits the otherness of the text: 'literary works have their eyes on you' (p. 7). The acceptance of the otherness leads Hawthorn to thematise the lack involved in reading any text, the lack of full meaning (p. 13). He insists that the project of reading is both an alienation from and an integration of the text: 'literature is, then, permanently in the process of being recontextualised' (p. 13). Similarly, Kiernan Ryan has recently argued for the importance of keeping otherness in play and of positing new historicism as a fluid process that refuses to stabilise the other:

> The trouble [...] is that too many exponents of cultural poetics and cultural materialism are curbed by their remorselessly diagnostic attitude to literature, hamstrung by their invulnerability to the work's enigmas and mutations.
>
> Hence the importance, if this radical historicist movement is to remain vital, of developing more dialogic forms of criticism, which respect the power of texts from the remote and recent past to call our

> deepest preconceptions into question, disclosing insights into its world and our own that hindsight deemed impossible. If that means acknowledging something incalculable, something indecipherable in the most appealing works that defies appropriation, so much the better. (p. xvii)

A dialogic relationship between text and context does not necessarily have to be an extreme and reductive radical indeterminacy, which is the parodic suggestion made by Greenblatt.[14] Rather, such dialogism might constitute an ethics of reading other-wise which refuses to exorcise, romanticise or reify the strangeness in a text. Representing or forming a paradigm for the dialogism as a critical methodology seems not to be the best way of proceeding, however, for the alterity in the process of recovering dead voices, and in the transference and countertransference between the reader and the text, is a process of discovery not of identity. As Thomas Docherty asserts: 'I contend that we must "hear" alterity, that we must undergo alterity as an event'.[15] This is a methodological manoeuvre that avoids totalising the spectral voice and its readerly effects.

Feminism and the voice

New historicism is not the only critical school with an investment in the recovery of the voice. I now turn to investigate what a problematisation of the voice offers feminist interest in the recuperation of neglected texts. Feminist concerns to give a voice to women oppressed and silenced by patriarchy are exemplified by, and to some extent originate with, Tillie Olsen's *Silences*.[16] Olsen offers a litany of literary examples which illustrate how cultural, social, and racial codes have impeded women writers. *Silences* marked a new emphasis in feminist literary criticism. As well as inspiring research which tries to explain why women's writing is marginalised – an example being Joanna Russ's *How to Suppress Women's Writing* – Olsen laid the groundwork for the recuperation of the marginalised, for listening to the silences.[17]

Tensions between feminism and the new historicism have often been noted, with particular attention paid to the latter's stress on the historicised human subject as decentred, fragmented and subjected to a multitude of conflicting ideological discourses which denies feminists the full subjectivity they seek in the struggle for equality.[18] But, for feminists, the new historicism's interest in listening to and recovering the voices of the dead has a particular validity and, indeed, I argue that both types of critical recovery in praxis are predicated upon the voice as a stable monolithic origin. For Anglo-American feminist literary critics such as Sandra Gilbert and Susan Gubar, the female voice and female power are equivalent because, as Tilly Olsen also argues, silence equals oppression and subjugation. Toril Moi, along with other commentators, points out that the valorisation of the voice as power is a fantasy of an authorial origin, that could be perceived as running counter to new historicism's post-modern foundations. Moi comments that: 'for Gilbert and Gubar, [. . .] the female voice is a duplicitous, but nevertheless true, and truly female voice'.[19] This is, however, for Moi the weakness of *The Madwoman in the Attic*: 'Gilbert and Gubar's belief in the true female authorial voice as the essence of all texts written by women masks the problems raised by their theory of patriarchal ideology. For them, [. . .] ideology becomes a monolithic unified totality that knows no contradictions; against this a miraculously intact "femaleness" may pit its strength' (p. 63). Thus, for Gilbert and Gubar, female voice is an origin that inscribes power, subjectivity, and the body and intentions of the female author.

Gilbert and Gubar would not necessarily style themselves new historicists. The problems which their valorisation of the female voice raise, however, suggest a certain methodological overlap between their brand of Anglo-American feminism and the new historicist project of recovery. Any feminist methodology which voices the silent, in fact, is caught up in an impossible double bind. On the one hand, in the logic of recovery, literary voices that have been silenced, repressed, or muffled from within the representational scheme need to be recovered in order to understand their contextual positions and to interrogate the construction of canonicity that marginalised them in the first place. This is the assumption behind, for example, Tricia Lootens' *Lost Saints* which analyses the Victorian construction of the canon. But, on the other hand, the result is to project a voice onto what has culturally become the voiceless: an act of critical ventriloquy which overturns, yet leaves in place, the methodological binary voice/silence upon which the literary canon is constructed.[20] But, if we remember that, in psychoanalytical terms, the voice as origin is a fantasy which both produces and covers over a hole in representation, the act of voicing the silent adds a supplement, a third term to the binary, an uncanny remainder.

In her study, *Ventriloquized Voices: Feminist Theory and English Renaissance Texts*, Elizabeth Harvey argues that ventriloquism is inherently part of all historical literary readings, but suggests that this can be appropriated positively by feminist critics:

> Historical reconstructions are always a kind of ventriloquisation [...] a matter of making the past seem to speak in the voice that the present gives it. Rather than suppressing this enabling twinship, I foreground it by pairing texts of the early modern period with late twentieth-century considerations of what I claim are analogous issues.[21]

For Harvey, ventriloquism constitutes an author's adoption of a feminine voice in a way that silences or marginalises women. By reading such acts of ventriloquy alongside feminist theory's formulation of the feminine voice's bodily origins, Harvey argues that the woman can nevertheless be recovered through the author's act of ventriloquy. By so doing, she shifts the usual constructionist debate, by reference to Diana Fuss's *Essentially Speaking*, to argue that essentialist notions of identity are the basis of constructionist historicist accounts of femininity.[22] But, despite her sophisticated theoretical model, and despite admitting that ventriloquism underlies all historical readings of texts, Harvey's attempt to validate ventriloquism as both a rhetorical misogynist fact of Renaissance texts and as a feminist reading strategy has no room for questioning whether the female body and its voices can be recovered as something pure and separate from the critic's will to power. In addition, in psychoanalytic terms, the body cannot be recuperated from the voice, from which it is always already divorced.

The voice is particularly associated with women's poetry. In the collapse of woman into experience into text, which categorised nineteenth-century notions of female creativity, the voice is taken to be the pure expression of the poetess, directly associating lyric cries with the author. Late nineteenth-century representations of Christina Rossetti frequently invoke her lyric voice as an index of the historical personage. Her poetry has a 'strong and tender' voice[23] and sings with 'the ultimate music of the communicating word'.[24] The experience of hearing the author's voice is often remarked upon; for William Sharp, her voice is 'resonant crystal', and she has 'singularly clear, rippling laugh', a 'spontaneity', and is 'unusually distinct'.[25] As Yopi Prins observes, the nineteenth-century ideology of lyric reading is predicted on the figure of the voice.[26] Isobel Armstrong reads this ideology in relation to expressive theory which evolved from Romantic sensibility, becoming a poetics of the feminine which associates the lyric voice with exhalation and expiration, as well as secrecy and contextlessness in Rossetti's œuvre.[27]

Leaving aside Christina Rossetti for a moment, an intriguing case study is afforded by Elizabeth Siddal, which exemplifies the problematics of recovering a silenced voice in feminist and new historicist critique. In particular, Siddal is a paradigm for the fantasy of an origin which underlies the project of recovery. This origin manifests itself in praxis as the critical attempt at forging a direct access to the historical personage Lizzie Siddal. Recovering Siddal's silenced voice, on the contrary, exposes the gap or hole within the representational axiom that made her silent in the first place. It is true that Siddal is an extreme example. As Dante Gabriel Rossetti's model, mistress, and then wife, she was positioned as an appendage to the Pre-Raphaelite Brotherhood, the circle of artists and poets in which she was excluded by virtue of gender, and yet worshipped for her unusual beauty. Yet, as Elisabeth Bronfen argues, Siddal exists within a cultural logic that determines her art and life. Bronfen sets up Siddal's life as a dramatisation of Dante Gabriel Rossetti's investment in an aesthetic that equates women with death.[28] Valued in the nineteenth-century for her status as muse, any recovery of her art and poetry is inevitably bound up within the ideology that both produced and silenced her work.

This has not, however, prevented such recoveries from taking place. The first collected edition of Siddal's poems and drawings was published in 1978 by Wombatt Press in Canada.[29] In a review, Maggie Berg praises the edition for its recovery of Siddal's work from neglect (indeed, the title of her article is 'A Neglected Voice') and from the editorial hand of her brother-in-law, William Michael Rossetti. The assumption is that such a recovery can restore Siddal from the prevalent interest in her biography.[30] Commensurate with such a restoration of the neglected voice, however, is precisely the fantasy of a biographical subject that the editorial recovery strives to dispel. Berg depicts Siddal's work as a voice which encapsulates the Pre-Raphaelite aesthetic ideal and Siddal's own personal emotion:

> Subsequent assessments cannot ignore this book of *Poems and Drawings of Elizabeth Siddal*, if only because they represent the voice of the Pre-Raphaelite ideal. Although the themes of world-weariness, early death, and frustrated love which regards heaven as union with the loved-one are all typically Pre-Raphaelite, and the guilt and lack of commitment to the religious imagery are Rossettian, these poems nevertheless derive originality from their manifestly personal nature: the Pre-Raphaelite motifs do not conceal vacuousness as in so much minor Pre-Raphaelite verse: they are inevitable expressions of genuine emotion. (p. 155).

This response to the edition has it both ways: the poems and drawings are both quintessentially Pre-Raphaelite and also autobiographical. Thus, the complete edition of Siddal's œuvre, so crucial to the project of recovering 'neglected voices', according to Berg reveals a voice which echoes the aesthetic which marginalised her in the first place and her true, originary, female voice. Rather like the logic that Fuss describes in *Essentially Speaking*, the recovery of Siddal reveals new historicism's essentialist basis: the belief in the voice as source and origin.

Other projects of uncovery also demonstrate how difficult it is to separate Siddal from the Pre-Raphaelite ideal that silenced her. The catalogue of an exhibition held at the Ruskin Gallery in Sheffield in 1991 offers an account of Siddal's biography written by Jan Marsh. Although attempting to divorce biography from legend and hagiography, the account demonstrates how difficult it is to separate the two.[31] The use of anecdote in particular, the mainstay of biographical narrative, discloses the biography's debt to legend and Victorian hagiography. For example, in the very opening of the biographical background, we learn that: 'she was said to have first discovered Tennyson by reading a poem on paper wrapping a pat of butter, and to have had only a chilly bedroom in which to draw' (p. 11). Such unconfirmable details ('she was said...') are part of the Siddal mythology, which structures her as an ill-educated working class girl whom Dante Gabriel Rossetti rescues from obscurity and poverty.

Another anecdote which Marsh repeats, citing Arthur Hughes who shares a studio with Millais, is the famous incident in which Siddal almost catches pneumonia as a result of modelling for Millais's *Ophelia* in 1852:

> Miss Siddal had a trying experience whilst acting as model for 'Ophelia'. In order that the artist might get the proper set of the garments in water and the right atmosphere and aqueous effects, she had to lie in a large bath filled with water, which was kept at an even temperature by lamps placed beneath. One day, just as the picture was nearly finished, the lamps went out unnoticed by the artist, who was so intently absorbed in his work that he thought of nothing else, and the poor lady kept floating in the cold water till she was quite benumbed. She herself never complained of this, but the result was that she contracted a severe cold and her father wrote to Millais, threatening him with an action of £50 damages for his carelessness. Eventually the matter was satisfactorily resolved. (pp. 12–13)

As Bronfen notes, this is apocryphal (p. 169); the anecdote offers no verifiable and factual access to the historical personage Elizabeth Siddal. What we get instead is further evidence of her status as a representation, and a representation which invests her persona in death itself:

> Her deanimation occurred on two levels. In his numerous portraits Rossetti painted her sitting, sewing, reading, resting at her easel, but always as an enigmatic woman, her gaze withdrawn into herself, the eyes semi-closed, averting the spectator's gaze. Her continual illness seems to have predestined her for these portraits that render her as a languid, aloof, withdrawn woman, with almost translucent pallor, in the weakness and flickering febrile flightiness of the consumptive ill woman, supportive of the conventional notions of the transitory nature of feminine beauty, femininity as virginal and vulnerable, ideal and tainted. (p. 170)

Jan Marsh, in her ground-breaking biography of Siddal, admits that her life is inseparable from the myths and legends surrounding her. In addition, Marsh's *The Legend of Elizabeth Siddal* begins by firmly associating Siddal with not only death, but with absence and irrecoverability, for Marsh tells of her initial contact with Siddal when she fruitlessly searches for her overgrown grave at Highgate Cemetery.[32]

In two recently published anthologies of Victorian women's poetry, Siddal's entry is prefaced in each case with an introduction which weaves biographical details inextricably with mythology and anecdote.[33] In particular, they include an account of the Ophelia incident as part of our understanding of Siddal's historical persona.[34] Both editions implicitly participate in the project of recovering neglected and forgotten voices. The introduction to Armstrong and Bristow's anthology opens:

> Over the last two decades, researchers have gradually begun to rediscover the work of women poets in the nineteenth and earlier centuries. This process of rediscovery has been one of the most intellectually exciting developments within the field of literary history, and its significance cannot be underestimated. As a consequence, the contours of the literary past begin to change as new relations emerge, both between newly read poems and the largely male canon, and between women poets themselves. (p. xxiii)

The vocabulary here of rediscovery repeats a familiar logic of retrieval: the re-shaping of the canon, the realisation of new configurations of literary influence. And yet the editors do not address the inclusion of biographical information. Although the introductory remarks to each poet offer valuable factual information, the inclusion of biography raises certain methodological questions. Most importantly, as is the case with Angela Leighton's landmark *Victorian Women Poets: Writing Against the Heart*, there is a certain tension between biography and literary text.[35] This is particularly true of Victorian women's poetry, written out of the sentimental tradition which prescribed female creativity to be limited to the private sphere of experience and emotion. Thus, as we have already seen, woman is experience is text. By appending biographical information to the poetry, the anthologies are in danger of encouraging a biographical context to readings which re-inscribe Victorian gender ideology. But all recovery of marginalised and silent voices is in danger of this process. The trope of the voice as a source of origin means that recovery of voices and of contexts is predicated upon the historical personage of the poet. Such a critical manœuvre re-deploys the naive intentionality of autobiographical readings that new historicism was meant to counter.

An important article by Deborah Cherry and Griselda Pollock confronts our problematic access to the historical personage Elizabeth Siddal.[36] They describe and elucidate her construction as a Pre-Raphaelite icon, whose very surname is altered on entry into their circle from Siddall to Siddal (p. 208).[37] Cherry and Pollock consider the difficulty in assessing Siddal's active role as a producer of art because of the mythology and hagiography within the contemporary narratives. One option they consider is the recovery of Siddal as a producer, to try to enable the historical personage to emerge:

> The first impulse is to challenge the dominant knowledge system by providing more information about the artistic activities of Elizabeth Siddall, attempting thereby to position her as a creative individual by reassembling an oeuvre, and producing an authorial identity for it. (p. 209)

Such a project, however, fails because of the 'masculinist paradigm' of art history, for Siddal has come down to us exclusively in relation to Dante Gabriel Rossetti to whom she will always be secondary. 'Attempting to restore Elizabeth Siddall in this empirical and monographic manner cannot effect the necessary alteration of the gendered discourses of art history' (p. 211).

The second option which Cherry and Pollock consider is also problematic:

> This second strategy involves a more sophisticated scrutiny and cross-referencing of all the available documentary material which might reconstitute a history of Elizabeth Siddall both inside and beyond the Pre-Raphaelite circle. It is possible to collate material from the Pre-Raphaelite literature of diaries, letters, journals and memoirs with records such as censuses, post office directories, parish records, the register of births, marriages and deaths, articles in parliamentary papers, contemporary newspapers and journals, etc. This project is based on the assumption that the accumulation of a more extensive range of documentation will itself be sufficient to dispel the enigma of 'Siddal' and reveal, hidden from history, a more complex identity for this working-class woman who became a painter and poet.
>
> (p. 210)

This project is aligned to the new historicist recovery of context, in which Siddal would emerge from history, dissolving her status as an enigma with a verifiable historical identity. Interestingly, Cherry and Pollock admit that this option is positioned partly within the Pre-Raphaelite aesthetic, for it would reveal a Siddal 'inside and beyond the Pre-Raphaelite circle'. But it is precisely this dependency upon, this relativity to, the Pre-Raphaelites that dooms the strategy: 'but such a project does not necessarily produce and alternative version of "Siddal" with different factual attributes; indeed it may well reproduce the character of the melancholy, fatally ill, wife of Rossetti' (p. 210). In other words, because of her position in the aesthetic in relation to the Pre-Raphaelites, any recovery of her historical personage would inevitable recirculate that aesthetic. Pollock and Cherry conclude by emphasising that the historical 'Siddall' must be separated from the enigma 'Siddal', and that any attempt to expose the constructedness of the latter still precludes rescuing 'Siddall' as an independent producer of art, so pervasive is the aesthetic.

Cherry and Pollock's argument reveals the impossibility of recovering the person labelled 'Siddall' outside the Pre-Raphaelite aesthetic. Their response is to investigate the creation of 'Siddal', accepting that it constitutes no window to the past. This rather elides the issue of the recoverability. And, as we've seen from other recoveries of her œuvre, such an investigation in praxis rests upon the assumption that there is an autonomous historical figure underneath the ideological complexities operating as a pure origin of meaning. One way of dealing with this might be to accept, as Diana Fuss does, that this is an inevitable result of the binary essentialism/constructionism. This would mean that historical recoveries of women writers, making their silenced voices speak, would involve a concept of the voice as both a fantasmatic source of originary plenitude and as a ventriloquism divorced from the historical body of the author.

In fact, such a strategy of combining the voice as presence and as fragmentation is employed by Hélène Cixous, which has often been misunderstood and dismissed by feminists as hopelessly contradictory. On the contrary, Cixous's paradoxically double conception of the voice testifies to her Lacanian and Derridean heritage. Cixous's most significant discussion of the voice occurs in *The Newly Born Woman* in which she gives her account of women's archaic associations with the voice. Cixous insists upon the special association of the feminine with the voice and with writing:

> First I sense femininity in writing by: a privilege of *voice*: *writing and voice* are intertwined and interwoven and writing's continuity/voice's rhythm take each other's breath away through interchanging, make the text gasp or form it out of suspense and silences, make it lose its voice or rend it with cries.[38]

Writing the feminine, however, is no mere reiteration or mimesis of the voice's rhythm and presence. This is because the origins of the association between the feminine and the voice are in the Imaginary. In the Symbolic, which is of course our only conscious access to the Imaginary, the voice however continues to haunt us: 'feminine writing never stops reverberating from the wrench that the acquisition of speech, speaking out load, is for her' (p. 92). The voice even in the Real Symbolic maintains a connection with origin, with the with m/other:

> The Voice sings from a time before the law, before the Symbolic took one's breath away and reappropriated it into language under its authority of separation. The deepest, the oldest, the loveliest Visitation. Within each woman the first, nameless love is singing. (p. 93)

But, because we only know of the voice through the medium of symbolic structures or the Symbolic, Cixous here insists that the voice is also disruption, loss, agony, and fragmentation: 'voice: unfastening, fracas. Fire! She shoots, she shoots away. Break. From their bodies where they have been buried, shut up and at the same time forbidden to take pleasure' (p. 94). Cixous's writing of the feminine, or *écriture feminine*, involves both the proleptic utopia of recovery, in which the voice is pure self-presence and self-identity, and the realisation that in the Symbolic this will involve the writing of the other.[39] Toril Moi, who notes the doubleness within Cixous's discussions of the voice as both origin and detachment, accepts that Cixous is aware of the contradiction. Moi is, however, too eager to emphasise in Cixous's writing her utopian and idealistic project of recovering the voice (pp. 113–21, 126).

Hélène Cixous's insistence upon writing the feminine as both an inscription of the voice's status as presence/origin and as detachment/fragmentation has a number of important contributions to make to the recoverability of the dead voice in new historicist and feminist praxis. Firstly, Cixous demonstrates and performs the inevitable intertwining of voice as both loss and as a fantasy of origin. In academic critique, this would suggest the importance of confronting and motivating the project of recovery as one predicated upon a fantasy of origin. The historical personage of the author, as the example of Elizabeth Siddal indicates, is not accessible through the archaeological project of unearthing textual information or producing authoritative editions. In fact, moving back to Žižek's argument that the voice is both hole and rim, the historical personage as textual voice is precisely signified by the excess or remainder of representation. Historical recovery must acknowledge the fact that its methodology is grounded upon the spectral presence of the voice that speaks from the dead.

But how to motivate the voice's complexity and doubleness? One possibility is to open up as a subject of investigation the voice as the fantastic origin of authorial authenticity, historical personage and Imaginary self-presence. This might initiate a fruitful rapprochement between feminist theory and new historicist praxis. It might also aid the scholarly use of the recently published anthologies of Victorian women's poetry, by analysing the role of biographical information as a preface to the reading of recovered texts. In addition, an investigation of the voice might address the nineteenth-century construction of the voice in Victorian sentimental or expressive women's poetry as a voice of both loss and presence, for the tradition figures women's poetry as music or song that articulates sadness and loss.[40] Much of the contemporary theoretical exploration of the voice has its origin in Freud, whose narratives in turn are in many ways a product of nineteenth-century ideologies. Secondly, awareness in academic discourse, and in classroom discussion, should fall upon the act of critical writing itself as part of a process of reading other-wise, as a confrontation and communication with the other which refuses to master or exorcise dead voices or textual traces. This would move towards the dialogic criticism urged by Ryan and Hawthorne. But an attention to the process of critical writing would also open up opportunities for writing what Cixous terms the feminine as a mode of academic discourse; in other words, exploring the critical voice as one that intertwines presence and loss in its engagement with a text. Above all, we must resist trying to stabilise and master the other, and instead learn to listen to its voice as one inhabiting our reading and our writing and that tells us what representation leaves behind.

3
Christina Rossetti in Effect: Reading Biographies

> If only my figure would shrink somewhat! for a fat poetess is incongruous, especially when seated by the grave of buried hope.
>
> Christina Rossetti to D.G. Rossetti, 4 August 1881
>
> (*Letters* 2: 289)

> Wrapt in fire, indeed, was that pure and perfect spirit, that disembodied soul of song.
>
> William Sharp on Christina Rossetti[1]

History

Who was Christina Rossetti? The biographies and reminiscences present us with a character at once enigmatic and prosaic, but always inherently contradictory. Dichotomies ascribed to Rossetti – passion/repression, aestheticism/asceticism – define for Georgina Battiscombe, and for most of Rossetti's biographers, what is distinctive in her life: 'outwardly, Christina Rossetti's life was an uneventful one; inwardly, it was a continual conflict'.[2] W.M. Rossetti authorises this interpretation with his comment on his sister's limited sphere of activity:

> It does not seem necessary, in this brief Memoir, to dwell upon any of the other incidents in her life – all in themselves insignificant. It was a life which did not consist of incidents: in few things, external; in all its deeper currents, internal.[3] (*PW: CR* p. lviii)

The mythically constructed split character of Christina Rossetti allows the biographer to move the normal goal posts of the genre. Instead of presenting a factual account of the life of an historical personage, the subject for the biographer becomes a wholly interior life, an emotional drama. Edward Boyle, for example, admits that she lived among the Pre-Raphaelites and yet 'even in youth Christina lived a life apart. If she appears, it is in spite of herself. [. . .] [L]ittle [is] said about her. She was merely there.'[4] The shift of emphasis within still represents Christina Rossetti as an historical personage, but this has become an ambiguous position: with the shift comes an insistence that the personage is also ahistorical, that she is removed from history by virtue of living an entirely emotional life and acquiring a status as a feminine ideal, a saintly poetess.[5] This doubleness – the insistence upon an historical subject and the concurrent insistence that the subject is ahistorical – agitates the stability and presence of the biographical subject.

Conventionally depicted as a devout spinster whose lyrical poetry directly transcribes her unrequited love, the biographical representation of Rossetti subscribes to the aesthetic construction of femininity while attempting to place such an operation under erasure. Writing about the surge of biographical interest at the centenary of Rossetti's birth (5 December 1930), Virginia Woolf begins to explore the problems of biography as a genre:

> As everybody knows, the fascination of reading biographies is irresistible. [. .] Here is the past and all its inhabitants miraculously sealed as in a magic tank; all we have to do is to look and to listen and to listen and to look and soon the little figures – for they are rather under life size – will begin to move and to speak and as they move we shall arrange them in all sorts of patterns of which they were ignorant, for they thought when they were alive that they could go where they liked.[6]

Woolf expresses dissatisfaction with the biographical mode that positions and frames people and events in artificial patterns, while she also relishes the various Rossetti anecdotes. An apocryphal anecdote is recounted of a tea party at which, possibly in response to some remark about poetry, 'suddenly there uprose from a chair and paced forward into the centre of the room a little woman dressed in black, who announced solemnly, "I am Christina Rossetti!" and having so said, returned to her chair' (p. 240). The anecdote might well have the same source as that offered by Ellen Proctor in her *Brief Memoir of Christina G. Rossetti*. During a tea party, Proctor spoke at length to a lady whom she was later surprised to learn was Christina Rossetti:

> I turned to my late companion, and said, 'Are you Miss Rossetti?' 'Yes', she said cheerily, 'I am'. 'Miss Christina Rossetti?' I continued. 'Christina Rossetti at your service!' was the reply. She was smiling now, and her face seemed to say, 'What a wonder you make of me!'[7]

For Woolf, Christina Rossetti's name denotes something more than a name: it signifies a poetess trapped and framed by the biographies but nevertheless removed from cultural, social and historical shapings: 'years and the traffic of the mind with men and books did not affect you in the least' (p. 242). Proctor, however, tells of how Rossetti's use of her own name undermines the value Proctor herself has put on it. By inscribing into her account the supposed puncturing by Rossetti of the significance of her own name, Proctor insists upon the actual historical existence of Rossetti, rendered as her prosaic ordinariness, while also constructing her name as a signifier for something more than a name. The signification process whereby the name exceeds its own designation as a name bears within it the attempted erasure of this process, the mask of its operation. The presentation in the biographies of a complete and unified historical personage emerges plainly as a fallacy, an illusory by-product of the text. To critique this fallacy, furthermore, is to see that Christina Rossetti as understood in the biographies is a trope.

For a woman who lived to be 64 and was associated with a literary and artistic coterie, there are surprisingly few anecdotes about Rossetti in circulation. The source of much information is the first full length biographical and critical study, by Mackenzie Bell, which utilises explicitly the information given him by W.M. Rossetti and from which subsequent biographers have taken much of their detail.[8] Across the biographies the material is retold in a similar pattern and the same incidents are repeated with an almost tedious regularity.[9] We are told of Rossetti's impressive vocabulary as a child, illustrated on the occasion when, less than six years old, she remarked to a visitor that: 'the cat looks very sedate'; the young poet's first verse: 'Cecilia never went to school / Without her gladiator';[10] and her canary dream, told to D.G. Rossetti (who planned to paint it) and passed down by William Sharp, in which Christina Rossetti saw a yellow cloud of escaped canaries converging over London rooftops and later returning to their cages.[11] There are other, more apocryphal anecdotes: her unwillingness to step on a scrap of paper on the street in case it had written upon it the Holy Name;[12] her habit of carrying her cat, Muff, on her shoulders around the house in Torrington Square;[13] finally, her method of dealing with a young poet who wished to discuss his work with her: upon seeing the manuscript in his pocket, Rossetti denounced modern poetry so vehemently that he was terrorised from producing it.[14]

The Rossetti family's habit of destroying material made possible their control of information in the tropic construction of Rossetti.[15] Although, like Elizabeth Siddal, Rossetti is represented as a trope, she is also, due to her status as a published poet, theoretically more historically recoverable. But, because she is a relatively independent figure, and a producer of meanings in her own right, the value of the fallacy of historicism in biographies increases in importance. Historical accuracy is masked as pleonasm, in excessively prosaic and excessively repetitious anecdotal material across the biographies. Mackenzie Bell was criticised by contemporaries for his attention to commonplace detail, and he is reported as defending himself to Godfrey Bilchet thus:

> Bell told me [...] that he gave so much prosaic matter of Christina Rossetti's because he wished to bring out her [...] absolutely practical everyday mind combined with the gift of the visionary, artist & poet; & Bell said his father had found the same combination in the Italians in the Argentine.[16]

As Bell seems to have suggested, anecdotal information is inserted as part of a wider tropic concern: here, Rossetti is portrayed as an Englishwoman who is quintessentially Italian, a duality widely presented as a facet of her characteristic ambivalence. The inclusion of so much detail is equivalent to what Elisabeth Bronfen terms, in a discussion of the female corpse, an attempt to parenthesise subjectivity: the subject as an 'accurate' historical personage is present but as an empty shell, bracketed or displaced to 'make room for the concept it is used to signify'. Consequently, 'the body is deprived of history [and] changed into a gesture'.[17] This presence-in-absence is fundamental to the mythological construction of the Christina Rossetti personage. The trace of displaced subjectivity, the notional inclusion of an emptied trope (Rossetti as an historical subject), is rendered biographically as her 'divided life', a duality of 'inner' and 'outer' lives, between 'natural' passion and imposed repression, between asceticism and aesthetics.[18] Her 'outer' life, or historical existence, is seen as a cover for her 'inner' turmoil. In other words, the trope Christina Rossetti is deprived of history and deanimated. The 'spirit of postponement', for which her poetry and her biographical personage are so famed, becomes a continual postponement of presence and materiality.[19] As Cherry and Pollock conclude in relation to Elizabeth Siddal (see Chapter 2), ultimately only a textual analysis of the biographical subject, rather than a recovery of the historical personage, can expose the construction given as Christina Rossetti.

Hysteria

As a fragmentary narrative which must have, in order to work, an epiphanic moment, the biographical anecdote discloses the cultural constructions of femininity behind its operation in a biographical text. The disclosures are most fruitful when the very point of the anecdote – its epiphanic moment – is explicitly in question. The anecdote then becomes self-consciously and excessively a pleonasm. Indeed, as an epiphanic moment, the anecdote encompasses in its revelation both plenitude and loss: a conflicted access to the meaning of the trope Christina Rossetti. The following example signposts an elision of data that agitates the binary construction (inner/outer, passion/repression) of the subject's supposed identity, when an ambivalent textual silence seems to expose the gap between sign (the person labelled Christina Rossetti) and signified (Rossetti as trope). Mackenzie Bell's biography and W.M. Rossetti's memoir cautiously describe Rossetti's adolescent crisis and last illness. In 1845, when she was 15, Rossetti's health became delicate. Bell briefly mentions that at this time she was attended by Dr Hare, whose opinion of Rossetti's beauty and filial love is recounted, but not his diagnosis (pp. 20–1). No further details are offered as to the cause of her illness, which later biographers tend to interpret as a form of breakdown which transformed her from a vivacious child into a solemn and sickly adult. In his memoir, W.M. Rossetti is also vague in his description of his sister at this period:

> Christina was, I think, a tolerably healthy girl in mere childhood; but this state of things soon came to an end. She was not fully fifteen when her constitution became obviously delicate. [...] There was angina pectoris (actual or supposed), of which, after some long while, she seemed cured; then cough, with symptoms which were accounted ominous of decline or consumption, lasting on towards 1867; then exophthalmic bronchocele (or Dr. Graves's Disease), which began in 1871, and was truly most formidable and prostrating. [...] All these maladies were apart from her last and mortal illness, of which I must say a few words in its place. I have naturally much more reluctance than inclination to dwell upon any of these physical ills; but any one who did not understand that Christina was an almost constant and often a sadly-smitten invalid, seeing at times the

> countenance of Death very close to her own, would form an extremely incorrect notion of her corporal, and thus in some sense of her spiritual, condition.[20]

W.M. Rossetti does not name the illness that began in 1845, but Bell's friend, Godfrey Bilchet, transcribed the following note in the back of his copy of Bell's book: 'the doctor who attended on Christina Rossetti when she was about 16–18 said she was then more or less out of her mind (suffering, in fact, from a form of insanity, I believe, a kind of religious mania)'.[21] Around 1845 the family were in great financial difficulty owing to the ill health of the father Gabriele, and preparations were made for Christina Rossetti to take up a post as a governess. It is also known, from her manuscript notebooks, that she was continuing to write poetry at this time. Marsh comments: 'it is perhaps understandable that her adolescent breakdown coincided with the reigning in of her spirited personality to fit the requirements of Victorian femininity'.[22] It seems likely that the contemporary diagnosis of the mysterious illness, which W.M. Rossetti and Bell would be naturally reluctant to mention, was hysteria.[23]

It is necessary to distinguish between definitions of hysteria. As Elaine Showalter argues in *The Female Malady,* the symptoms and cultural meaning of hysteria changed from era to era. For the Victorians, hysteria was a disorder of the womb and a sign of dysfunctional femininity for which the prescribed cure was rest, marriage or motherhood.[24] The Victorians, in a much documented ambivalence, also construed women's illness as an affirmative sign of femininity; hysteria then becomes a sign of excess which challenges this cultural code, a sign for extremes of emotion and of physical symptoms. The significance of hysteria has subsequently evolved through the work of Freud and Breuer, and feminist readings of their *Studies on Hysteria* and Freud's *Fragment of an Analysis of a Case of Hysteria*[25] which develop its designation as a neurotic illness communicated through the hysteric's body into a gender ambivalence that emerges in the hysteric's discourse. Thus, hysteria as the excessive sign for what the Victorians understood as 'feminine' becomes in hysterical discourse a vacillation between masculine and feminine, both an acceptance and refusal of the feminine position as dictated by society. The biographical representation of Christina Rossetti emerges as an illusory historical personage presented as both historically accurate and removed from the workings of history; the suggestion and biographical suppression of her hysteria helps unravel this paradox.

As Kathleen Jones notes in her biography of Rossetti, hysteria would almost certainly have been mentioned as a cause of her illness: she was seen by a gynaecologist and one symptom was described as a suffocating sensation, typical of psychosomatic illness (pp. 19–20). W.M. Rossetti's comment that to understand that his sister was an invalid is to understand her 'corporal, and thus in some sense her spiritual, condition' (see above) suggests that illness is both the sign of a suffering saint and the outward sign of a psychical or spiritual malaise, two different notions attesting to the Victorian ambivalence towards illness and femininity. At a time when she had extreme reluctance to become a governess[26] and an increasing poetic output, we witness in the seminal biographies intimations of hysteria when her behaviour could not be presented in line with nineteenth-century concepts of femininity. The suggestion of hysteria is even more pertinent when one considers the contemporary interrelationship of writing, motherhood and disease, for both literary output and nervous illness were thought to originate in the womb.

Another relevant passage occurs in Bell in an uncharacteristically explicit description of Rossetti's last illness, breast cancer, which caused her much pain and distress:

> Her brother has said to me, and wishes me to mention, that about 'a couple of years' before her death Dr. Stewart told him 'she was very liable to some form of hysteria'. For a while in her final illness, though appreciably less in her last fortnight of life, such symptoms were apparent, particularly during semi-consciousness, chiefly manifesting themselves in cries, not so much, as far as could be observed, 'thro' absolute pain' as 'thro' some sort of hysterical stimulation'.
>
> (p. 170)

Bell's tentative reference to hysteria, which W.M. Rossetti refuted,[27] is further amplified by a previously unpublished letter quoted in Packer's biography, in which a neighbour complains of Rossetti's 'distressing screams that sound clear from her drawing-room to mine' (p. 399). To label her understandable distress during the closing stages of her illness hysteria *and* to suppress this diagnosis indicate another incident when her behaviour could not be accounted equivalent to the assigned 'character' of Christina Rossetti.[28]

Furthermore, it is possible to apply contemporary theories of hysteria to the biographical texts themselves. By both fetishistically stating and refuting the diagnosis that Rossetti was a hysteric, these texts are haunted by the other they wish to deny – the trope Christina Rossetti as historically constructed. To include and withdraw the designation of Rossetti as an hysteric (in the sense understood by the Victorians) is to intimate an ambiguity and vacillation of sexual identity – particularly in the insistence that a saintly asexuality and a perpetual sickness is concurrent with her femininity. The texts thus refuse the 'ordering' of a sexuality construed as normal: the classic symptom, the classic failed repression, of the twentieth-century's definition of hysteria. The ensuing uncanny duplicity is both a denial and an affirmation not only of the diagnosis of hysteria, but also of the biographical subject as a feminine subject. As Bronfen asserts, the hysterical textual voice is a function of the cultural equivalence of femininity and death:

> The hysteric's is a superlatively uncanny position, and as such another aspect of death's figure in life. Precisely because of the hysteric's doubleness between self and image and her oscillation between sexual signifiers, she uses her body to collapse the difference between opposite terms like masculinity/femininity, object/agent of spectatorship, confirmation/disclosure of cultural values, only to pose undecidable questions. (p. 282)

The biographical *representation* of an alleged clinical hysteric subscribes to the same operation; the textual appropriation of the included and refuted hysterical feminine subject positions the text within an hysterical discourse.

In a discussion of Lévi-Strauss's analysis of woman as a commodity for exchange within culture, Bronfen notes that 'Woman-as-sign', 'also marks a self-reflexive moment within the process of signification to become a signifier for exchange itself'. She is both body and trope, and her historical existence and subjectivity are different from the way she is spoken of 'in figure' (p. 225). Thus, 'Woman' comes to represent in herself the meaning process she is part of. This semiotic function is inherently associated with the feminine subject represented within a discourse that positions the subject as hysterical, for by definition the hysterical symptom is histrionically somaticised and dramaticised by the subject in an enactment of the self-doubling that comes with the resistance to gender identity and the disjunction inscribed into the textual position. The explicitly unknown and unknowable trope of Christina Rossetti in the biographical texts emerges as both a figure of represented 'Woman' and a figure for the actual process of representation, for the self-enacting and histrionic nature of the trope.

That Christina Rossetti is a sign for representation is suggested most forcefully in a recurrent biographical anecdote of her stay at Penkill Castle, the home of Alice Boyd in Ayrshire, in the summer of 1866. Quotation from five of the principal biographies will suggest not only a tendency of the authors to repeat similar material and even similar phrases but also a tendency to literally and figuratively frame Rossetti as object and as trope. Christina Rossetti as a reflexive narrative effect, it transpires, infects the genealogy of biographies.

> Mr. Arthur Hughes, in the course of conversation, has described to me in a very vivid manner the little four-cornered window of Christina Rossetti's bedroom at Penkill, which commanded a view over an old-fashioned garden, and in which, according to Miss Boyd, as quoted by my informant, she used to stand, leaning forward, 'her elbows on the sill, her hands supporting her face' – the attitude in which she is represented in Dante Gabriel's drawing of 1866, just alluded to. 'The little window exactly framed her', added Mr. Hughes, 'and from the garden she could be seen for hours meditating and composing'.[29]

> At Penkill the room assigned to the shy, dark-haired lady from London looked out upon an old garden and had a little four-cornered window at which that lady used to stand for hours together, 'her elbows on the sill, her hands supporting her face', lost in meditation. How she must have looked standing there we may guess from Dante Gabriel's chalk drawing made about this time and used by Mr. Mackenzie Bell as the frontispiece to his monograph. [. .] The wistful look of the earlier Christina has given place to an aspect at once passionate and austere. Here is the image of the woman who wrote:
>
> My heart goes singing after swallows flown
> On sometime summer's unreturning track.[30]

> From the old-fashioned garden below, Christina was often seen standing in front of the little four-cornered window which, Arthur Hughes tells us, 'exactly framed her'. Her habitual position was to lean forward, 'elbows on the sill, hands supporting her face', and she could be seen for hours 'meditating and composing'.
>
> But she could see as well as be seen. Her room commanded a view of the garden with its sundial, moss-covered stone benches, and lattice arbours overarched by roses, of the dark leafy depths of the glen, of Girvan stretching out into the distance, and further, beyond the town, the sea and Ailsa Craig.[31]

> In spite of these occupations, however, much of her time was spent alone in her room, the topmost one in the tower, and originally known as 'the ladies' bower'. From its windows she could see the distant sea and the rocks of Ailsa Craig. She would stand for hours on end, her elbows on the window-sill, her chin cupped in her hands, looking out over the garden and the more distant landscape, 'meditating and composing'.[32]

> Alice told Arthur Hughes that it [Rossetti's room at Penkill] had a 'little four-cornered window... which commanded a view over an old fashioned garden...' where Christina stood leaning on the sill for hours at a time 'meditating and composing'. Or so Alice Boyd thought. It was more than likely that Cayley was the object of her thoughts. At Penkill she wrote another haunting, allusive lyric.[33]

The repetition of a 'little four-cornered window' at which Rossetti was to be seen is highly suggestive of the frame of a portrait, as if Rossetti was herself a living 'framed' picture,[34] for she both looks out and is seen. The tropic construction that yokes representation *of* 'Woman' and the sign for representation *as* 'Woman' becomes also in these descriptions part of the contemporary discourse of the creative female as both object and subject, as both surveyed and spectating. Both Bell and Stuart follow their description of Rossetti at the turret window with a reference to D.G. Rossetti's 1866 drawing of his sister to provide an index to how she actually appeared at the window. As Cherry and Pollock have shown with reference to Elizabeth Siddal, representations of Pre-Raphaelite women cannot be taken as simple reflections of their appearance. Such a myth of the accuracy of Pre-Raphaelite representation does, however, prevail in the biographies and was instigated principally by W.M. Rossetti's memoir in the posthumous edition of his sister's *Poetical Works* where he explains the extent of the likeness of each portrait of Rossetti to the model. Significantly W.M. Rossetti declares the 1866 coloured chalk drawing (which Bell and Stuart refer to) to be the best of all the portraits:

> This is a beautiful drawing, showing a face very chaste in outline, and distinguished in expression; it would be hard for any likeness to be more exact. I have seen it stated somewhere (and I believe it à propos of this very drawing) that one cannot trust Rossetti's likenesses, as he always idealised. Few statements could be more untruthful. Certainly he aimed – and he succeeded – at bringing out the beauty and the fine

> expression of a face, rather than its more commonplace and superficial aspect; but his likenesses are, with casual exceptions, very strict transcriptions of the fact.[35]

To confuse actual appearance and representation, sign and signified, at the very site where Christina Rossetti watches and is herself watched suggests the process by which the iconic image of Rossetti is mistaken for that which it represents. To present Rossetti at a window in an act of composition and contemplation is also to involve her poetics in the trope of representation, for poetry here becomes an act of perceptual cognition, a reflex of sight. The biographies compound this trope by giving a description of the view that Rossetti would have seen.

Interestingly, contemporary commentators claim that her poetry describes an identifiable locale.[36] Edmund Gosse writes:

> Unless I make a great mistake, she has scarcely visited Italy, and in her poetry the landscape and the observation of Nature are not only English, they are so thoroughly local that I doubt whether there is one touch in them all which proves her to have strayed more than fifty miles from London in any direction.[37]

Arthur Symons declares that her style is 'sincerity as the servant of a finely touched and exceptionally *seeing* nature'.[38] Bell also quotes W.M. Rossetti's analysis of his sister's poetics: 'there is no poet with a more marked instinct for fusing the thought into the image, and the image into the thought: the fact is always to her emotional, not merely positive, and the emotion clothed in a sensible shape, not merely abstract' (p. 328). We are presented with a poetess whose work is believed to constitute a direct collapsing of thought into image, perception into poetry. What Lynne Pearce terms the Victorian anxiety over the 'slipperiness' of signification[39], or the difficulty of fixing sign to signified, manifests itself as a sequence of mirrorings of life into art and of sight into poetry.

The object of the gaze can, of course, gaze back. Thus, while Christina Rossetti at the window is a representation and a sign for the process of representation, her own subjectivity is potentially recuperated through her own framed look out of the window. But accounts of her gaze emphasise its passivity, its direct collapsing of what is viewed with the viewer. Lacan defines the gaze as an excess of seeing, as desire and not just a perceptual mode. To the subject (defined as that which is capable of being seen and shown), the possibility of being seen has primacy over the recognition that a reciprocal gaze is possible. Thus, the potential for subjectivity emerges as only a trace: this is apparent in the suggestion that Rossetti's gaze (delimited already within the aesthetics of biographical representation) is secondary to and predicated on the spectacle of viewing her.[40] Despite being figured as looking out of a window in this paradigmatic biographical anecdote, her agency is spectacularly diminished.

Histrionics

Over an analysis of the Victorian construction of the feminine subject always falls the shadow of the Lady of Shalott, reformed by the Pre-Raphaelites into their own parable for feminine transgression: an attempt to reinstate displaced subjectivity is an attempt that ends in death.[41] Rather than being a critical dead-end, however, this topos of death is highly pertinent to an interrogation of the representations of Christina Rossetti: death as both a literal threat (Rossetti as an almost constant invalid from her adolescence, positioning her literally as in-valid) and figural (death as non-existence, a no-place from which the subject of Rossetti's poetry is predominantly positioned).

The highly ambivalent subject position of the trope Christina Rossetti emerges from the concept of 'Rossetti' as both a sign of the representation of 'Woman' and a sign for that signification process itself. This self-reflexive doubleness blurs the distinction between the socio-economic and semiotic functions of the trope, and the resultant indeterminacy becomes one of the signifieds of the sign. 'Woman' may thus turn into the subject and producer of this operation, thereby blurring the difference between active and passive.[42] The dualism of Rossetti as an historical personage and as a sign for representation emerges in the depiction of Rossetti as a living saint, as dead before her death; thus the subject is always already posthumous and conceptually disembodied.[43] The dichotomy is apparent in the descriptions of her appearance, which posit her as both 'real'/historical and outmoded (or always outmoded and thus ahistorical). There is a widespread biographical interest in her unfashionable appearance (and thus non-contemporary, not of her time and therefore situated outside of her historical context), and in her illnesses which are inscribed in the text to re-figure Rossetti as trope, to present her as literally equivalent to the subject position of death that the trope occupies. Emphasis is placed upon her manner of dressing, particularly in her later years when she was heralded as a virginal suffering saint. Max Beerbohm's cartoon wittily presents the ambivalence of

Rossetti as a Pre-Raphaelite heroine and as an old-fashioned plain dresser (Plate 2). Rossetti, dressed in black, is remonstrated with by D.G. Rossetti for her dowdiness, and he offers other, more fashionable material, declaring: 'What *is* the use, Christina, of having a heart like a singing bird and a water-shoot and all the rest of it, if you insist on getting yourself up like a pew-opener.'[44] She is distinctive by virtue of her inappropriate dress (her face could be that of any female, whereas D.G. Rossetti is clearly identifiable) – if she was to wear the cloth he offers, she would no longer be identifiable as Christina Rossetti. Katherine Tynan Hinkson tells how she was initially disappointed with Rossetti's appearance:

> I remember that it was something of a shock to me to receive at my first sight of Christina an impression of short-petticoated sturdiness. [...] Doubtless it was a mortification of the flesh or the spirit to wear, as she did, thick boots and short rough grey skirts. As far as they could they made her almost ugly, for the spiritual face, with the heavy-lidded eyes, had nothing to do with those garments fit for a ten-mile walk over ploughed fields. [...] Something of a death-in-life, it seemed to the girl coming in from the outside, to be shut up in an ill-lit house in Torrington Square, with two or three old ladies getting up their centuries. (p. 186)

Similarly, Gosse complains about a 'absence of style' in Rossetti's dress which distresses him. Her ignorance of fashion is linked with her apparent ignorance of the outside world: 'common topics of the day appeared entirely unknown to her' (p. 158). And yet her removal from the world transforms her into a formidable 'Sibyl whom no one had the audacity to approach' in a noisy drawing-room (p. 158).

William Sharp recounts the story of his first encounter with Rossetti during his visit to the home of friends. As he sat in the twilight he was conscious of a laughing, musical voice which attested to the right to prefer London to the countryside. A servant entered announcing the arrival of a guest and bearing a light, and the woman who had just spoken swiftly and mysteriously covered her face with a veil and left (pp. 736–8). The reclusiveness and preference for the anonymity of twilight is explained in Rossetti's correspondence as the result of Graves' disease, which dramatically altered her appearance. Most noticeable was a darkening of the skin and protruding eyes along with other distressing unseen symptoms.[45] Rather than representing her as disfigured, however, the change in appearance is taken by biographers and commentators to signify spiritual beauty in suffering. Sensitivity to her symptoms would doubtless explain the use of the veil, but it also becomes part of the enigma of Rossetti as an idealised feminine figure in a play between what is seen and what is elusively covered up. Rossetti belongs comfortably to the twilight and must veil the visual signs of her illness. In physical suffering she is represented as supremely non-physical. The descriptions of her debilitating illness, and her own documented acute awareness of and attempts to conceal it, enact the nineteenth-century aporia of illness as the superlative sign of the feminine and illness as a sign of spiritual malaise.

Other references to Rossetti's appearance emphasise her unfashionable plain dress (which W.M. Rossetti comments was a family tradition),[46] the link between her clothes and separation from the outside world (which Hinkson aptly terms 'death-in-life'), and the correlation of her dress with domestic and pious passivity. All serve to construct Rossetti as a saint – dehistoricised, decontextualised – and, as a saint that is alive yet also posthumous, to posit her intrinsic identification with death.[47] Roland Barthes in 'The Iconography of the Abbé Pierre', declares: 'the saint is first and foremost a being without formal context; the idea of fashion is antipathetic to the idea of sainthood'. He comments upon the ambivalent haircut of the Abbé Pierre, which seems to be neutral, unfashionable, 'a sort of zero degree of haircut', but concludes that 'neutrality ends up by functioning as the *sign* of neutrality, and if you really wished to go unnoticed, you would be back where you started'.[48] An attempt to exempt oneself from fashion becomes a statement about fashion. For representations of Christina Rossetti, her unfashionable clothes do not simply decontextualise her but also place her relative to her context and become a statement about her difference, her spirituality, her asexuality and saintliness; her dress becomes an excessive sign, one that theatricises her, renders her histrionic. This ambiguous attempt to decontextualise is also true of depictions of Rossetti as an invalid, which seem to be a figure for the process whereby she is immobilised, fixed semantically and socio-historically as an identity: reclusive poetess, devoted daughter, pious spinster. The essence of feminine purity is couched ahistorically, beyond outside influences, and the feminine identity of Rossetti is constructed in terms of the fallacy that it transcends history.[49]

The biographical hysterical discourse insists on the body as a site of signification, and the body as physical entity and as presence is thus represented as a literal or actual portrayal in order to disembody Rossetti conceptually. Emphasis upon her literalness is ironic, for the inclusion of details supposedly attesting to her historical identity only serves to dehistoricise. It is significant that the literal serves a special purpose. Comments upon Rossetti's thought processes – her analysis of the Scriptures, her non-intellectual faith, her spontaneous and 'natural' poetry – all serve to construct her thought as literal, feminine, and non-participatory in masculine literary tradition and masculine symbolism.[50] In contrast, Elizabeth Barrett Browning's public and political poetry was interpreted by contemporaries as a transgression of the scope of women's poetry, and she was denounced by some as a hysteric and as masculine.[51] The biographies widely claim Rossetti's literalness in her interpretation of the Scriptures[52] and circulate the anecdote of how she disapproved of cremation because of her literal notion of the Resurrection.[53] They also recount the anecdote given in Rossetti's *Time Flies* of how her sister Maria would not visit the Mummy Room at the British Museum because 'it would be very unseemly if the corpses had to put on immortality under the gaze of mere sightseers'.[54]

The significance of assigning the literal as inherent to femininity is explored by Lacan. The mother is connected, in Lacanian semiotics, to the literal and the absent referent: both the feminine and the literal in language are always located elsewhere and represented in terms of displacement. Thus to conceptualise literality as inherent to femininity becomes part of the tropic construction of 'Woman' as the sign for representation itself, and 'Woman' in this way figures the subject displaced in the aesthetic into a position which is constantly fading (Lacan's *aphanisis*).[55] To construct Christina Rossetti's mode of thought and poetry as non-participatory in a dominant masculine signification process and her physical entity as actual and literal is to reposition her as already posthumous: a fading and elusive presence-in-absence. There is, of course, an irony: Victorian biographies are conventionally written after the subject's death, but Christina Rossetti's death is the crescendo of her representations.

The complex and paradoxical nature of such representations is suggested by Mackenzie Bell's account of Rossetti's deathbed, in which the literal and the abstract become confused.[56] Bell narrates how he arrived one afternoon at 30 Torrington Square to find that Rossetti had died earlier that day. He is told of the events of her last hours and is shown upstairs to see the body:

> As I entered what had formerly been Christina's drawing room I thought how unchanged yet how changed was the room. All the

> pictures, and well-nigh all the pieces of furniture, even to the miscellaneous articles which stood usually on the large drawing-room table, were in the same places as I had been in the habit of observing them. This, paradoxical as it may seem at first sight to say so, added vastly to the sense of impressiveness, just as the contrast between the commonplace – almost the prosaic – details and the supernatural element indissolubly enlinked with the poem, adds to the impressiveness of that lyric by Christina which her brother Gabriel named for her 'At Home'. (pp. 174–5)

When Bell enters Rossetti's home after her death he describes in that feminine and (literally) private sphere a paradoxical emotion that exposes the uncanniness of the biographical feminine subject. He aligns the strangeness of the house – 'changed and yet unchanged' – with the *unheimlich* juxtaposition of the commonplace and the supernatural in 'At Home', and in this way transposes Rossetti's text onto his own in a rhetorical move that abducts his subject.[57] The repetition of 'impressiveness' recalls Freud's technique in the treatment of the clinical disease, whereby the hysteric was pressed – and literally pressed on the forehead – in order to overcome the block in articulation that constitutes the malaise.[58] Here, the biographical subject's intrinsic identification with death is re-enacted *at* the subject's death. This critical scene of recognition puts pressure on the discourse and exposes the aporia of the posthumous subject within representational axioms and also the subject's uncanny otherness from Bell, which he counters by abducting the subject through her text.

The site of abduction is, aptly, also accomplished through citation of D.G. Rossetti's artistic appropriation of his sister's poem, which he revised for publication in *Goblin Market and Other Poems* (1862) by changing the title from 'After the Pic-nic', a re-location of the poem to an interior, domestic space.[59] Bell then continues to describe the room and again uses D.G. Rossetti as a medium for articulating and appropriating the subject: 'with the sharpening of the perceptive faculties that comes to us sometimes, at moments like these, I thought I had never before seen Dante Gabriel's large chalk drawing of his sister – that drawn in 1866 – appear so lovely' (p. 175). He then describes the face:

> I saw that, though slightly emaciated, it was not greatly changed since the last time I had beheld it in life. Perhaps I was hardly so much struck with the breadth of her brow – I mean in regard to its indication of intellectual qualities – as I had been often when

> conversing with her, but on the other hand I was struck more than ever before both by the clear manifestation of the more womanly qualities and by the strength of purpose shown in the lips. [...] My spirit was moved by the contrast I felt between the holy – almost the saintly atmosphere of the house and its common-place surroundings. (p. 175)

The juxtaposition of spiritual and prosaic and the collapsing of poetry and portrait into life which dramatise and negotiate the rhetorical impasse, suggests that death itself signifies Christina Rossetti's feminine biographical subject position.

Rossetti's face in death, in fact, is acknowledged as the 'true' representation and a figure for feminine purity. As the epitome of absence, the corpse of Rossetti is the ultimate trope for displaced subjectivity and for a disembodied historical personage. Under the guise of an authoritative chronicle, Bell's account, prompted by W.M. Rossetti and repeated through the genealogy of Rossetti biographies, subscribes to cultural notions of femininity which insist upon the absence of subjectivity and historical identity, but it nevertheless purports to place Rossetti within the framework of historical reference. In Bell's description of the deathbed scene, the attempted repression of historical identity is epitomised by the inert figure of Rossetti. Other commentators repeat his formulations. Gosse, for example, declares upon her death: 'this great writer, who was also a great saint, passed into the region of her visions' (p. 162). The biographical subject, only precariously inhabiting the world in which it is a female paragon, now comes fully to be that which it has represented – the disembodied, denatured, and ideally feminine.

The inability to obtain an historical purchase on Rossetti suggests an unbreachable gap between the historical personage and the textual subject, and the gap is figured as absence or loss *per se*, or, in other words, the feminine. William E. Epstein argues that *all* biography marks the absence of the subject: 'as an expression of difference, the biographical subject has no metaphysical presence in the ordinary sense; rather, it occupies the epistemological gap between presence and absence, singular and plural, self and other'.[60] Christina Rossetti's superlative position in the representational axioms – specifically, as a Pre-Raphaelite muse, model, and artist in her own right – makes the problematics of her biographical representation more acute. This is not a reason to elide the genre in an analysis of Rossetti's poetry, but in fact it exposes the need to critique the biographical representation as a producer and product of the trope Christina Rossetti which so inhabits our criticism.[61] It is no accident that a sudden upsurge in biographies of Christina Rossetti coincides with the rise of new historicism.[62]

In Chapter 5 I go on to suggest that the scopic is the site at which Rossetti herself contests the aesthetic which so deanimates and dramatises the feminine. In representations of Rossetti the unknowable nature of the historical subject is most forcefully brought home, as Bell's account of Rossetti's deathbed suggests, in visual apprehensions. In fact, visual representations of Rossetti were marketed in such a way as to control the circulation of her image and also to contain the unknowable nature of the 'Rossetti' subject.[63] In 1877, aged 47, D.G. Rossetti depicted his sister in a chalk drawing which reproduces the familiar Pre-Raphaelite iconography (see Plate 3). In the same year, Christina Rossetti had a studio photograph taken (Plate 4), which, W. M. Rossetti reports, she 'was accustomed to call "the idiot", and indeed it is sufficiently vacant-looking'.[64] I would not claim, as W.M. Rossetti does with reference to an 1856 photograph, that this medium gives us unproblematical access to how Rossetti actually looked, by virtue of 'the irrefutable evidence of the sun'.[65] The difference between the two representations suggests, however, how a particular image of Christina Rossetti has been circulated as a Pre-Raphaelite icon in contrast to the photograph, not reproduced in biographies until fairly recently, although Bell claims in his biography that it is well known through reproduction (p. 53).[66] Of the portrait, W.M. Rossetti notes: 'anything more close than the drooped head to the features and the sentiment of my sister's face in her advanced years [...] cannot well be imagined' (*PW: CR* p. lxv). Of the photograph, however, Bell remarks that there is 'considerable fidelity to external fact [...] but in it her soul's beauty, so to speak, is altogether lacking' (p. 53).[67] In other words, Christina Rossetti's essence, or her tropic value, exceeds photographic legibility. One could say the same for her biographical representations: although the subject is deanimated, her presence-in-absence continues to haunt critical readings of her work, much like the posthumous speaker in 'At Home' who is so paradigmatic for biographers, and who cannot resist returning to the scene of her absence, 'sad / To stay and yet to part how loth' (Crump 1: 28).

4

Defining the Feminine Subject: Fraternal Revisions I

Tracing the subject

In a copy of *Goblin Market*, dated December 7 1893, Christina Rossetti notes her obligation to D.G. Rossetti for his assistance with *Goblin Market and Other Poems* and *The Prince's Progress and Other Poems*: 'and here I like to acknowledge the general indebtedness of my first and second volumes to his suggestive wit and revising hand' (Crump 1: 234).[1] In an unpublished letter five years earlier, she insisted: 'in poetics my elder brother was my acute and most helpful critic'.[2] The extent of D.G. Rossetti's revisions to his sister's manuscripts is now fully apparent with Rebecca Crump's recently completed variorum edition of the poems. Christina Rossetti's poetry has come down to us as a series of textual ellipses, for the canon conceals significant deletion of stanzas and changes to titles and has been enshrined by W.M. Rossetti's posthumous 1904 edition.[3] On occasion these can be directly attributed to D.G. Rossetti, either by his handwriting on the manuscript or by cross-referencing a manuscript change with suggestions made in correspondence with his sister; for others there is indirect evidence of his amendments where changes correspond to the pattern of his identifiable alterations. The configuration of D.G. Rossetti's revisions to the first two volumes, and to the second edition of *Goblin Market* (1865), suggests the imposition of an aesthetic upon Christina Rossetti's work and the revised poetry consequently is predicated on his definition of the feminine.[4]

The revisions are crucial to an understanding of Rossetti's relation to the Pre-Raphaelite Brotherhood and in particular her relation to the work of her brother, for they assign to (or, to use a phrase of D.G. Rossetti's, 'superscribe' upon) her work the aesthetic of the feminine

which, in turn, obscures and diminishes the poetry's own exploration of and responses to this dominant Victorian patriarchal discourse.[5] In fact, the revisions dramatise Rossetti's entrenchment within the representational system, for they demonstrate the various ideological pressures that constitute the poetic subject: both the power relations behind the production of the poetry and the manoeuvring of the subject within those relations. Rossetti's aesthetic and artistic affinity with the Pre-Raphaelites has been extensively documented but there has been no analysis to date of the patterns of D.G. Rossetti's alterations to her poetry.[6]

Nineteenth-century ideologies of female poetic creativity assume the act of writing is spontaneous, natural, immediate. William Michael Rossetti, in his 'Memoir' of his sister, declares:

> her habits of composition were entirely of the casual and spontaneous kind, from her earliest to her latest years. If something came into her head which she found suggestive of verse, she put it into verse. It came to her (I take it) very easily, without meditating on a possible subject, and without her making any great difference in the first form of the verses which embodied it.[7]

Although he concedes that she sometimes made small changes 'with a view to right and fine detail of execution', he immediately reiterates the spontaneity of her art: 'if the thing did not present itself before her, as something craving a vesture of verse at her hands, she did not write at all'. Furthermore, her poems were immediately circulated amongst the family in her 'impeccably neat' manuscript notebook – into which, presumably, the first and final perfect draft was inscribed – although, he assures us, the circulation was not immodest display nor an invitation for 'help, counsel, or co-operation' (p. lxix). Late nineteenth-century commentators on her poetry make similar claims. For Alice Meynell, the poetry conceals the process of composition, which she terms 'the unapparent history of a poem'. She argues '[Christina Rossetti] has no unhandsome secrets of composition, or difficulties of attainment' and 'all she touches is fine poetic material'.[8] Paul Elmer More's review of the *Complete Poetical Works* emphasises Rossetti's passivity in the use of her poetic powers which, he continues, 'makes her to me the purest expression in English of the feminine genius'.[9] For Edward Boyle, writing three decades into the twentieth-century, 'the probability is that her poems were written merely because she felt impelled to write them. There was no underlying purpose but merely a subconscious instinct'.[10]

Lootens comments that, in accounts of her unconscious artistry, 'Rossetti is to some extent lost.'[11] It would seem, then, that an exploration of Christina Rossetti's process of writing would uncover the mechanics of its production, the materiality of her poems, and dispel the mythology surrounded her 'artless art', as Dante Gabriel termed it.[12] I do not offer this contextual recovery, however, as a paradigmatic new historicist voicing of the silenced mechanics of literary production. As other chapters demonstrate, one of the potential dangers of revisionary historicist readings is to align the text to a stable coherent context, in the assumption that each illuminates, determines, and even constitutes the other. This betrays the same rhetorical tendency as that of nineteenth-century autobiographical readings of women's poetry, which, in a self-sustaining circularity, produce the life as evidence for textual interpretation and the text as evidence for biography. Rossetti's collusion with her brother's alterations offers a paradigm for reading contextual information, for it suggests a poetic subject that desires to elude the text altogether in an anti-literary urge towards self-deletion.

This impossible desire to re-locate the subject outside of the text produces poetry that oscillates uncannily between presence and absence and between affirmation and denial of the feminine aesthetic, just as the fact of revisions and power relations behind the textual production do not merely inscribe D.G. Rossetti's signature onto the text of a poetic subject that has already become less than a subject. This does not propose an abandonment of new historicist interpretations, which have so dominated Rossetti studies, but a more sophisticated and self-conscious understanding of the way in which context signifies in a text.

Andrew and Catherine Belsey usefully discuss feminine subjectivity within Pre-Raphaelite aesthetics and its relation to Christina Rossetti's poetry. They describe a 'double lack' endowed by patriarchy upon unmarried women, 'the double displacement, the double uncertainty of a woman's hold on subjectivity in a world where women were barely subjects', which penetrates Rossetti's poetry to the effect that she 'seeks instead to repudiate subjectivity itself, to be less than an object'.[13] The trace of the feminine as subject is, however, necessarily always present:

> If it is the inability of the subject to be fully present to itself that generates desire, the double displacement of women from the symbolic order, their construction as doubly lacking, has the effect of reinforcing their desire. But if desire is ultimately the desire for presence, to be the thing you speak of, then patriarchy itself, precisely by withholding subjectivity from women, in practice impels them

> towards it. Resistance is inseparable from the patriarchy which forbids it. (p. 46)

D.G. Rossetti's aesthetics position the feminine as less than a subject, but also inscribe, within such a displacement, the feminine subject as a trace and fully present subjectivity as a female desire. His representation of female figures at times employs a mirror to play with the figure as both subject and object. In 'Body's Beauty', from the *House of Life* sonnet sequence, Lilith (Eve's precursor and the primordial woman) is 'subtly of herself contemplative' and, it is implied, this self-reflection both attracts and destroys male onlookers, for it, 'Draws men to watch the bright web she can weave, / Till heart and body and life are in its hold.'[14] In the corresponding painting *Lady Lilith*, however, the woman's hand glass is held so as to conceal this dangerous image; Lilith's self-contemplation and possession of her own mirror-image is presented so that the sign of her status as a subject is repressed.[15] J. Hillis Miller sees the projected mirrorings of the male gazer upon female object, of the female upon herself, of text upon painting, and of poetic tradition upon poem as a series of mismatchings, so that 'the mirrored image undoes what seeks its image there'.[16] Within this series of reflection and distortion, the mirror-image of a woman is figured as a false sign of her presence, a misrepresentation. This is a symptom of the male gazer's anxiety, intensified when the woman is engaged in self-contemplation, for it suggests that the woman is in possession of her own image and is independent from masculine perception. Hillis Miller asks (although with an unfortunate critical complicity: he does not speculate on the consequence of a female viewing the other gazing into a mirror): 'why is it that when we men contemplate not ourselves in the mirror but our incongruous other self, a desirable woman contemplating herself, our own integrity is mutilated, destroyed?' (p. 334). To D.G. Rossetti, this seeming independence, the woman's possession of her own image, is, by implication, an assertion of her status as an autonomous subject and a challenge to the masculine creator. In 'Jenny' there is a telling passage in which the speaker defensively positions the prostitute's mirror image as firmly relative to his own perception and transcription of that image:

> And yonder your fair face I see
> Reflected lying on my knee,
> Where teems with first foreshadowings
> Your pier-glass scrawled with diamond rings.
>
> (ll. 321–24)

A description of her mirror image is not given, but we have instead the suggestion of its mysterious distortion by virtue of the scrawl 'superscribed' upon the glass.[17] The image of Jenny is depicted as an adjunct of the speaker and is overlapped by the text upon the mirror.[18]

The secret of the mirror's various (mis)matchings of the subject and its reflection is, J. Hillis Miller argues, that there is no secret, that there is instead a sign of loss behind images of difference (pp. 336–7). The mirror does, however, hold an unarticulated and unrepresentable secret, an intimation of the 'double lack': that of the woman as subject.

Revising hands

The feminine subject has a precarious position, subordinated to masculine creativity within Pre-Raphaelite discourse and also positioned beyond that discourse, repudiated and also inhabiting the text as a trace or fleeting presence. It is this delicate and provisional position that is unsettled by D.G. Rossetti's revisions of his sister's poetry. In his revisions and suggested revisions, D.G. Rossetti attempts to mould Christina Rossetti's literary persona and poetry to his requirements in an effort to redefine her poetic form, style, metre and subject matter. Ultimately, it is the signature of the poetry that is in question, for the revisions disclose that the poetry always/already exists in an afterlife that divorces it from authorial origins.

This is apparent in 'Seeking rest', which first appeared in W.M. Rossetti's 1896 edition as a poem in five stanzas.[19] Crump's textual notes indicate that the original version numbered eleven stanzas and that the revisions were almost certainly D.G. Rossetti's. The first four stanzas are deleted after which is written 'Begin here', in, according to Crump, 'what appears to be Dante Gabriel Rossetti's hand' (Crump 3: 429). Two further stanzas are deleted, that following line twelve, and the last stanza. As W. David Shaw puts it, the final version seeks 'the greater objectivity of the ballad' in its reduction of the poem into a dialogue between the speaker's Mother and Sisters, followed by the speaker's own lament.[20] The Mother, in the first stanza of this version, describes the speaker as a child whose 'inward joy' has animated her:

> My Mother said: The child is changed
> That used to be so still;
> All the day long she sings, and sings,
> And seems to think no ill.
>
> (Revised version; Crump 3: 180, ll. 1–4)

The subject has become animated into an inspired lyrical female, but her song is not transcribed. In the following stanza the Sisters urge the speaker to reveal to them the secret which has prompted this change from inertia, but a revelation is not forthcoming. Succeeding this is another transformation, again indicated by the Mother, from joy to sorrow:

> My Mother says: What ails the child
>   Lately so blythe of cheer?
> Art sick or sorry? nay, it is
>   The Winter of the year.
>
> (Revised version; ll. 13–16)

The images of illness are pertinent, for the speaker – who enters the poem only in the last stanza – describes herself, in a continuation of the winter metaphor, as solitary, silent, and forever in 'the Winter of the year':

> My Spring will never come again;
>   My pretty flowers have blown
> For the last time; I can but sit
>   And think and weep alone.
>
> (Revised version; ll. 27–30)

Thus the revised poem ends in a reification of the speaker's total surrender to the unarticulated secret. This version positions the poem as lyrical-confessional, but in this mode the speaker is expelled in a catalogue of elisions – the Mother's relation of the speaker's song of joy, the speaker's exclusion from the dialogue between the Mother and Sisters, the mysterious withheld secret. The poem culminates with a sense of loss: 'I can but sit / And think and weep alone'. What had once caused her to sing now renders her a figure for death-in-life; the speaker is portrayed as an inspired lyrical female but in the non-specific and impersonal balladic framework her song is silenced. The poem thus inscribes the conventional role of a poetess while also deleting her song. Further, throughout the simple balladic structure of the final version the speaker is objectified as merely a function of the missing referent which silences and alienates her. As Shaw asserts, balladic objectification has been attained, but it is at the hand of D.G. Rossetti.

The original poem may be reconstructed from Crump's textual notes (Crump 3: 429). It is far more complex and unsettling than the revised poem.[21] The deleted stanzas are part of a fragmented and disjunctive first person narrative in which, it is suggested, the secret has a wholly interior existence:

> There was a hope I cherished once,
> A longing, a vain dream:
> I dreamed it when I thought that men
> And things were what they seem.

A lost belief in the literal seems implied here, in the truth of 'seemings', in a correspondence between signifier and signified, 'When the clouds had no gloom for me, / No chill the pale moon-beam'. Such a belief allows the joy of the secret to be experienced passively, 'I never questioned my own heart'. The secret is portrayed as further entrenched in the heart than is suggested by the final version, and so further removed from identification:

> But evermore I kept my joy
> Hidden in mine own heart; –
> I could not show them my life's life: –
> So now I bear the smart
> Of disappointment; and I strive
> To hide it with vain art.

This stanza was originally inserted after the Sisters' first speech as part of the transition between the speaker's joy and sorrow, but the transition is ambiguous. The 'So' in the fourth line may imply that the consequence of interiorising the secret is the speaker's sorrow, or that the sorrow itself must be hidden because the joy was not shared. Such ambiguities are typical of the fragmented narrative that unsettles the reader's sense of the figurative, for nouns such as Mother, Sister, Winter and Spring seem to oscillate between literal and figurative denotations. But it is the secretive heart that is most suggestive of this linguistic ambiguity.

As in 'L.E.L.' (which D.G. Rossetti also revised), the heart is again given as the locale of the secret, a locale whose secret must 'with vain art' be concealed.[22] The secret is, however, also 'my life's life': vague, reflexive, circular, and enigmatic.[23] Paradoxically, we are invited to define that which is portrayed as beyond definition. The invitation to decode the 'vain art' is also to entice a lyric-confession reading and so to see the secret as an actual experience or event. The very opacity of 'my life's

life', however, suggests the missing referent is non-experiential. In the deleted stanzas of 'Seeking rest', the Mother becomes Mother Earth, in which the speaker longs to reside and thus transpose the heart's secret to the grave, in an echo of Chaucer's Pardoner: 'She knocked at the Earth's greeny door: / O Mother, let me in'. The vague 'greeny door' and the Earth as Mother suggests a wish to further displace the subject into a vague and liminal place, a non-experiential realm. The heart is a suggestive locale that prefigures this realm, for it is both an actual 'place' and traditionally a site for femininity and emotion. It is also depicted as the place of a semantic secret: the missing referent, the textual ellipsis which is protected, by virtue of its very absence, against objectification. Further, the heart is the place of a linguistic secret, for it implies that the withheld referent is beyond articulation: it is a 'vain dream', a 'vision', a 'secret store / Of unimagined bliss'.

Angela Leighton's *Victorian Women Poets: Writing Against the Heart* analyses the metaphor of the heart as a product of the relation between female creativity and cultural and aesthetic constructs which delimit that creativity: 'Victorian women's poetry [...] grows out of a struggle with and against a highly moralised celebration of women's sensibility. [...] The attempt [is] to overcome that dissociation by writing not from, but against the heart.'[24] Leighton sees the implications of emotional self-betrayal as also, 'the story of imaginative creation, which is, very often for Victorian woman, a death story, as well as the story of fantasy, invention, imitation, dream' (p. 6). Following from Jerome McGann's statement that Rossetti 'employs the symbol of the personal secret as a sign of the presence of individuality', Leighton suggests that the secret, as an intimation of individuality, either may or may not be disclosed by Rossetti for it implies in the poem 'a self fully in control of its own game'.[25] In the full version of 'Seeking rest' the heart's secret is the sign whose signified is 'my life's life', which may be translated as a trope for the displaced feminine subject, depicted as one move away from the experiential and estranged from the text. It is not a party to what Leighton terms 'a world of sceptically disordered moral and linguistic reference' (p. 3). Its very displacement from the text, however, implies that it can never be fully present and, rather than being a function of the poet's will, the secret can never be wholly disclosed. For all the speaker's seeming coquetry, the secret – as a sign whose signified is feminine subjectivity – never fully inhabits the text. The suggestion that the withheld secret denotes the feminine subject is also implicit in the parodic self-reflexivity of 'Winter: My Secret' (Crump 1: 47) and, as in 'Seeking rest', the speaker plays with the possibility of disclosure: 'I tell my secret? No indeed, not I:/Perhaps some day, who knows?' (ll. 1–2).

As we have seen in the Introduction, the conditions upon which the speaker may reveal the secret are endlessly modified and withdrawn:

> Perhaps some languid summer day,
> When drowsy birds sing less and less,
> And golden fruit is ripening to excess,
> If there's not too much sun nor too much cloud,
> And the warm wind is neither still nor loud,
> Perhaps my secret I may say,
> Or you may guess.
>
> (ll. 28–34)

The emphasis is constantly upon the conditional nature of the secret and the speaker's possession of the (absent) referent: 'Only, my secret's mine, and I won't tell' (l. 6), 'Suppose there is no secret after all, / But only just my fun' (ll. 8–9). The very existence of the secret is in question and, as a trope for the feminine subject, the secret is neither fully present in the text nor wholly absent.

The traditional balladic and lyric-confessional framework of the revised version of 'Seeking rest' arouses conventional expectations that a female poet directly transcribes personal experience. The sentimental tradition, within which Rossetti works, specifies this experience as failed love. Despite the suggestion in the original version of 'Seeking rest' that the secret is non-experiential, in nineteenth- and early twentieth-century critiques the missing referent in the revised poem is traditionally read as an actual event in Rossetti's life, the concealment of her cherished love for James Collinson.[26] The sign of the personal secret located in the heart is taken to signify love relations which, in turn, signify a representation of an actual event. Upon Rossetti's poetry is thus 'superscribed' a lyric confession. W.M. Rossetti, in his notes to the 1904 edition, is everywhere at pains to give the poetry a relation to an actual event. He categorises the poems as 'Personal Experiences and Emotions' and, when the evidence seems to be against assigning biographical data to a poem, W.M. Rossetti suggests his knowledge may not be comprehensive. For example, of 'A Birthday', he writes,

> It is, of course, possible to infer that the *Birthday* is a mere piece of poetic composition, not testifying to any corresponding emotion of its author at the time; but I am hardly prepared to think that.[27]

Furthermore, D.G. Rossetti's revisions to the first two volumes in general attempt to transpose his sister's poetry into the realm of the experientially knowable. In particular, his identifiable title changes impose a suggestion of stasis and place where, in the original, the subject is stressed. The titles 'After the Pic-nic', 'A Peep at the Goblins', and 'A Yawn'[28] – all indicative of the presence of a subject – become at his hand, respectively, 'At Home' (Crump 1: 238),[29] 'Goblin Market' (Crump 1: 234), and 'By the Sea' (Crump 1: 298). The subject has thus become an object in relation to something else. Similar changes (although there is no direct evidence that they were all at her brother's instigation) are made to 'Something Like Truth', 'A fight over the body of Homer', and 'Nonsense', which become 'Sleep at Sea' (Crump 1: 262), 'The Lowest Room' (Crump 1: 301), and 'Winter: My Secret' (Crump 1: 247), all of which transfer the subject in the title to an actual locale. Paradigmatic of the subject's exclusion from the titles is another title change suggestive of D.G. Rossetti's influence, but for which no direct evidence exists: 'What happened to me' is changed to 'Shut Out' (Crump 1: 252). Of 'Something Like Truth', D.G. Rossetti writes:

> Maria showed me the other day two poems of yours which are among the best you have written for some time: only the title of one – *Something like Truth* – seems 'very like a whale'. What does it mean? The latter verses of this are most excellent; but some, which I remember vaguely, about 'dreaming of a lifelong ill' (etc. etc. *ad libitum*), smack rather of the old shop. I wish you would try rendering either of narrative or sentiment from real abundant Nature, which presents much more variety, even in any one of its phases, than all such 'dreamings'.[30]

The advice is to locate the poem in the knowable, in the natural, and to omit imaginative 'dreamings'. The subject is thus to be erased and replaced by reflections of 'real abundant Nature'. To 'shut out' the subject is to replace it with an feminine figure whose subjectivity is put into question. The aesthetics of the feminine, however, posit the objectified figure as deanimated:

> The construction of masculinity and of the masculine artist is made not only in opposition and in precedence to a feminine body caught in the process of fading, but also in opposition and in precedence to absent femininity, because the feminine figure functions as a sign whose signified is masculine creativity.[31]

While imposing the experiential and the natural, stasis and closure, the manuscript revisions disembody the poetry from its authorial origins. Both the feminine subject in the poetry and the feminine signature of the poetry are removed from the text and become always already posthumous. By imposing closure in his various revisions and deletions, Dante Gabriel Rossetti positions the poetry as inherently posthumous, always and only existing in its afterlife.

Commentators have detailed the revisions to *The Prince's Progress*, for which much of the direct evidence exists in the correspondence between D.G. Rossetti and his sister.[32] D.G. Rossetti advised, cajoled and bullied in his attempt to influence the selection of poetry and its arrangement. The following poems were omitted from *The Prince's Progress* on his advice: 'I will lift up mine eyes unto the hills',[33] 'Tomorrow',[34] 'By the Waters of Babylon', 'Last Night', 'Margery', and 'Three Nuns'.[35] She also requests: 'please don't throw away what pieces you turn out of vol. 2., but kindly preserve them for me'.[36] D.G. Rossetti also supervised the proof reading and oversaw the physical form of the volume (including colour of the cover, the designs and illustrations), and also the negotiations with the publisher.[37] Crump's edition of the poems, however, reveals direct manuscript evidence for D.G. Rossetti's intervention in the earlier *Goblin Market* volume, evidence which is suggestive of the more systematic process of revision in *The Prince's Progress* whereby the manuscripts were either directly altered by him,[38] or his suggested changes implemented. Instances of revision also appear as a change unattributable in the manuscript but for which other suggestions of his influence exist, such as the title 'Goblin Market' which was changed from 'A Peep at the Goblins' and the deletion of the original title of 'At Home'.

The general tendency of these revisions is towards an imposition of a more regular verse form, metre and rhyme. Most spectacular, perhaps, are the alterations to 'L.E.L.', which begins with a misquoted reference to Elizabeth Barrett Browning's poem on her ill-fated precursor, Letitia Landon, 'L.E.L.'s Last Question' (Crump 1: 153, 288). The manuscript has a note of thanks by the author: 'Gabriel fitted the double rhymes as printed, with a brotherly request that I would use them.'[39] The changes to the *Prince's Progress* version have the first and third lines rhyme in every stanza. In the manuscript and the poem's first published version, in *The Victoria Magazine* (May 1863), the poem is not only less regular but is also explicitly associated with a female poetic tradition. Furthermore, *The Victoria Magazine* was an explicitly feminist enterprise, and Rossetti's poem appeared in the first volume and also, as Marsh tells us, she went to the launch party.[40] Indeed, D.G. Rossetti's version compounds the poem's removal from female precursors with the deletion of Barrett Browning's name which was originally alongside the misquotation and Browning was, of course, known for her irregular metrics. In a letter to her brother, Christina Rossetti thanks him for the 'enormous improvement' to 'L.E.L.', but adds 'I am glad you retain my title.'[41] Despite his alterations, the poem retains one explicit link to its poetic heritage. Christina Rossetti's revision of the poem's title, for its first publication, from the original title, 'Spring', reverses the changes of Dante Gabriel, who as we have seen turns titles into identifiable, and often natural, locales.

In his earlier attempts to find a champion for her verse to ensure its publication, D.G. Rossetti approached Ruskin, who famously dismissed 'Goblin Market' as irregular:

> no publisher – I am deeply grieved to know this – would take them, so full are they of quaintness and other offences. Irregular measure (introduced to my great regret, in its chief wilfulness, by Coleridge) is the calamity of modern poetry. [...] [Y]our sister should exercise herself in the severest commonplace of metre until she can write as the public like. Then if she puts in her observation and passion all will become precious. But she must have the Form first.[42]

Despite his disagreement with Ruskin's analysis, D.G. Rossetti's revisions to Christina's manuscripts[43] suggest an attempt to soften what he terms the 'metric jolt', 'screech', her 'queer rhyme' and 'groans'.[44] He forges simpler poetic forms out of more complicated unsettling poems, such as the construction of a ballad from 'Seeking rest'. There are also other examples: the reduction of 'There remaineth therefore a rest' to the simple dirge of 'The Bourne' (see below); 'A Yawn' is turned into a brief description of the sea in 'By the Sea'; and, at his instigation, a dirge is turned into a narrative poem, 'The Prince's Progress'.[45]

D.G. Rossetti disapproved of certain kinds of contemporary women's poetry, especially poetry which encroached upon the masculine public and overtly political sphere, and suggested that such writing was an inappropriate model for Christina Rossetti to follow:

> A real taint, to some extent, of modern vicious style, derived from that same source [Mrs. Browning] – what might be called a falsetto

> muscularity – always seemed to me much too prominent in the long piece called *The Lowest Room*. This I think is now included for the first time, and I am sorry for it. [. . .] Everything in which this tone appears is utterly foreign to your primary impulses. [. . .] If I were you, I would rigidly keep guard on this matter if you write in the future; and ultimately exclude from your writings everything (or almost everything) so tainted.[46]

'The Lowest Room' (Crump 1: 200–7) attempts to formulate a feminine heroic ideal using literary history as a model. Originally entitled 'A fight over the body of Homer', the poem presents two versions of the feminine role. The speaker desires Homeric action, for 'A shame it is our aimless life' (l. 81). Her sister, however, is content with the contemporary definition of a woman's place. D.G. Rossetti's objection seems directed towards the speaker's wish to overturn contemporary feminine roles and the implicit relation such attempts bear to the function and vocation of contemporary women poets. Christina Rossetti wrote to D.G. Rossetti on 13 March 1865:

> *Lowest Room* pray eject if you really think such a course advantageous, though I can't agree with you: still it won't dismay me that you should do so; I am not stung to obstinacy even by the Isa [Craig] and Adelaide [Anne Proctor] taunt in which I acknowledge an element of truth.[47]

Finally in the poem, the wish to revise gender roles is superseded by a desire for the afterlife which will overturn the unsatisfactory hierarchy of the poem's present social time. The speaker is portrayed 20 years later as a spinster, now 'Content to take the lowest place' (l. 271) whilst she also, in typical Rossettian fashion, awaits the Second Coming, 'When all deep secrets shall be shown, / And many last be first' (ll. 279–80). W.M. Rossetti's notes to the poem register surprise at his brother's reading, for he interprets the revisionary metaleptic deferral of perfection in the speaker as 'the final acceptance [. . .] of a subordinate and bedimmed position – [which] is clearly the very reverse of "falsetto muscularity"'.[48]

The radical poetic strategy, whereby aesthetic constructs of the feminine are both included in the poetry and evaded, is suppressed in both brothers' readings of the poem. D.G. Rossetti's wish that his sister avoid the 'modern vicious style', that she omit all stylistic commerce with her contemporary women poets, is part of his wider attempt to re-feminize her poetry and to revise its place within literary and social time in accordance with his ideal of the feminine. His title change to 'Goblin Market' suggests a similar pattern. The original title 'A Peep at the Goblins' was, as Rossetti herself states in a note in a volume of the poems, 'in imitation of my cousin Mrs. Bray's "A Peep at the Pixies"' (Crump 1: 234). The poem in manuscript, as the note also states and as Crump verifies, 'was inscribed to my dear only sister Maria Francesca Rossetti herself long afterwards the author of "A Shadow of Dante"'. There is no evidence that D.G. Rossetti also deleted this dedication, but the erasure of the references to two literary women is significant. The pattern of manuscript changes attributable to her brother suggests that Rossetti's relation to a female literary tradition is at stake.

In another poem subject to multiple revisions and also using for part of its title the keyword 'rest', there are marks made upon the manuscript by Christina, W.M. and D.G. Rossetti, who all indicate their rearrangement of the original. 'There remaineth therefore a rest' is published in *The Prince's Progress and Other Poems* as 'The Bourne'. This version is D.G. Rossetti's, for on the manuscript in his handwriting is written 'Take two stanzas' and he numbers those he wishes to make up his version.[49] W.M. Rossetti also denotes with the letters 'a' to 'e' those stanzas he published in his 1896 and 1904 editions.[50] Finally, we are left with the original version and with the poet's own indication on the manuscript of the two final stanzas she was to publish in *Verses* (1893) as 'There Remaineth therefore a Rest to the People of God' (Crump 3: 226–8, 448). The original poem may be seen as a linguistic attempt to apprehend the subject and to articulate self-autonomy, but such an attempt, the poem suggests, is a necessarily doomed poetic venture within the aesthetic and cultural discourses available to Rossetti. 'There remaineth therefore a rest' begins with an attempt to describe the last resting place: 'Very cool that bed must be / Where our last sleep shall be slept' (ll. 1–2). Starting with a definite locale ('that bed') and a definite event ('our last sleep'), the whole process of the poem is to undo stable and fixed denotations and locales.[51] Social hierarchies are meaningless: 'In the grave will be no space / For the purple of the proud' (ll. 16–17), and 'High and low and rich and poor, / All will fare alike at last' (ll. 26–7). The very place of the grave, 'Underneath the growing grass' (l. 6), becomes vague as boundaries and limits are rendered opaque and elusive. The first seven stanzas slowly lead us into this liminality in which all margins are unstable and dissolve into the dreams of the sleeping soul:

There no laughter shall be heard,
  Nor the heavy sound of sighs;
  Sleep shall seal the aching eyes;
  All the ancient and the wise
There shall utter not a word.

(ll. 31–5)

In the eighth stanza, however, fragments of the material world suddenly enter the text.

Yet it may be we shall hear
  How the mounting skylark sings
  And the bell for matins rings;
  Or perhaps the whisperings
Of white Angels sweet and clear.

(ll. 36–40)

The sounds of the skylark and matin-bell enable the perception of the material to be transfigured into a glimpse of the afterlife for the sleeping soul, which then may witness the angelic voices. The inclusion of the seemingly literal, which allows the afterlife to be perceived, is followed by an increasing misalignment of signifier and signified as words veer towards opaque meanings beyond their capacity.

Sun or moon hath never shone
  In that hidden depth of night;
  But the souls there washed and white
  Are more fair than fairest light
Mortal eye hath looked upon.

(ll. 41–5)

The misalignment is, paradoxically, semantically enabling. Comparatives – 'sun or moon' – and superlatives – 'more fair than fairest light' – struggle to convey this vision of the afterlife which remains unclassifiable and shapeless precisely because it bears no relation to the empirical. The linguistic blockage is a triumph: not only is it a dramatic struggle of representation, not only does it indicate what W. David Shaw terms Rossetti's 'skeptical conviction that meaning is always in excess of anything she can say',[52] but it also suggests how the poetic subject is located beyond the linguistic bounds of the text.

Furthermore, the final stanzas show that such a relocation of the subject rests on the authority of belief, not experience:

Fear and hope and chastening rod
  Urge us on the narrow way:
  Bear we still as best we may
  Heat and burden of the day,
Struggling panting up to God.

(ll. 56–60)

The poetic subject is spiritually transfigured and thus beyond possible articulation. In a seeming anti-literary act, the event is anticipated in which true autonomy will be attained; thus Rossetti turns from poetess to prophetess. By locating subjectivity outside of the text, the text itself is made secondary to its own linguistic aims.

The heavy reliance upon belief over experience, furthermore, deftly evades the trap of the lyric-confessional mode by which much nineteenth-century women's poetry was interpreted. In D.G. Rossetti's version, however, two stanzas are taken from the first portion of the poem which, out of its original context, suggest that the subject is bounded, inert, dead:

There a very little girth
  Can hold round what once the earth
  Seemed too narrow to contain.

('The Bourne', Crump 1: 142, ll. 8–10)

'The Bourne' ends thus with an image of the speaker bounded by death when once life could not contain her. Christina Rossetti's originally radical poetics are thus repositioned into an unresisting equivalence with conventional notions of femininity. In this way the process whereby Rossetti negotiates and evades these conventions is obscured.

Self-erasure

Antony H. Harrison employs the term 'poetics of conciseness' to denote her poetry's terseness, the absent referents, the brevity, deceptive simplicity, dense literary allusions, deletions of stanzas and emphasis upon style over subject matter. Conciseness, he also argues, informs the aesthetics of the poetry.[53] Harrison's detailed account of the poetry's context and intertextuality, however, assumes an unproblematic commerce between D.G. Rossetti and Christina Rossetti and assumes the latter's total artistic autonomy, without an acknowledgement of the power structure that informs the revisions, and which informs in particular the aesthetic of the feminine, the discourse within which the poetry of both Rossettis operates. Christina Rossetti was not unwilling to submit her work for revision. Her letters to her publisher show an active concern with the preparation for publication, and the surviving letters to her brother reveal that she resisted some changes and forcefully argued over others.[54] The extent of her submission to D.G. Rossetti's advice suggests something more than the attempt to shape a poetic identity within an artistic circle; it suggests, in fact, a complicity with dis-figuring the feminine subject that lies at what she herself terms the 'heart' of her poetry. (It is, of course, a paradoxical centrality in a poetics that undermines all notions of a centre, of placement, of locale.) D.G. Rossetti's critique of 'Under the Rose', later titled 'The Iniquity of the Fathers Upon the Children', is based (so far as Christina Rossetti's reply indicates) on the premise that the speaker's experience of illegitimacy is foreign to Christina Rossetti's own experience, thus assuming her poetics could be only confessional, could only reflect experience. She replied to this criticism:

> As regards the unpleasant-sided subject I freely admit it. [. . .] But do you know, even if we throw *U. the R.* overboard, and whilst I endorse your opinion of the unavoidable and indeed much-to-be-desired unreality of women's work on many social matters, I yet incline to include within female range such an attempt as this. [. . .] [A]nd whilst it may be truly urged that unless white could be black and Heaven Hell my experience (thank God) precludes me from hers, I yet don't see why 'the Poet Mind' should be less able to construct her from its own inner consciousness than a hundred other unknown quantities.[55]

Juxtaposed with the assertion that meaning may be generated beyond the sphere of experience is her acceptance of D.G. Rossetti's wish to remove unspecified flaws in the poem, for the above plea is prefixed with '*U. the R.* herewith [. . .] I meekly return to you, pruned and re-written to order.' Her paradoxical stance may be explained by reading D.G. Rossetti's deletions and revisions as further displacing and estranging the subject from the text. This is diminishment taken to the extreme, an act of textual and self-deletion at another's hand, a function of the 'double lack' which Andrew and Catherine Belsey see as determining her poetics. Rossetti's poetry always suggests that the subject resides, or is fully present, elsewhere. The text is superfluous to its own ends, and the revisions merely further inscribe this self-protective strategy into the poetry.

Indeed, in her own rearrangement of the poems for the *Verses* volume (1893), only those stanzas suggestive of a metaleptic deferral of signification and projection of the feminine subject into perfection in the afterlife are reproduced. Rossetti herself sees fit to present, for a devotional volume, only the fruits of her exploration of subjectivity, giving the subject a firmly non-empirical locale in a realm that perfects gender relations by transforming them into divine love, such as in 'As a king, ... unto the King', which, out of a poem originally seven stanzas long, preserves only the final two stanzas (Crump 2: 248, 426).[56]

The irony of the poetry's confrontation with the aesthetics of the feminine is that the resulting figure of the speakers as mute self-contemplative women who anticipate a fully present subjectivity in some future time mimics the contemporary stipulation that women must be still, inert, silent.[57] Christina Rossetti's collusion with her brother's attempt to re-define the feminine in her early publications was however far from a submission. The linguistic operation of the poetry works to position the feminine subject as less than an object, a displacement beyond the text into the amorphous realm of the sleeping soul, itself an anticipation of the Second Coming. This doubleness – the speaker's desire for Soul Sleep and the Sleeper's desire for the Resurrection – eludes the revisions that would re-inscribe Rossetti's text within Pre-Raphaelite feminine aesthetics and obscure her parodic mimicry of that discourse.

The urge towards self-erasure displaces the subject beyond the text, and the subject is left as a trace, as presence-in-absence. This uncanniness makes the poems in the early volumes disruptive of social norms, for the subject refuses to be located in a fixed position, and thus eludes definition and identification (despite D.G. Rossetti's efforts to re-feminise the poetry), even as this mimics nineteenth-century feminine attitudes. This double within the feminine, as both known and unknown, within and beyond, produces poetry at once conventional and subversive. But, together with the disruption of social norms, the poems also resist critical readings which determine their historical contexts. Even a recovery of the conditions of their revisions, which this chapter partly offers, withholds the recovery of a historicised literary subject. The poetry thus lends itself to a reading not of determined identities but of positionalities; not *who* is the subject but *where* is she.

5
Spectres and Spectators: Fraternal Revisions II

Sister to the Brotherhood

In an article published in 1893, Edmund Gosse praised Christina Rossetti as one of the 'obscure group of boys and girls who called themselves Preraphaelites', for:

> association with men so learned and eager, so daring in experiment, so well equipped in scholarship, gave her an instant and positive advantage. By nature she would seem to be of a cloistered and sequestered temper, and her genius was lifted on this wave of friendship to heights which it would not have dreamed of attempting alone. On the other hand [...] critics have taken for granted that she was a satellite, and have been puzzled to notice her divergences from the type.[1]

Two years after her death in 1894, Gosse felt it necessary to add an anecdote at the end of this article in preparation for its publication in *Critical Kit-Kats*. He describes, on his first meeting with Christina Rossetti at around 1870, how he found her style of dress deeply disappointing:

> She is known to the world, and very happily known, by her brother's portraits of her, and in particular by the singularly beautiful chalk drawing in profile, dated 1866. [...] [B]ut, as I suppose, an ascetic or almost methodistical reserve caused her to clothe herself in a style, or with an absence of style, which was really distressing. [...] The high stiff dress ended in a hard collar and plain brooch, the extraordinarily ordinary skirt sank over a belated crinoline, and these were inflictions hard to bear from the high-priestess of Preraphaelitism. (pp. 157–8)

Gosse's attempt to integrate Rossetti into the Pre-Raphaelite Brotherhood is fraught with tension. On the one hand, as we have seen in the previous chapter, her familial associations with the Brotherhood helped launch her into the literary marketplace. She was the first writer associated with the Brotherhood to publish a volume of poetry, which led Swinburne to term her melodramatically 'the Jael who led the hosts to victory'. And yet she is also seen as an inappropriate member of a fraternal artistic group by virtue of her gender. A Jael, a high-priestess, a consummate model for her brother, Christina Rossetti is nevertheless associated with the Pre-Raphaelite Brotherhood in a highly ambivalent way. Her historical position, in fact, is one of uncanny alterity: both belonging and excluded, she is the 're-mark' of the group, the focus of their aesthetic and the point at which it recedes.[2] Brought face to face with Christina Rossetti's duplicitous position, no wonder Gosse is distressed.

Contemporary reviews tend to inscribe the alterity by employing visual language in the assessment of her poetry. While this annexes her uncomfortably with the Pre-Raphaelite Brotherhood, it is also associated with Victorian constructions of women's poetic creativity as a direct and spontaneous reflex of experience or sight. Thus, the early maxim of the Pre-Raphaelite Brotherhood, the rejection of contemporary representational axioms in painting and a concurrent return to nature, becomes, for the reviewers, a passive visuality. The unsigned review of the *Goblin Market* volume in *The Athenæum* (26 April 1862), suggests the visual artlessness of Rossetti's poems:

> These lays by Miss Rossetti have the charm of a welcome surprise. They are no mere reflections and echoes of previous beauty and music, but, whatever their faults, express both in essence and form the individuality of the writer. To read these poems after the laboured and skilful, but not original, verse which has been issued of late, is like passing from a picture gallery, with its well-figured semblance of nature, to the real nature out-of-doors, which greets us with the waving grass and the pleasant shock of the breeze.[3]

The *Saturday Review*'s comments on *The Prince's Progress and Other Poems* (23 June 1866) also compares the poetry to the visual: 'all her visions of social and moral truths seem to come to her through pictures, and to stay in her mind in the pictorial shape. Instead of analysing her ideas, she embodies and dramatises them'.[4] Similarly, Arthur Christopher Benson responded to the 'haunting sense of locality in which the mood dreams itself out', as distinct from a purely descriptive pictorial poetry:

> Christina Rossetti's *mise-en-scène* is a place of gardens, orchards, wooded dingles, with a churchyard in the distance. The scene shifts a little, but the spirit never wanders far afield; and it is certainly singular that one who lived out almost the whole of her life in a city so majestic, sober, and inspiriting as London, should never bring the consciousness of streets and thoroughfares and populous murmur into her writings. She, whose heart was so with birds and fruit, cornfields and farmyard sounds, never even revolts against or despairs of the huge desolation, the laborious monotony of a great town.[5]

Benson's appreciation is caught in the aporia that, conventionally, female poetry is experiential, but, as a city dweller, Rossetti's experience of nature was minimal. He escapes the contradiction by figuring the city as industrialised and masculine, and the country as natural and feminine. William Sharp describes a social gathering at which Rossetti was asked if her inspiration came from the country, to which she reportedly replied:

> Oh dear, no! I know it *ought* to be so. [...] I don't derive anything from the country at first hand! Why, my knowledge of what is called nature is that of the town sparrow. [...] And, what is more, I am fairly sure that I am in the place that best suits me. After all, we may enjoy the magic and mystery of ocean without ever adventuring upon it.[6]

The biographical subject Christina Rossetti, as we saw in Chapter 3, is represented as having a wholly interior existence, which enables any tension between her experience, her poetry, and the conventions of women's writing to be attributed to the spontaneity of her spiritual and imaginative existence.

Rossetti's poetry does, as the language of the reviews implicitly suggests, have an important correspondence with Pre-Raphaelite visual aesthetics, but the effect is not merely to reiterate their conventions and nor is her poetry wholly determined by the aesthetic of the Brotherhood. Jerome Bump argues that, while the Brotherhood by its very appellation excluded Christina and Maria Rossetti, the former was fully qualified in her artistic concerns and productions to be a Pre-Raphaelite.[7] Such a re-assessment aims to restore through historical revisionism Rossetti's place in a movement from which she was excluded by virtue of her gender. The danger with this critical praxis is the erasure of the alterity which, far from being debilitating, enables a subtle exploration of Pre-Raphaelite aesthetics from a superlative subject position in the representational axiom. Sharon Smulders argues that Rossetti saw herself as the representative woman.[8] Indeed, 'Woman', in the Lacanian paradigm of gender, occupies an ambivalent position as both the ground and vanishing point of phallogocentrism. But Rossetti's position was excessively ambivalent thanks to her construction as both representative of her gender and yet also eccentric. Both Marina Warner and Julia Kristeva refer suggestively to Caelius Sedulius, who writes of the Virgin Mother that 'She . . . had no peer / Either in our first mother or in all women / Who were to come. But alone of all her sex / She pleased the Lord'.[9] Christina Rossetti, model for the Virgin in her brother's first two pictures, was similarly culturally constructed as 'alone of all her sex': feminine *par excellence*, and yet also exceeding her gendered identity.

Rossetti engages most obviously and directly with D.G. Rossetti's visual aesthetics in two sonnets, 'In an Artist's Studio' (1856) and 'An Echo from Willowwood' (date of composition unknown; published 1890). Her poem 'The Queen of Hearts' (1863) may also refer to his two *Regina Cordium* pictures (1860 and 1861) that predate it.[10] In addition, her short story 'The Lost Titian' (1855) and sonnets 'The P.R.B.' (1853) and 'The two Rossettis (brothers they)' (1853) refer satirically to the Pre-Raphaelite Brotherhood.[11] The concern with her brother's art is, I will argue, informed by two paintings for which she sat as a model for the Virgin Mary,[12] *The Girlhood of Mary Virgin* (1849) and *Ecce Ancilla Domini!* (Behold the Handmaid of the Lord; 1850), later re-titled *The Annunciation* (Plates 5 and 6). The difficulty of interpreting these pictures has been traditionally attributed to the painter's stylistic immaturity and his interest in the Art-Catholicism.[13] The paintings benefit, however, from acknowledging their interpretative difficulties as part of an early expression of D.G. Rossetti's feminine aesthetics which his sister's position of alterity – both within and without the Brotherhood, both model and artist – unsettles in her explicit commentaries on his art.[14]

'Alone of all her sex'

It is a critical commonplace that the Pre-Raphaelites thrived artistically on the configuration of word and image, but for D.G. Rossetti the verbal/visual combination is both appealing and problematic. Technical deficiencies, in particular with perspective and the fresco technique,[15] make both *The Girlhood of Mary Virgin* and *The Annunciation* especially difficult to interpret in any satisfactory and coherent way. Indeed, at the same time as the pictures didactically insist on a symbolic interpretation, they unsettle the viewer and undermine the semantic project. This is most obviously true of the earlier *Girlhood* which is littered with spiritual symbols that clutter the domestic space of the interior, attest to the purity of the Virgin and proleptically hint at her visitation by the angel Gabriel, represented in *The Annunciation*. Attached to the frame of *The Girlhood* are two sonnets that leave us with no doubt as to their overtly didactic message. The first poem describes the spiritual qualities of 'that blessed Mary, pre-elect / God's Virgin' (ll.1–2) and points towards the imminent Annunciation. The Virgin is emphatically defined as spiritual, passive and feminine.[16] In the second sonnet, the symbols of her purity in the painting are explained:

> These are the symbols. On that cloth of red
> I' the centre is the Tripoint: perfect each,
> Except the second of its points, to teach
> That Christ is not yet born. The books – whose head
> Is golden Charity, as Paul hath said –
> Those virtues are wherein the soul is rich:
> Therefore on them the lily standeth, which
> Is Innocence, being interpreted.
>
> The seven-thorn'd briar and the palm seven-leaved
> Are her great sorrow and her great reward.
> Until the end be full, the Holy One
> Abides without. She soon shall have achieved
> Her perfect purity: yea, God the Lord
> Shall soon vouchsafe His Son to be her Son.
>
> (Surtees 1:10)[17]

It could be argued that this explicit didacticism in *The Girlhood* is produced by the artist's frustrations with improperly learnt rules of composition; for the anxiety is that difficulties with the application of technique may confuse the viewer, who would then bring alternative and improper interpretations to the picture. D.G. Rossetti also admitted to difficulties with the execution of *The Annunciation*: he called it 'the blessed white eye-sore' and the 'blessed white daub',[18] and Frederic Stephens and John Millais are reported to have assisted with the perspective of the whitewashed interior.[19] I would suggest, however, that the didacticism is also an attempt to control the indeterminacy produced by the verbal/visual doubling in *The Girlhood*. *The Annunciation* is also implicated in this, for the frame was originally covered with Latin phrases, as noted in the Tate catalogue:

> In 1874 it [*The Annunciation*] was once more in Rossetti's hands when its frame was altered to the present one. The original frame evidently bore Latin mottoes, copies from a brass or brass-rubbing owned by F.G. Stephens, which were 'Popish' in sentiment. They must have increased the didactic quality of the picture. (p. 73)[20]

Furthermore, the sonnets attached to *The Girlhood* offer an interpretation of this later visual text, and, like that painting, it also has another obvious verbal source: the Bible.[21]

The effect of the didactic configuration of picture and poems is to present both mediums as one and the same, a project that Lynne Pearce has described as the '"will" to monolithic meaning' (pp. 37–8)[22] that denies the difference between the mediums and imposes a coherent and unitary interpretation upon the spectators. Stamping such a convincing and unquestionable meaning on the pictures, however, fails by virtue of its own excessiveness. Both pictures have a symbolic content that leaves them claustrophobic and stultifying; the visual text is over-burdened with moral meaning and the signifiers are exhausted.[23] Paradoxically and at odds with the didacticism, the end result is to leave the viewers with an unsettling sense of exclusion from the act of interpreting the paintings. Further, the explicit didacticism calls attention to its attempt to suppress alternative readings, and so the attempt to forge a monolithic relation between the visual and the verbal is exposed and undone.[24]

The tight and clinical structuring of *The Girlhood of Mary Virgin* and *The Annunciation* forcefully suggests both the attempted refusal to acknowledge the gap between art forms, and the associated attempt to control the gaze of the viewer. In the earlier painting, the vertical lines of the lily and that of its embroidered counterpart, the criss-crossing of the lattice, the edging of the floor tiles, the seven-thorned briar and the palm leaf and the frozen angularity of the figures all suggest the tight structuring of space along linear principles. In *The Annunciation*, the cramped and narrow depiction of the Virgin Mary's chamber is even more austere and angular and is heightened by the stark predominant whiteness.[25] All the details in *The Annunciation* loom large within a domestic interior and the effect is to make the Angel Gabriel seem disproportionate. The bare interior is in contrast to the many symbols that fill up the space of *The Girlhood*, but the effect is still claustrophobic.

Further, both pictures are marked by the contrasting faintness of the outside scene.[26] In *The Girlhood*, the lattice marks the division between outside and inside while the towering unproportional figure of St Joseph tending the vine has a contrasting faintness of colour: his dusty purple-blue clothes blend with the sky and the horizon, while the faint vertical lines of the tree trunks also seem disproportionate. There is a similar visually disturbing quality induced by the view from the window in *The Annunciation*, for the outside is depicted as a small portion of blue sky and an unfocused tree in the top left hand corner, in direct contrast with the interior, as if this was a token of the exterior. In both pictures, with the exception of St Joseph tending the vine, the sacred symbolism is fully concentrated within the domestic space; the outside does not fully engage with the symbolic content of the picture nor heighten any sense of geometric perspective as one would expect in traditional Renaissance Annunciation pictures. In fact, the depiction of the exterior does not appear to serve any conventional technical or symbolic function. The fading, imprecisely drawn outside, making up only a small portion of both paintings, seems to mark a refusal to engage with what is external to the delineated signifying 'space' of the visual text. The status of the viewer, whose independent participation in the picture is already diminished by the explicit didacticism, seems to be symbolised by this representation of the exterior, which while necessarily included is at once also cornered off and made extraneous, reinforcing the anxiety that the viewer will undermine the attempt to impose a single interpretation.

The resistance to any acknowledgement of the spectator's independence from the didacticism is all the more disconcerting when perspective is considered.[27] Perspective presupposes and is organised by the viewpoint of a single spectator. It is constructed with reference to both this *singular* line of vision and to the concept of a *masterful* point of reference, a centre. Further, as Gombrich notes, the illusion of perspective brings about a monolithic reading practise, for it: 'consists [...] in the conviction that there is only one way of interpreting the visual pattern in front of us'.[28] According to W.M. Rossetti,

> [D.G.] Rossetti never paid any attention, worth speaking of, to perspective, and indeed – so far as his own interest in matters of art was concerned – was at all times almost indifferent to the question whether his works were in perspective or out of it. Mr. Stephens did

> something to arrange the perspective of Rossetti's picture (1849–50) of *The Annunciation*, now in the National Gallery, and in 1850 gave him a few lessons – and would not have minded giving many more – in this bugbear science.[29]

Despite this declaration of indifference to perspective, the overall effect of the perspective in the paintings is unsettling and functions as part of D.G. Rossetti's visual aesthetics.

While denying the spectator the semblance of geometric perspective beyond the domestic space, there is a suggestion of disturbed perspective in the treatment of the lily, used in both paintings as a symbol of the phallus and of purity. In *The Annunciation*, we find that from the spectator's viewpoint the lily points to the Virgin's womb, but from the Archangel's perspective it seems to point to the wall. As the dominant vertical line in *The Girlhood*, the lily is the only point that immediately attracts our gaze as the displaced centre of the picture, balanced but split in the Virgin's embroidery on the anachronistic High Church stole. Ultimately, the clutter and clatter of symbols and the disturbed perspective distract the spectator. Meaning is enclosed within the claustrophobic domestic space and the lines of vision which we seem invited to follow frustrate the text's claim to accuracy (both of history and of perspective). In addition, any semblance of perspective is confined to the domestic interior; overall, the paintings thus suggest a depthlessness and a two-dimensionality which denies the corporeality of the figure of the Virgin, who seems consequently to be flattened and deanimated.[30]

The denial of difference between mediums and between the artist's didactic intention and the spectator's threatening independence has its origins in sexual difference. D.G. Rossetti acknowledged this in a note, subsequently transcribed by W.M. Rossetti: 'picture and poem bear the same relation to each other as beauty does in man and woman: the point of meeting where the two are most identical is the supreme perfection'.[31] This problematic assertion first genders genre (in its widest possible sense as types of artistic medium) in keeping with literary tradition, only to deny difference at a certain imagined point of intersection between image and word.

The eradication of sexual difference is complicated by Pre-Raphaelite aesthetics, which give priority to the male artist over an objectified feminine figure, upon which his identity is predicated. The representational system positions the feminine as both ground and vanishing point of the aesthetic. Indeterminacy is thus connoted as feminine. Toril Moi usefully summarises Luce Irigaray's point, in *Speculum of the Other Woman*: 'if one imagined that the woman imagines anything at all, the object (of speculation) would lose its stability and unsettle the [male] subject itself'.[32] Elisabeth Bronfen gives the rhetorical implications:

> The ambivalence of Woman's position is that she is supplement to man and point of an original unity. She is fluid, undifferentiated, yet her function is to define man and she serves as the limit or boundary at which difference is drawn and confirmed. She is not whole, a sign for human mortality, yet also the body over which man and culture can be defined as being whole. [...] The allegory of the female body is an ambivalently coded figure and the rhetorical figure of ambivalence *per se*; a figure thematising difference and a rhetoric[al] enactment of difference.[33]

The attempt to control the viewer's gaze in *The Girlhood* and *The Annunciation* thus emerges as an effect of the scopic basis of sexual difference, 'by which the sex one can *see* becomes the gender one must *be*'.[34] In addition, according to this formalist logic, a theory of sexual difference based on the gaze perceives the female as being a gender defined by its anatomical lack. Thus, while the gaze assures difference between genders, it also carries a reminder of the threat of castration which then leads to the mobilisation of the fetish. In such a representational axiom, to view the figure of 'Woman'[35] both affirms and denies her difference, as the mark of fetishism both affirms and denies women's castration. In D.G. Rossetti's earliest paintings, then, the mastery of the gaze that is an imperative of geometric perspective as well as the 'logic of the Same' is undermined by the acknowledgement that these generic doubles bring about an indeterminacy that is (culturally) encoded as feminine, and that re-inscribes difference and loss. Most obviously, this is evident in the depiction of the Virgin as a vaguely delineated physical body in both pictures, the former as a wooden adolescent and the later picture as an amorphous shape underneath the night-dress.[36] The physicality of the Virgin is indefinite and uncertain at the very point at which it represents the feminine. Further, this indeterminacy is represented by the viewer's gaze which challenges the artist's didacticism by its very difference in position, threatening D.G. Rossetti's 'supreme perfection' of art.

Within the signifying space of the visual texts it is the rhetorical figure of the Virgin Mary that attempts to counteract the dangerous threat to monolithic meaning produced by indeterminacy. In rhetorical tradition the figure of the Virgin signifies wholeness, completion and stability of meaning. In Christian tradition, the Virgin was depicted as the counterpart of Tuccia, the vestal virgin who proved her virtue by miraculously carrying water in a sieve. This potent image for a sealed whole as opposed to a penetrated body was attached to the Virgin Mary, whose maidenhood was described allegorically with images of cinctures or closed vessels drawn from the Old Testament. In particular, she was seen as figured in the verse from the Song of Solomon: 'a garden inclosed is my sister, my spouse; a spring shut up, a fountain sealed' (6.12).[37] Significantly, this very passage is echoed in W.M. Rossetti's Memoir of Christina Rossetti, to suggest the one flaw in her character:

> Over-scrupulosity made Christina shut up her mind to almost all things save the Bible, and the admonitions and ministrations of priests. [...] Her temperament and character, naturally warm and free, became 'a fountain sealed'. Not but that affection continued to flow in abundant measure, and the clear line of duty told out all the more apparent from receiving no side-lights. Impulse and élan were checked, both in act and in writing, but the most extreme spontaneity in poetic performance always remained.[38]

W.M. Rossetti describes his sister as a contained and closed personage, suggesting repression, wholeness and completion. Depicted by the Pre-Raphaelites and by subsequent biographers as 'Santa Christina',[39] in Gosse's words 'cloistered' from society (see above) in her celibate and purely emotional life, Christina Rossetti would seem to be the perfect choice for the model of the Virgin. Both pictures were finished shortly after her own mysterious and unexplained transformation, recounted in the biographies, from a lively child into a solemn and sickly adult (see Chapter 3). D.G. Rossetti commented to Charles Lyell that her appearance was: 'exactly adapted to my purpose'; and to Frederic Stephens, D.G. Rossetti acknowledges the saintliness of his own sister when he described *The Girlhood* as: 'a symbol of female excellence, the Virgin being taken as its highest type'.[40] G.P. Boyce describes the representation of the Virgin as: 'one of, if not the most[,] exquisite conception I have yet seen [...] full of intense thought and awakened and growing religious awe, almost my ideal of a woman's head'.[41] And Holman Hunt described the sitter as: 'exactly the pure and docile-hearted damsel that her brother portrayed God's pre-elect to be'.[42]

As the Second Eve, the Virgin Mary participates rhetorically in the attempt to convert the picture and poem to the status of a unitary and single text which strives to frame and structure interpretation and to tightly control the reader's response. In Christian tradition, the Virgin Mother is a paradoxical feminine ideal that emerges from the cultural impasse that women are defined by both their maternal function and their sexual purity. As the mother of Christ she brings forth and enables Redemption and thus the healing of original sin. She is the mediator between the human and the divine who heals the split between signifier and signified brought about by Eve.[43] As the iconic woman she is also disembodied,[44] as Elisabeth Bronfen remarks, for her body is not subject to the decay and death that Eve typifies. In her heavenly reanimation:

> conceptually a collapsing of first and second burial occurs, which completely circumvents a dissolution and corruption of the body, and by implication places her from the start outside the 'feminine' realm of material time and bodily decay and into the 'masculine' symbolic realm of eternal unchanged forms. (p. 68)

Thus, while the Virgin Mother is ideally feminine, she is also a figure for translation, for feminine perfection carried over to the masculine realm. Culturally made to mediate 'the underhand double of explicit phallic power',[45] the Virgin Mary is *ideally* feminine but not *merely* feminine.

The gender ambivalence inscribed into the cult of the Virgin is suggested by the lily in both *The Girlhood* and *The Annunciation*. In the latter the Angel Gabriel holds the lily as a symbol of virginity and faith while the Virgin Mary stares anxiously at the stem which sharply separates her from the Archangel. The erect lily is 'the symbolic instrument of impregnation' and the means of the Virgin's 'transformation from sexual innocence to sexual awareness'.[46] In this way, the lily incorporates masculine and feminine significances and thus becomes the appropriate symbol of the Virgin, who in the earlier *Girlhood* picture is shown embroidering the lily onto a stole, supervised by Saint Anne. Here, the Virgin is engaged in a typological act of self-representation as she embroiders the image of herself.[47] She copies from a real lily which towers close in front of her on top of books denoting the cardinal virtues. The frame on which she works rests tight up against her and suggests that she is hemmed in by this ecclesiastical anachronism. In *The Annunciation*, the narrowness of the canvas emphasises the cowering Virgin's entrapment; and, again, both the lilies hold the figure in her place. The Virgin's representative status as a female figure – in *The Girlhood* as a pious daughter, and in *The Annunciation* as a vulnerable adolescent – heightens the sense that the phallic lily's function is to rein in the feminine.

As a figure for mediation between gender differences, the rhetorical figure of the Virgin Mary enters the symbolic masculine domain and promises to repress the challenging indeterminacy of verbal/visual doubles which are encoded as feminine. In D.G. Rossetti's attempt to posit an effacement of difference between poem and picture and man and woman, the Virgin is the perfect bearer. As the healer of the unstable language split and the mediator from feminine to masculine, she is rhetorically figured as potentially stabilising gender and genre difference.

One wonders what effect D.G. Rossetti's representation of his sister has had on receptions of her poetic signature as a trope. We have seen that discussions of key biographical episodes, such as her bedroom window at Penkill Castle and her deathbed scene, and of her poetics, emphasises Christina Rossetti as both an object of gaze and also an author of poems that directly transcribe her sight. As Stephen Heath argues: 'where a discourse appeals directly to an image, to an immediacy of seeing, as a point of its argument or demonstration, one can be sure that all difference is being elided, that the unity of some accepted vision is being reproduced'.[48] In fact, Christina Rossetti emerges as a meta-figure, the figure of the figure of containment, Tuccia's miraculous sieve, the Virgin's sealed fountain. Yet the figure for the figure for containment is a doubled figure of absence, of an empty trope of a trope. Julia Kristeva's meditation on the Virgin in 'Stabat Mater' points out how excessive her representation in Western rhetorical tradition; indeed, such an excess is part of its failure to contain feminine abjection for twentieth-century women. Indeed, as a paradigm for virgin maternity, the Virgin Mary is also, in the words of Anna Smith, an 'enigmatic, sublime kind of identity' which overwhelms language with the unnameable.[49] The creation of the myth of the Virgin, as exemplified for Kristeva in Pergolesi's *Stabat Mater*, is to ward against closure by substituting archaic sameness: 'man overcomes the unthinkable of death by postulating maternal love in its place – in the place and stead of death and thought'.[50] This love is, however, a 'surge of anguish at the very moment when the identity of thought and living body collapses' (pp. 177–8). One of the reasons why the myth of the Virgin is an insufficient discourse of identity for women today is because its monolithic shield against death denies for women the 'remainder' of feminine otherness, the 'strange fold that changes culture into nature, the speaking into biology' that 'concerns every woman's body' (p. 182).

Indeed, the failure of D.G. Rossetti's aesthetics to erase difference through the figure of the Virgin and her body testifies to the fracture in the rhetorical tradition. *The Girlhood of Mary Virgin* fails to contain difference despite figuring the Virgin's mother Saint Anne as his own mother Frances Lavinia Rossetti in a doubled attempt to substitute a maternal ideal in order to contain difference. The historical personage and literary signature Christina Rossetti – another fold of culture into nature and speaking into biology – motivates the maternal, as we shall see in the next chapter, to articulate feminine identity as otherness. In several sonnets which refer explicitly to her brother's aesthetics, however, Christina Rossetti deftly unravels her brother's denial of difference and alterity.

'Not as she is, but as she fills his dream'

A sonnet that overtly refers to D.G. Rossetti's aesthetics is the posthumously published 'In an Artist's Studio', composed 24 December 1856, which has become emblematic of the relationship between Elizabeth Siddal as model and D.G. Rossetti as male artist. Elisabeth Bronfen, in a case study of their legendary relationship, uses Christina Rossetti's entire sonnet as her epigraph without further comment, implying that the sonnet merely inscribes the legend (p. 168). J.B. Bullen misinterprets the poem's parodic undoing of D.G. Rossetti's aesthetics and critiques the poem for, as he sees it, suggesting that the artist finds a positive and satisfying reflection in the model.[51] W.M. Rossetti, the first to publish the poem posthumously, notes only that: 'the reference is apparently to our brother's studio, and to his constantly-repeated heads of the lady whom he afterwards married, Miss Siddal'.[52] Rather than a reinscription of the D.G. Rossetti and Elizabeth Siddal myth, however, the sonnet challenges the semiotic fixing of the female model into D.G. Rossetti's pictorial representation.[53] This is achieved in the sonnet by establishing an apparently stable frame of reference which is then challenged by the doubleness of the model and her representation. It is this doubling of the poem's representation of the 'real' model and her other that emerges as radically unstable.

The poem begins with a refusal to distinguish between the model and her representation:

> One face looks out from all his canvasses,
>   One selfsame figure sits or walks or leans;
>   We found her hidden just behind those screens,
> That mirror gave back all her loveliness.
>
> (Crump 3: 264; ll. 1–4)

The screens are those behind which the artist's model changed, and so the third line introduces the 'real' Elizabeth Siddal whose 'parenthesised subjectivity'[54] is literally depicted by her 'actual' fleeting presence, as she hides behind her representations. The use of 'selfsame' is ironical: the same as *which* self? The vanishing figure's presence, both displayed and hidden, is almost wholly disavowed even as it is affirmed, when the narrator mimics the convention of equating model with her image (l. 4). The poem then slips back to the representations, the many poses of the model – queen, nameless girl, saint, angel – which repeat: 'The same one meaning, neither more nor less' (l. 8). The second part of this line is a pleonasm which reaffirms the fixity of meaning imposed onto the various representations of the model. In the final sestet, however, we are unsure who is referred to by the personal pronoun 'she', the model or her image:

> He feeds upon her face by day and night,
>   And she with true kind eyes looks back on him
> Fair as the moon and joyful as the light:
>   Not wan with waiting, not with sorrow dim;
> Not as she is, but was when hope shone bright;
>   Not as she is, but as she fills his dream.
>
> (ll. 9–14)

The vague, transient images of moon and light further unsettle as the attempt to describe the model/image's returning look (and also, by implication, her identity) flounders. The feminine figure is represented with reference to her own reflection and to that of the moon's reflected light.

A vanishing spectral image of precarious feminine subjectivity, an image that mimics and menaces the gesturing imposed by the artist, is thus evoked. The sexual images of consumption ('He feeds upon her face') suggest a literal disfigurement in the representation that undercuts the 'mirror' of the canvas. Along with the uncertainty implicit in 'she', there is a suggestion of the presence of the model's marginalised subjectivity as the poem acknowledges her as spectator – 'And she with true kind eyes looks back on him'. The use of the word 'true' and 'kind' here is unsettling. 'True' may be understood as faithful to the artist or as suggesting that what is seen is genuine, real (as in 'seeing truly'). Further, 'kind' has similar paradoxical overtones, 'kind' as compassionate or as natural. In both senses of 'true' and 'kind' there is a fissure between a notion of the subject as autonomous and the subject as constructed with reference to the artist: if her eyes see truly and 'naturally' they do not reflect the artist's consuming passion. There is a disjunction between that which is seen and that which is figured as being reflected back, between object and subjectivity.

The repetition of qualifying negatives in the final three lines disturbs a sense of time scale between 'is' and 'was', which increases the displacement of the model from her representation and which, ultimately, suggests that she exceeds her own representation as she fluctuates between presence and absence. The half rhyme 'dream' in the final line further disturbs both the sense of rhyme (and therefore of time) and comes with an acknowledgement that although the model exceeds the attempt to equate her with her representation and to suppress her subjectivity, she can nevertheless only be 'seen' relative to the artist: 'Not as she is, but as she fills his dream'. We have a sense of the model's 'real' presence, constructed in terms of negatives and as a mimicry of D.G. Rossetti's aesthetics, but this 'real' is itself a further representation. The poem confronts the dilemma that the model is presented to us as already a linguistic construct. The text which is read as an adumbration of the model's image is thus ekphratic – a representation of a representation.

The poem's relation to the visual works in other ways. The narrator is posited as a voyeuristic spectator who intrudes upon a spectacle – 'We found her hidden just behind those screens' (l. 3). The model and her other are both gazed upon and gaze back, an activity which disrupts the distinction between the passive model as object and image, and the woman who inhabits her own subjectivity. The verbal/visual interchange is also something that we, as readers, participate in for the poem, as a visual shape on the page, is itself an object of our gaze. Compounded with this is the status of the sonnet as a poetic form associated with the scopic and which, from Petrarch to D.G. Rossetti, is conventionally the masculine medium through which the speaker predicates his subjectivity upon a female beloved. Furthermore, the model is seen in the act of vanishing into her representation, blurring with her image, dramatising her parenthesised subjectivity by hiding behind the screens and canvases. The inability of the visitors to the studio to focus on the model's person – the model 'as she is' rather than 'as she fills his dreams' – both allows them a voyeuristic gaze and, at the same time, allows them to challenge the fetishisation of the feminine. In this way, the poem is both predicated on an authentic origin, the source of the representations (Siddal the model) *and* serves to deny us direct access to her. The event of the poem is the subject and object of this process, arresting the gaze on the anaphoric iteration of images and yet also exposing the fear of loss and absence that perpetuates them. 'In an Artist's Studio' is truly a paradigmatic poem for, in a way that recalls Barthes's meditation on photography in *Camera Lucida*, which we encountered in Chapter 1, the lost object is restored, the woman engendered, the Symptom dissolved: and yet her presence eludes us. This is truly a 'mad image'.[55]

In Christina Rossetti's version of her brother's visual aesthetics, the depiction of the model as a male representation of the feminine is fleeting, spectral, but marks a difference between the model and her image – as Christina Rossetti, the spectator, in the act of writing the sonnet, marks a difference from herself as her brother's model. The effect of 'In an Artist's Studio' is to intimate a precarious feminine subjectivity by mimicking and exceeding her brother's aesthetics which attempt to impose a unitary and stable aesthetic over the instability of verbal/visual doubles. In this way, Christina Rossetti explores differences *within* the trope 'Woman' that displace the concern with the difference *between* genders and genres.

This intervention in her brother's aesthetics exploits his anxiety that the spectator and the model may, by mere act of looking, challenge the perfection of an art based upon a repression of difference. Both the subject in the poem and Rossetti herself have a superlative feminine position of alterity in the representational scheme as both observed and observer. In a dynamic of presence and absence, parodying the conception of female poetry as a direct experiential reflex, her poem speaks from the position of the fading feminine subject which Pre-Raphaelite art so compulsively depicts. As the speaker in her famous crocodile dream-poem coyly asks, after giving a blatantly uninterpretable account of her dream:

> What can it mean? you ask. I answer not
> For meaning, but myself must echo, What?
> And tell it as I saw it on the spot.
>
> ('My Dream', Crump 1: 40; ll. 49–51)

Like 'In An Artist's Studio', Christina Rossetti's 'An Echo From Willowwood' makes explicit reference to her brother's art, in this case the four 'Willowwood' sonnets from the *House of Life*.[56] This sonnet sequence exhibits the same concern with structure as his earliest pictures: as well as referring to architectural structure and first of the twelve 'houses' of astrology, the term also denotes the primal house of life, the womb. As I have argued elsewhere, the sequence is memorial to otherness, 'To one dead deathless hour',[57] but the attempt to engender the other ends up effacing difference itself through an appropriation of the beloved as a doubled loss, the absence of her image.[58]

In the micro-sequence of the four 'Willowwood' sonnets, the figure of the speaker as masculine is fundamental to the achievement of this perpetual union of addressee and beloved.[59] But already we are faced with a paradox: to stress the masculinity of the speaker is to inscribe a gender difference onto the aesthetics which thrives on the attempt to *efface* difference in type (be it gender or genre).[60] Indeed, the erasure of difference is predicated on masculinity. Willowwood is the place of doomed love, a forest of grief circumscribing Love's fountain. In this enchanted place – enclosed and also liminally transient – the union between lovers is fleeting and momentary. The brief meeting is, however, dependent upon the fading and provisional nature of the female beloved. The speaker's own reflection in the 'woodside well' (Sonnet 1, l. 1) brings forth the lover as mapped onto a reflection of him, a 'superscription':[61] the speaker looks into the pool at the personified Love's image, 'and my tears fell // And at their fall, his eyes beneath grew hers' (Sonnet 1, ll. 8–9). His beloved is only seen as an image in the pool: she is not a spectator, but merely a reflection. Further, she appears in the place of Love: Love transforms into lover, figuration becomes a personage, which turns out to be an image, another figuration. Love sings and warns of the danger of meeting a dead beloved: 'Better all life forget her than this thing, / That Willowwood should hold her wandering!' (Sonnet 3, ll. 13–14). It is her intangibility, her death, which allows a momentary union, but at the end, when the two are depicted in Love's aureole, the masculine speaker has consumed and subsumed the beloved:

> Only I know that I leaned low and drank
> A long draught from the water where she sank,
> Her breath and all her tears and all her soul.
>
> (Sonnet 4, ll. 9–11)

The union is achieved, precariously and at a cost: the dead beloved is imaged as a feminine figure constantly in the process of fading, a dangerous wandering signifier, an embodiment of the cultural cliché that 'Woman' is man's symptom, and she is unified with the masculine upon the assumption that the male creator has primacy. It seems that the attempt to efface gender difference becomes a further attempt to displace and efface the provisional feminine figure.

Christina Rossetti's sonnet in response uses the suggestive word 'echo' in the title which is fundamental to the notion of translation and interchange between the texts, whilst also suggesting diminution (in the sense of both diminishment and a diminutive). The reference to her brother's sonnets seems self-deprecatory, but, as with 'In An Artist's Studio', the poem's initial appearance as a reinscription of her brother's aesthetics emerges as ironical. The echoic quality of this poem is the reverse of D.G. Rossetti's palimpsestic 'superscription', but nevertheless for Christina Rossetti the mimicry exceeds its counterpart. Furthermore, as Angela Leighton points out, the trope of the echo even predates D.G. Rossetti:

> The scene of willows and water was that of her own Sappho's forgetful, curative twilight after her suicidal leap. [...] Echoes, for [Christina] Rossetti, are not so much signs of poetic imitation as of hollowed-out memory; they represent something that has been secondary for so long that it has almost lost its literary or biographical origins. As a figure for poetry, the echo points to that element of fiction which is no longer tied to life or feeling, but which sets up its own meaning beyond their gravity.[62]

Christina Rossetti's echo trope undoes the narcissistic aesthetic of her brother and also reconfigures her intertextual relationship to that art as both secondary to a primal Sapphic fragility and as a relationship so secondary that it is under erasure. Yopi Prins, who unravels the echoic quality of the Victorian Sappho, argues that '[Christina Rossetti's] Sappho poems put on display [...] the figurality of the figure' of Sappho as part of her poetics of postponement and erasure; so much so, that 'it is difficult to distinguish between the "sham utterances" and the "real poetry" of Christina Rossetti, or between the "poetess" and the "Woman poet."'[63] In fact, I argue, the troping of the trope suggests that Rossetti's poetic identification with Sappho serves both to parodically highlight the emptiness of her own poetic signature and biographical personage and, in addition, to motivate this absence as a superlative position from which to unravel her secondary relation to her brother's aesthetics.

In D.G. Rossetti's 'Willowwood' sonnets, the beloved is seen only as an image, a reflection on the water, and is devoid of a fully present subjectivity. Christina Rossetti's version depicts the two lovers looking upon each other's image: 'Two gazed into a pool, he gazed and she', and 'Each eyed the other's aspect, he and she' (Crump 3: 53; ll. 1, 5). The repetition of 'he and she' and the anaphoric repetition of 'each' in the following lines (ll. 5–7, 10) suggest that the gaze is reciprocated and so by implication both are affirmed as subjects. To the duality of the gazers is added another spectator: the narrator, who in D.G. Rossetti's version is the male lover. The threefold viewpoint of this spectacle undermines the corresponding text's attempt to efface gender difference. Further, the third person, the narrator, introduces figures of aporia and liminality which exceed the images of transience in the original version. The excess is that of meaning itself, and a third term is inscribed onto the original doubleness of spectator/narrator and feminine image that gestures toward a threshold of meaning to which feminine subjectivity had been implicitly marginalised in the original.[64] 'Not hand in hand, yet heart in heart, I think' (l. 2) is emblematic of this linguistic operation: moving from D.G. Rossetti's physical union in the lovers' kisses to the heart which is both literal and metaphorical, and finally the 'I think' which introduces the spectator's gaze to the intertextual translation between texts and the intersubjectivity of the lovers. Images of thresholds also denote excess: 'brink' is repeated (ll. 3, 4, 8) and first denotes the edge of the pool and later 'of life's dividing sea' (l. 8), and the strange perspective which submerges the reflections: 'Lilies upon the surface, deep below / Two wistful faces craving each for each' (ll. 9–10). The shadowy intangible 'Willowwood' is translated into that which exceeds even its own provisionality.[65]

The sonnet emerges as a key space in which to engage Dante Gabriel Rossetti's aesthetics: the space, as 'Monna Innominata' makes clear, for the unnamed lady, the beloved of the Petrarchan tradition (epitomised by Laura to whom Christina claims a direct genealogical link). It is a space which renders her the absent and mute beloved, and a space within which the silenced projects her voice. A sonnet which reverses the topos of a dead female beloved is 'Love Lies Bleeding'.[66] Here, a lost and ghostly beloved is confronted who does not recognise the female speaker; the result is the denial of an intersubjectivity:

> Love that is dead and buried, yesterday
>   Out of his grave rose up before my face;
>   No recognition in his look, no trace
> Of memory in his eyes dust-dimmed and grey.
>
> (Crump 1: 210; ll. 1–4)

The fading male is menacing, just as the model of 'In an Artist's Studio' menaces the artist, but here the sonnet proceeds to make safe and counter, rather than celebrate, the transitoriness of the figure who is less than a subject and who has usurped the posthumous feminine position. The disruption in the discourse is suggested by the confusion between literal and figural. The dead beloved is love personified, but the bleeding corpse is also a metaphor for a past love and what might be termed a negative resurrection. The title is the name of a drooping red feathery flower and perhaps a reference to Wordsworth's poem of the same name, which describes the flower as appearing to be constantly in the process of dying: an apt figure for the feminine position in masculinist discourse.[67] The end of the poem poses a question which allows us to doubt the reality of the encounter: 'Was this to meet? Not so, we have not met.' The 'event' occurred yesterday: a displacement of time which the sonnet proceeds to intensify in order to make safe the linguistic blockage in the speaker, the male figure's threat to dialogue and intersubjectivity.

At the speaker's acknowledgement that there is no remembrance in the male figure, there follows a sequence of images which figures her recalled memory as displaced fragments:

> [...] I, remembering, found no word to say,
> But felt my quickened heart leap in its place;
> Caught afterglow, thrown back from long-set days,
> Caught echoes of all music passed away.
> Was this indeed to meet?
>
> (ll. 5–9)

With this sense of internal displacement comes a reversion to the female self: difference seems to be located internally, in the distinction between the speaker's remembrance of the beloved and the description of the encounter. The highly suggestive word 'echoes' was employed in Christina Rossetti's 'Willowwood' sonnet where the precursor is inscribed before underwriting (rather than 'superscribing') a difference of meaning onto D.G. Rossetti's own sonnets.[68] Here, the dialogical operation is explicitly *internal*, figured as a function of the workings of memory, and this overcomes the rhetorical impasse or aporia caused by the reversal of the aesthetic.

In contrast, 'Venus's Looking Glass' (Crump 1: 209), the sonnet intended to precede 'Love Lies Bleeding' and printed before it in *The Argosy* as the first sonnet in a pair and in *Goblin Market, The Prince's Progress, and Other Poems* (1875), presents the speaker as spectator to the splendour of Venus and her court in Spring. Venus is the personification of love, but in this sonnet there is no action: nothing happens except verbal play, a glory in poetic artifice, suggested by the alternative title 'Love-in-Idleness'.[69] Venus seems an empty trope but nonetheless one upon which the poem is dependent. Together, these sonnets are more than an inversion of D.G. Rossetti's denial of difference. His aesthetics are negotiated in terms of their implications for intersubjectivity. The claustrophobic pastoral scene of Venus, in which the only motion is that of verbal play, and a fading masculine figure underscore the supremacy of the narrator as spectator; but nevertheless the subjecthood of these figures is dependent upon the cultural cliché of 'Woman' as man's symptom (Venus) and an inversion of that cliché (the dead male beloved). 'Love Lies Bleeding' ends with an attempt to refuse the textual encounter – 'Not so, we have not met' – in a mimicry of D.G. Rossetti's own refusal of intersubjectivity, but it is ambiguous. The repetition of the question 'Was this to meet?' (ll. 9, 14) opens up a figure of doubt and a sense of incompletion, as well as heightening the confusion between literal and figural – of course, they *have* met, but the sense of what constitutes a meeting is never defined. 'Love Lies Bleeding' exists in this vague, liminal realm which both mimics and challenges D.G. Rossetti's attempt to erase difference. What prevails is the image of the dead male beloved – hovering between literal and figural, forever gesturing towards the aesthetic that he inverts but which the sonnet exceeds.

Out of focus

As a conclusion, I turn to the shared resonances, unseen in the critical tradition, between the photography of Julia Margaret Cameron and Christina Rossetti's commentary on D.G. Rossetti's aesthetics of the feminine. As Chapter 1 explicates, the photographic technique of Cameron is caught up in the aesthetic transformation of the visual referent that links the emerging photographic technologies with literary signatures and that, furthermore, provides us with new figures of reading verbal and visual signs. Cameron's work, like Rossetti's, does not simply reiterate the representational registers of the Pre-Raphaelite aesthetic, despite her reputation as a Pre-Raphaelite photographer. For example, Graham Ovenden, in *Pre-Raphaelite Photography*, explains her divergence from the Pre-Raphaelite aesthetic as an effect of the technical deficiency of photography in general:

> If the influence of the Pre-Raphaelites painters' search for realism contradicts Mrs. Cameron's sense of spiritual romanticism, it is because the camera is unable to interpret as readily as paint the

> complex emotional strain that make up the strength and weakness of mid-nineteenth century English art. Often, but not inevitably, the sublime hovers on the brink of the absurd.[70]

Ovenden compares Cameron's depiction of women with D.G. Rossetti's photographs of Jane Morris, for certain pieces of Cameron's work: 'give greater depths to our understanding of the languid sensuality of ideal Victorian womanhood' unlike 'the fantasy of the decaying, dope-ridden mind' suggested by portrayals of Siddal (p. 13).

Although the seminal biography by Mackenzie Bell makes no mention of Rossetti's relation to Cameron, it is known that the two women enjoyed some degree of social contact. On 13 May 1862, Cameron wrote to W.M. Rossetti to give effusive thanks for the gift of the *Goblin Market* volume:

> If you and your Sister have judged of me by my seemings, you must both have thought me unworthy and ungrateful of the book which is really precious to me. It has given me a great *longing* to know your Sister; but you don't know and won't understand how much this discourse of her soul makes me feel as if I *did* know her now, and always affectionately as well as admiringly.[71]

Cameron's social gatherings seem to have given Rossetti the opportunity to make the acquaintance of literary celebrities (including 'a glimpse of Browning'), but the invitation to her house on the Isle of Wight, with the promise of meeting Tennyson, was never taken up.[72] There is also evidence that Cameron took a photograph of Christina Rossetti in profile which unfortunately is now lost.[73]

Cameron's photographic œuvre draws some of its specific subjects from Pre-Raphaelite painting,[74] poetry,[75] and also includes portraits of literary and artistic personages.[76] It is, however, her exploitation of perspective that subverts at the same time as it represents Pre-Raphaelite aesthetics. Perspective, as a way of structuring the visual from the fallacy of the spectator's unique centrality, was undermined with the development of photography. As John Berger points out:

> The camera isolated momentary appearances and in doing so destroyed the idea that images were timeless. [...] It was no longer possible to imagine everything converging on the human eye as on the vanishing point of infinity. [...] The camera [...] demonstrated that there was no centre.[77]

Nevertheless, as we have seen in Chapter 1, photography was motivated to preserve visual aesthetics. Lindsay Smith comments:

> From the beginning, the photographic definition of focus was made to serve existing systems of representation, and in particular to conspire with the dominance of geometric perspective, thus further confirming the sovereignty of the latter in various media. In one fundamental and immediate sense, photography could appear to guarantee the continued ubiquity of geometric accounts of space by seeming to represent geometric spatial mapping in the greatest degree of verisimilitude experienced in visual perception up to that time.[78]

Pre-Raphaelite art developed alongside the new art form of photography, and the relationship between them was explored through Cameron's most distinctive characteristic: the refusal of sharp focus. This famous 'blurred' quality was considered by some contemporary commentators to be so deviant from standard practice that it constituted a flaw: 'as one of the special charms of photography consists in the completeness, detail and finish, we can scarcely commend works in which the aim appears to have been to avoid these qualities'.[79] Cameron's blurred focus has rarely been attributed to an aesthetic, but rather to her camera or her poor eyesight. Cameron, however, defined her photography as an art form, similar to oil portraits. Ford comments that her negatives were untouched and unenlarged, and yet unusually large for her day (p. 19). Further:

> She appears to have had blinds fitted to her glass house so that she could cut off light from any direction, enabling the isolation of her sitters from their backgrounds, the revelation of depths of character in a face by a searching shaft of light from one side or another, the control of all the dramatic composition in a figure or group. She swathed her models in dark clothes, pushed her camera as close to their heads as she could and eliminated all extraneous details of clothing and furniture. (p. 20)

Cameron's subject fills up the entire space of the photograph, as with the portrait taken of Cameron's niece Julia Jackson in April 1867, the mother of Virginia Woolf (Plate 7). As in other photographs by Cameron, this portrait denies a sharpness of focus. Rather than geometric perspective, the sense of depth is given by light and shade falling on the subject's face and all extraneous background details are consigned to the darkness. There is a focused plane on Jackson's nose and lips, but the subject seems to recede from it, to fade away from sharpness. The detail of the neck of the dress, for example, varies in degrees of focus from the left side which is *almost* in focus to the right portion which is completely indistinct. The subject that fills up the space of the photograph thus conveys a presence in absence; the pose is static (partly due to the lengthy exposure time) but the figure, in an enactment of loss and indeterminacy, seems to vanish into indistinctness as there is no secure point of the photograph, no obvious point of sharpness, that attracts the gaze.

Cameron's response to criticism of her blurred negatives forms a statement of her aesthetics. In a letter to Sir John Herschel, December 31 1864, she famously comments on her non-experiential mode of photography and attempts to define her principle of representation. She wishes that Herschel:

> had spoken of my Photography in that spirit which will elevate it and induce an ignorant public to believe in other than mere conventional topographic Photography – map making & skeletal rendering of feature & form without that roundness and fullness of force & feature that modelling of flesh & limb which the focus I use can only give tho' called & condemned as *'out of focus.'* What is focus – & who has a right to say what focus is the legitimate focus – My aspirations are to ennoble Photography and to secure for it the character and uses of High Art by combining the real & Ideal & sacrificing nothing of Truth by all possible devotion to Poetry & *beauty*. (pp. 140–1)

The combination of structure of space, locale and representation in topography is rejected by Cameron as a false literalness which does not depict the desired 'roundness & fullness of force & feature'. Further, the exclusion of all but the subject is, in relation to the conventional photographic insistence on sharpness and detail, a (synecdochal) attempt to represent a subject in terms other than with reference to an experiential depiction of a locale or background. Cameron's insistence on the aesthetic value of her 'out of focus' photography also suggests that the subject is fading, transitory and elusive:

> I believe that what my youngest Boy Henry Herschel [...] told me, is quite true, that my first successes viz. my out of focus pictures, were 'a fluke.' That is to say that when focusing & coming to something which to my eye was very beautiful I stopped there, instead of

> screwing on the lens to the more definite focus which all other Photographers insist upon.[80]

The quotation is often taken as an statement of the accidental and arbitrary nature of her blurred focus, but she qualifies her 'fluke' with an assertion that she catches a Paterian moment of beauty that is fragile, delicate and fleeting.

As we have seen in Chapter 1, Cameron's photographic techniques critique representational axioms, in particular the ideology of perceptual mastery. To read her photographs, as photographic historians have done, as the development of 'soft focus' – rather than unfocused – falsely aligns her practice with a painterly style and obscures her challenge to the representational system's masculinist scopic regimes.[81] Smith equates focus with the fetishisation of the gaze, for focus enables loss (castration) to be displaced. The denial of focus is thus the denial of the fetish, and so 'the female subject is here newly realised'. Cameron: 'represents the possibility of demobilising the whole mechanism of fetishism in the field of vision' (p. 257). The disturbance of geometric perspective in D.G. Rossetti's *The Girlhood of Mary Virgin* and *The Annunciation* conveyed problematics of the fetishistic attempt to deny difference of both genders and genre, and so to deny loss (or women's castration) and the corresponding aporia of 'Woman' in the representational axioms. The refutation of perspective and focus in Cameron's photography exploits the insecurity evident in D.G. Rossetti's verbal/visual aesthetics by an insistence on unfocused subjects that resist the denial of difference and resist the fetishisation of the gaze.

The juxtaposition of Cameron's photography and Christina Rossetti's response to her brother's early pictures reveals a shared concern with perspective and the represented subject. Cameron's 'unfocused' female subjects have a similar spectral quality to Rossetti's; both representations of the excessively feminine, fleeting, and posthumous, they dramatise the feminine as both the ground and vanishing point of the aesthetic, and enact 'Woman' as man's symptom. But this is not a mere re-inscription of 'Woman' as undefinable, as not there. Precisely *because* the figure vanishes within the aesthetic, the subject evades the masculinist frame and fetishistic gaze:

> If [...] we conceive the symptom as it was articulated in the late Lacan, – namely, as a particular signifying formation which confers on the subject its very ontological consistency, enabling it to structure its basic, constitutive relationship towards *jouissance* –

> then the entire relationship is reversed: if the symptom is dissolved, the [male] subject itself loses the ground under its feet, disintegrates. 'Woman is the symptom of man' thus comes to mean that *man himself exists only through woman* qua *his symptom*: all his ontological consistency is suspended from his symptom, is 'externalised' in his symptom. [. . .] Woman, on the other hand, does *not* exist, she *insists*, which is why she does not come to be through man only. There is something in her that escapes the relation to man, the reference to the phallic signifier.[82]

Although vanishing spectral figures in Rossetti's poems discussed above are feminine, within the ideology of the scopic it is ultimately the identities of the masculine creator and beloved that dissolve with the fading figure in the poetry's engagement with her brother's aesthetic. Cameron's 'out of focus' photographs are a reminder of castration which frustrates the potency of the gaze of the masculine subject. This is not a declaration of feminine autonomy but an intimation of the potential for the undoing and un-fixing of the feminine from inside representational axioms and the potential for challenging the position of the masculine in the aesthetic. Always caught within the masculinist regime, Rossetti and Cameron nevertheless suggest that uncanny spectral feminine figures may dissolve as symptoms, and that they can unsettle the masculine gaze and have the ability to return the look. While they dissolve, they also reconfigure the material reality of the subject as that 'strange fold' between culture and nature, speaking and biology.

6
Father's Place, Mother's Space: Italy and the Paradisal

Strange homelands

We cannot fathom these mysteries of transplantation.

Edmund Gosse.[1]

In the nineteenth-century, Italy functions as a privileged trope, as the metaphorical site where issues of the past, political revolution and the exotic coalesce.[2] For Victorian women poets, however, Italy is also invested with particularly acute and gender inflected questions of identity and homeland. Angela Leighton reads this concern as the reaction of female poets both to the post-Romantic formulation of the home as a stable feminine sphere and the associated feminisation and interiorisation of poetry. Summarising Felicia Hemans' reaction to this discourse of Italy as homeland, Leighton argues that 'In many of her poems, home is either empty of its main figurehead, the father, or else home is somewhere else: in Italy, in the south – paradoxically, in one of those places still subject to the convulsions of political change.'[3] Leighton's anthology of Victorian women poets, edited with Margaret Reynolds, demonstrates the fascination with and importance of Italy as a reclaimed alternative feminine home. Elizabeth Barrett Browning's conception of Italy as a homeland in *Aurora Leigh* and *Casa Guidi Windows* is well documented, but other poets pursue the connection further and in different ways. Poems such as Alice Meynell's 'The Watershed', for example, testify to the transformative and enabling potential of this trope to forge a replenishing sense of feminine place and belonging as an alternative to the patriarchy of Victorian Britain:

But O the unfolding South! the burst
Of Summer! O to see
Of all the southward brooks the first!
The travelling heart went free
With endless streams; that strife was stopped;
And down a thousand vales I dropped,
I flowed to Italy.[4]

The images of warmth, fluidity, and *jouissance* occasioned by travel into Italy here connote the maternal, an association also made by other writers of the period. Mary Elizabeth Coleridge declares of her journey to Italy 'I feel as if I'd come not to a Fatherland but to a Motherland that I had always longed for and had never known.'[5]

For Christina Rossetti, however, Italy proves a more problematic trope. Her poetry conceptualises Italy as a homeland, but it is a homeland from which she is estranged. This double figure of home and exile provides a focal point for explorations of identity and heritage that emerge in multiple configurations of loss.[6] What interests me here is the relationship between the dominant figures that signify loss: the connection of the maternal and the beloved to Italy.

In the Freudian narrative of sexuality, the mother represents the original experience of loss, for the child must relinquish the pre-œdipal identity with the mother in order to take up a position in the Symbolic Order. As a result, the mother is the point to which all intimations of lost homelands, of absence and of exile, return.[7] By positioning her mother as a Muse, Rossetti speaks from the position of celebration and mourning as she remembers the 'homeliness' of the maternal body and marks her estrangement from it. But, in addition, her mother is also the primal love object, and Rossetti's sequence of Italian love poems to Charles Bagot Cayley, *Il rosseggiar dell'Oriente* (*The Reddening Dawn*), suggests that the Italian language itself is a vehicle that signifies not a familiar and homely 'mother tongue', but the loss of a maternal homeland remembered and rehearsed in her relationship with the beloved.

Rossetti's poetry, however, does not endlessly rehearse the painful trauma of loss. In the multiple configurations of absence and exile, she forges a personal space that signifies the paradisal by repressing the memory of separation from the mother. Such a space is both maternal and recuperative and gestures to the utopian possibilities of paradise as a re-found homeland.[8] Elisabeth Bronfen, in *Over her Dead Body: Death, Femininity, and the Aesthetic*, persuasively argues that femininity is the metonym for death, absence, grief and loss, for, in the dominant

representational scheme, the feminine signifies both the ground and vanishing point of the Symbolic Order. But, in her thematic concern with the mother, the beloved, and Italy, Rossetti's poetry does not merely re-inscribe the aesthetic's metonymical collapse of femininity with death. Rather, she gestures to alternative representational axioms which promise the restoration of the afterlife as a lost and refound maternal homeland, of which Italy is the imperfect earthly precursor.

Italy and the Italian language enjoyed priority for the Rossetti family by virtue of the father Gabriele Rossetti who was a political exile and Dante Alighieri scholar. Frances Rossetti, Gabriele's wife, was herself half Italian through her paternal line, the Polidoris. Christina, Dante Gabriel, William Michael, and Maria Rossetti were all bi-lingual, and the family had a double literary, cultural and linguistic identity. In the biographies, however, Gabriele is represented as quintessentially foreign and Frances as quintessentially English: he is eccentric, odd and flamboyant; she is modest, correct and 'full of common-sense'.[9] Marsh summarises the comparison thus: 'fatherly exuberance was balanced by maternal steadiness, and her firmness softened by his generosity' (p. 24). Although Christina Rossetti's Italian literary heritage is mediated by the paternal association with Dante Alighieri, in Rossetti's poetry, Italy is conceived as maternal.

Christina Rossetti's close association with her mother is circulated in the biographies as the distinguishing feature of her identity. Rossetti is depicted as the ideal daughter and is constantly equated with her mother. In the seminal biographical text, the memoir prefixed to his edition of the poems, William Michael Rossetti comments that

> for all her kith and kin, but for her mother beyond all the rest, her love was as deep as it was often silent. [...] To the latter (Frances Rossetti) it may be said that her whole life was devoted: they were seldom severed, even for a few days.[10]

The first biographer, Mackenzie Bell, tells how Rossetti's doctor remembers her most for her love for her mother, which was 'a feeling shown by every word and look. In the whole course of his life he had never known an instance of affection more absorbing in itself or more touchingly evinced'.[11] This excessive identification with her mother marks Rossetti as an eternal daughter, forever identified securely as feminine. As her mother's companion, and after her mother's death the companion of her aunts, Rossetti is always socially dependent, never independent. The ideal domestic, feminine sphere she inhabited with her mother secures and refines her spinsterly status into the reflection of the highest love, maternal love, and also enables Rossetti's asexuality, in line with her saintly persona, to be sustained.[12] As Deborah Gorham asserts, the contradiction inherent in the Victorian notion of female sexuality – the ideal of asexual feminine purity and the active sexuality required for motherhood – is resolved by the emphasis upon the daughter and her childlike dependency, transposed from the mother.[13] In fact, Bell quotes from Watts-Dunton's review in *The Athenæum*, 15 February 1896, of the posthumously published *New Poems*: 'all that is noblest in Christina Rossetti's poetry, an ever-present sense of the beauty and power of goodness, must surely have come from the mother' (p. 116).

Christina Rossetti believed that the maternal love was the highest of earthly love, the ideal to which all other love recurs. In a famously contradictory letter to Augusta Webster, she responds the question of women's suffrage with a statement of the value of maternal love:

> I take exceptions at the exclusion of married women from the suffrage, – for who so apt as Mothers – all previous arguments allowed for the moment – to protect the interests of themselves and of their offspring? I do think if anything ever does sweep away the barrier of sex, and make the female not a giantess or a heroine but at once and full grown a hero and a giant, it is that mighty maternal love which makes little birds and little beasts as well as little women matches for very big adversaries.[14]

In a letter to Caroline Jenner, dated 26 January 1875, Rossetti states her belief that 'the Maternal Type is to me one of the dear and beautiful things which on earth help towards realising that Archetype which is beyond all conception dear and beautiful'. The 'Maternal Type', she asserts, typifies divine love.[15] In *Seek and Find: a Double Series of Short Studies of the Benedicite*, Rossetti develops her conception of the ideal love by exploring her belief that Christ's love is maternal.[16]

As well as her reiterated assertion that maternal love is the ideal, Rossetti also spoke from the position of the mother in what can be seen as an experimental subject position, suggesting the possibility of a total identification with the maternal. Along with *Sing-Song*, the volume of nursery rhymes which adopt the mother's voice, there is also another, more autobiographical instance. As an appendix to her *Family Letters*, W.M. Rossetti gives extracts from a diary she kept on behalf of her mother between 1881 and 1886, and he notes that

> This, as the wording shows, purports to be the diary of Mrs. Rossetti, our mother; but my sister, acting on her behalf, was, with a few exceptions in the earlier dates, the real writer of the diary, so far as handwriting is concerned, and no doubt the composition or diction is often hers as well.[17]

In the act of writing this diary, Rossetti adopts her mother's subject position and enacts discursively her close relationship with the maternal. Significantly, she continues speaking in her mother's voice while giving an account of Frances Rossetti's death: 'The night over, no rally: unconsciousness at last. [. . .] Mr. Nash prayed beside my bed-side, but I knew it not (?)' (p. 232). The parenthetical question mark exposes Rossetti's own subject position here as she speaks from and through the uncertainty of her mother's consciousness, literally (if tentatively) refiguring the maternal at the mother's death. Only in an afterword to the diary after Frances Rossetti's death does she assume her own voice as a daughter: 'I, Christina G. Rossetti, happy and unhappy daughter of so dear a saint, write the last words' (p. 232). The ventriloquised, and, in the final entries, prosopopœic, diary illustrates Christina Rossetti's ability to transpose subject positions between her own signature and that of her mother's. This dialectic translation from self to maternal and back again suggests a subject discursively engaged with the mother as other. Rossetti's diary entries adopt a subject-in-process that enjoys an intersubjectivity which questions the stability of identity, for the stability is established at the expense of exile from the mother necessitated by the entry into the Symbolic Order.

Despite Rossetti's close identification with her mother, however, the attempt to forge an intersubjective dialogue between the subject and (m)other in the poetry cannot completely free itself from androcentric axioms. Indeed, according to the Freudian masculinist definition of ego formation as separation, identity is established at the painful expense of a union with the mother. Instead of total identification, tropes of exchange disclose both difference from and sameness to the maternal. In Rossetti's poetic language, the mother is depicted as the origin of love, the perfect precursor, to whom all heterosexual love recurs. *A Pageant and Other Poems* contains a dedicatory poem which celebrates maternal love in a love sonnet:

> Sonnets are full of love, and this my tome
> Has many sonnets: so here now shall be
> One sonnet more, a love sonnet, from me

To her whose heart is my heart's quiet home,
To my first Love, my Mother, on whose knee
I learnt love-lore that is not troublesome.

(Crump 2: 59, ll. 1–6)

The poem both supplements the œuvre of love poems and also refers back to their origin. The speaker associates her mother with requited and restful love, whose heart is the resting place of the speaker's heart. In later lines the mother is the 'loadstar while I go and come' (l. 8), the point of a stability to be returned to, a guide. The reciprocity of the love means that the speaker will dedicate the volume to her mother: 'I have woven a wreath / Of rhymes wherewith to crown your honoured name' (ll. 10–11). And, in the final couplet, the maternal love is seen to transcend all that is changeable: the flame of love's 'blessed glow transcends the laws / Of time and change and mortal life and death'. Along with the idealised picture, the speaker's emphatic insistence on her position as a daughter responding to the mother's love associates her with the passive. The first maternal love is the ideal: all future love is imperfect and there is always a return to the perfection of the origin, to the mother.

Rossetti also wrote Valentines to her mother for each year between 1877 and 1886. The Valentines represent a sequence of love poems that celebrate the relation between mother and daughter as a pure and refined version of heterosexual love and that attempt to redefine the relation of subject to other on these lines. As a note in the manuscript explains,

> These *Valentines* had their origin from my dearest Mother's remarking that she had never received one. I, her CGR, ever after supplied one on the day= & so far as I recollect it was a *surprise* every time, she having forgotten all about it in the interim. (Crump 3: 487)

This note adds a narrative to the poems that attaches them through the anecdote to an origin, to the mother as the primal experience of love. The anecdote also suggests how the Valentines themselves form a repetitive pattern, as they are written for the same day each year and each year surprise Frances Rossetti. In fact, the theme of the poems establishes a repetition attached to seasonal repetition, while depicting maternal love as the superlative earthly love, pure and constant. As her entry in *Time Flies* for 14 February makes clear, St Valentine represents for Rossetti both the secular and the divine as inextricably a 'double aspect' which 'accords, or should accord, with heaven as well as earth'.[18] The feast of St Valentine is associated with the proximity of spring, with all its typical symbolic overtones for Rossetti: 'More shower than shine / Brings sweet St. Valentine' (1880; Crump 3: 316), 'Too cold almost for hope of Spring' (1881), and the feast day comes at Winter's first sign of Spring, 'When life reawakens and hope in everything' (1886). The topos of repetition also is evident in the Valentine for 1877, which describes the transformative effect of familial love:

> Own Mother dear
> We all rejoicing here
> Wait for each other.
> [. . . . .]
> Till each dear face appear
> Transfigured by Love's flame
> Yet still the same,–
> The same yet new,–
> My face to you,
> Your face to me,
> Made lovelier by Love's flame
> But still the same
>
> (Crump 3: 314–15)

The iteration of sameness despite the transfiguration tells of more than the retention of an individual's identity; for daughter and mother, sister and brother, are mirrored onto each other as the same and yet difference is retained between them, emphasised by the personal pronouns 'you' and 'me'.

The mother, as 'embodied Love', is the ideal precursor to which all subsequent love refers but cannot equal: 'A better sort of Venus with an air / Angelic from thoughts that dwell above' (1882). She represents domesticated asexual love to which the subject always returns. This suggests what Bronfen terms 'an economy of love based on repetition', for it endlessly repeats the experience of maternal love. This is, however, a repetition that hinges on a paradox: as well as returning to the primordial loss of the maternal body, the repeated act of return attempts to supplement and cover up the loss with a new love object. Repetition, according to this model, is the conflation of loss and addition, and 'describes a longing for an identity between two terms, even as it stages the impossibility of literal identity'.[19] The wish to return to a full pre-œdipal union with the mother is frustrated at the very point at which it is desired.[20]

The inability to sustain a total identification with the mother leads to the double figure of the maternal space as both homeland and exile which also emerges in the poetic treatment of Italy. The poem 'En Route' is paradigmatic of this double figure. W.M. Rossetti's note to '*En Route*' links his sister's relation to Italy with Gabriele Rossetti and suggests that, for both of them, the country is not wholly foreign: 'the passionate delight in Italy to which *En Route* bears witness suggests that she was almost alien – or, like her father, an exile – in the North'.[21] W.M. Rossetti's insistence that his sister's sense of partial exile from Italy identifies her with her father is part of the biographical insistence that the father represents all that is foreign in the Rossetti household. But, in 'En Route', Italy is associated with the mother. The speaker in the poem addresses Italy:

> Wherefore art thou strange, and not my mother?
>   Thou hast stolen my heart and broken it:
> Would that I might call thy sons 'My brother',
>   Call thy daughters 'Sister sweet';
> Lying in thy lap not in another,
>   Dying at thy feet.
>
> (Crump 2: 382–3)

The speaker expects Italy to be familiar and maternal; instead, it is 'strange'. The poem also, however, insists upon the familiarity of Italy, for 'With mine own feet I have trodden thee, / Have seen with mine own eyes.' In fact, the first line of the stanza cited above encapsulates the disturbingly double nature of the speaker's relation to Italy as both familiar home and unfamiliar exile. 'Wherefore art thou strange, and not my mother' has a peculiar logic. It suggests Italy's association with a maternal homeland, for the speaker expects the country to be familiar and therefore to be her mother. But by virtue of the zeugma, 'strange' refers to the mother as well as to Italy; the 'strange' homeland is not maternal, because the speaker is herself estranged from the mother. The zeugma, working here as the rhetorical figure of the repressed (the adjective 'strange' in the second clause of the line) marks the maternal as the trope *par excellence* of homeland, as well as of exile and loss. Freud, in his essay 'The Uncanny', suggests that the process by which the familiar becomes unfamiliar marks an uncanny moment, when the homely (*heimlich*) signifies the unhomely (*unheimlich*).[22] This poem marks an uncanny moment when Italy and the maternal are rhetorically acknowledged as both known and unknown.

In the following stanza, the departure from Italy, the 'land of love', prompts intense and excessive 'yearnings without gain'. Rather than simply a yearning for a return to that country, however, the desire is for something *never* possessed:

> Why should I seek and never find
> That something which I have not had?
> Fair and unutterably sad
> The world hath sought time out of mind;
> Our words have been already said,
> Our deeds have been already done:
> There's nothing new beneath the sun
> But there is peace among the dead.
>
> (Crump 2: 120, 383)

If the analogy of Italy to the maternal is pursued, this stanza suggests that the original and total identification with the mother has been repressed as 'That something which I have not had' because the fact of loss is so painful. Although the sense of loss in this stanza is provoked by the departure from Italy, the excessiveness of the loss and its lack of a referent ('that something') intimates an additional cause of grief. Earlier in the poem, the speaker suggests that her gender is the cause of her grief:

> Men work and think, but women feel;
> And so (for I'm a woman, I)
> And so I should be glad to die
> And cease from impotence of zeal,
> And cease from hope, and cease from dread,
> And cease from yearning without gain,
> And cease from all this world of pain,
> And be at peace among the dead.
>
> (Crump 2: 120)

The feminine is here equated with yearning, passivity, and loss, and death gives the only relief. The emphatically feminine speaker is estranged from a maternal homeland and her sense of loss will only be appeased with death, suggesting that death is the speaker's true homeland.

Part of the unpublished stanzas of 'En Route' is included in *A Pageant and Other Poems* (1881) as 'An "Immurata" Sister' (Crump 2: 120–1). In

1 Charles Dodgson, photograph of the Rossetti family (1863).

2 Max Beerbohm, cartoon of Christina and D. G. Rossetti.

3 Dante Gabriel Rossetti, chalk drawing of Christina Rossetti (1877).

4 Elliot and Fry, studio photograph of Christina Rossetti (1877).

5 Dante Gabriel Rossetti, *The Girlhood of Mary Virgin* (1849).

6 Dante Gabriel Rossetti, *The Annunciation* (1850).

7 Julia Magaret Cameron, photograph of Julia Jackson (April, 1867).

this revised version, the three stanzas that refer to Italy are deleted and new lines are added that seem to resolve the disturbing nature of the other, for they suggest that death brings a renewal and a mystical purification reminiscent of Vaughan's *Silex Scintillans* (1650):[23]

Hearts that die, by death renew their youth,
  Lightened of this life that doubts and dies;
Silent and contented, while the Truth
  Unveiled makes them wise.

(ll. 13–16)

Sparks fly upward toward their fount of fire,
  Kindling, flashing, hovering: –
Kindle, flash, my soul; mount higher and higher,
  Thou whole burnt-offering!

(ll. 25–8)

The addition of these lines, along with the deletion of those referring to Italy, resolves the sense of loss by portraying death as rejuvenation in a realm *beyond* language and *beyond* loss. The title of this version, furthermore, suggests a speaker removed, or literally walled off, from earthly concerns while awaiting a spiritual release in death. In this way, the sense of exile from a maternal homeland is deleted and replaced with the intimation of Paradise as a replenishing utopian space.

The revisions that produce 'An "Immurata" Sister' imply that desire for the homeland of Italy translates into, or substitutes for, a desire for the paradisal. This shift of longing is commensurate with the repression of loss from the maternal body, for paradise is enjoyed as a utopian and feminine space of union between speaker and (m)other that recalls the primary and pre-œdipal relationship of the child with the mother. In fact, the repression of loss is refigured in this poem as sisterhood, another feminine relationship. In the deleted section of 'Seeking rest' (Crump 3: 429), the space of the grave, the home for the sleeper who awaits the Resurrection, is also portrayed as a feminine space – but here it is maternal:

She knocked at the Earth's greeny door:
  O Mother, let me in;
For I am weary of this life
  That is so full of sin.

As the site for spiritual rebirth, the grave is here analogous to the womb. The implication is that these spaces 'outside' the Symbolic Order – the pre-œdipal and death – are both feminine versions of the paradisal.

The desire of the feminine subject to align itself with the maternal testifies to a yearning for an original perfect wholeness, prior to separation, that becomes the projected paradigm for all love. This is, however, also the utopian condition upon which the afterlife is desired; both origin and end, death and life converge in the association of the maternal unity with a feminine paradise. The fullest statement of this is 'Mother Country' (Crump 1: 222), published in *Macmillan's Magazine* in March 1868 and then added to *Goblin Market, The Prince's Progress and Other Poems* (1875). The poem begins with the question:

> Oh what is that country
>   And where can it be,
> Not mine own country,
>   But dearer far to me?
>
> (ll. 1–4)

Only the title identifies this land as firmly maternal and also a land of origin. The speaker does not belong to the place, and possession of it is deferred, 'If one day I may see' (l. 6). The attributes listed, however, suggest an exotic place, with spices, cedars, gold and ivory; but these are only intimated in a transitory and fleeting vision:

> As I lie dreaming
>   It rises, that land;
> There rises before me
>   Its green golden strand,
> With the bowing cedars
>   And the shining sand;
> It sparkles and flashes
>   Like a shaken brand.
>
> (ll.9–16)

The speaker now positions herself as dreaming and perceiving the land in glimpses. In the next stanza it becomes clear that she imagines herself as a sleeper in Hades who can catch the 'windy song' (l. 20) of the angels and understand their non-verbal communication, 'Like the rise of a high tide / Sweeping full and strong' (ll. 21–2).[24] The subject is involved in a double projection: she positions herself as dead and, as a sleeper who dreams of the Resurrection, she anticipates the time when the dreams become real. The following stanzas emphasise the space of the grave as a social leveller and as a separation from the material world: 'Gone out of sight of all / Except our God' (ll. 47–8). And then, in the final three verses, the subject depicts herself in a semiotic or pre-œdipal retreat from language and at a point of repetition, as the afterlife is both an end and a beginning:

> Shut into silence
>   From the accustomed song,
> Shut into solitude
>   From all earth's throng
> [. . . . .]
> Life made an end of,
>   Life but just begun,
> Life finished yesterday,
>   Its last sand run;
> Life new-born with the morrow,
>   Fresh as the sun:
> While done is done for ever;
>   Undone, undone.
>
> (ll. 49–53, 57–64)

The repetition in the language mimics the theme that life and death coalesce. The final stanza, however, reverses the repetition: if the afterlife is life then it is also real, and the material world is a dream:

> And if that life is life,
>   This is but a breath,
> The passage of a dream
>   And the shadow of death
>
> (ll. 65–8)

The poem works on the principle of repetition as a recurrence to a point of origin and, by imagining the afterlife as a utopia accessible through dream and non-verbal communication that juxtaposes life and death, also associates that land with the semiotic maternal body.

The utopian vision of a maternal, feminine paradise as homeland can be imagined only on the condition that loss is repressed. In 'Italia, io ti saluto', (Crump 2: 74–5; also published in the *Pageant* volume), however, the speaker refuses to repress her difference from Italy and the Italian language. Italy is imagined as only a partial identification and the result is a statement of Italy's difference from and sameness to the speaker. The speaker is resigned to leaving Italy: 'To see no more the country half my own, / Nor hear the half familiar speech, / Amen, I say' (ll. 6–8). The south and the north are firmly differentiated and set up as opposites: 'I turn to that bleak North / Whence I came forth – / The South lies out of reach' (ll. 8–10). The distance and loss are negotiated by swallows, whose migration back to the south reminds the speaker of 'the sweet South' and 'the sweet name'. As with Swinburne's 'Itylus', the swallows mediate between the two opposites, north and south, but the prevailing sense of Rossetti's poem is that of both assimilation and isolation from the 'half familiar' country and language (made more immediate when we remember that the members of the Rossetti family were all bilingual).[25]

Cor mio

To posit Italy as partially identifiable, as 'half familiar', suggests the conjugation of both loss and union, difference and sameness, which is the condition of the speaking subject predicated on the loss of the mother. But Rossetti, through the reiteration of the phrase '*cor mio*' in her poetry, attempts to forge a space of intersubjective exchange where difference and loss is expelled. '*Cor mio*' (my heart) signifies both the speaker's love *and* the beloved.[26] The phrase is a common platitude in the Italian language, but in Rossetti's poetry it is transformed to figure the intensely private space of the heart and, in fact, is used only in poems that remained unpublished during Rossetti's lifetime, probably because of their personal nature and because of fears that her non-native Italian would be criticised.[27] The concept of a private interior space that is both a physical reality and yet also beyond interpretation and language is to be found in much of her poetry (for example, in 'Winter: My Secret'). But the special significance of the Italian phrase '*cor mio*' is that it denotes *both* the speaker's heart *and* her beloved, and so suggests that the concept of Italy and the Italian language that the phrase represents are part of the subject and other. In fact, the rhetorical function of this Italian phrase indicates a movement of translation (literally, of course, carrying over) and exchange between subject and other, for it is a space of mediation. Further, this translation is an anticipation and an intimation of the utopian and paradisal union of subject and other that rehearses the pre-Œdipal intersubjective relationship with the mother which occurs in a space prior to the knowledge of difference.

In a posthumously published sonnet, which takes as its title the Italian phrase, the speaker addresses a beloved from her past whom she terms '*cor mio*'.[28] This phrase denotes the speaker of the poem as well as the beloved; as a result '*cor mio*' functions as part of the movement of exchange between subject and the beloved. By the articulation of '*cor mio*', the 'two divided parts' of the subject's heart are brought together:

> Still sometimes in my secret heart of hearts
> I say 'Cor mio' when I remember you,
> And thus I yield us both one tender due,
> Wielding one whole of two divided parts.
>
> (Crump 3: 346, ll. 1–4)

The naming of the beloved is located firmly within the subject's 'secret heart of hearts', within the interior security of a self-reflexive doubling that is prompted by memory. The ambiguous unity of subject and beloved is immediately suggested by 'one tender due', 'due' implying that the union is not actual but owed to them both, and also implying monetary value which the following lines emphasise in images of exchange. The union between subject and other becomes, in fact, not a union but an exchange between them. But the other is again already part of the subject, representing both the loss and re-finding of the primary love object, the mother. 'Would you have given me roses for the rue / For which I bartered roses in love's marts?' (ll. 7–8): in this rhetorical question, exchange works back on itself as the speaker posits the reversal of an earlier transference, figured, significantly, as occurring in the market place. The beloved is asked whether he would have *replaced* the roses that the speaker exchanged for rueful love, but this questions if the beloved would have *accepted* roses from the speaker in return for rue. The uncertainty as to what type of exchange is meant ensures that the beloved and the speaker are not given secure market-place positions, as producer or consumer of a commodity, and heightens the sense that exchange itself is not a transferral of equivalents, of roses for rue, love for pain, but a type of substitution of the subject for the other.[29]

The sestet, however, increases the speaker's alienation from the beloved as the emphasis moves back to memory, upon which the sonnet is predicated. Despite being her 'heart', the beloved forgets the speaker's sacrifice just as 'late in autumn one forgets the spring' (l. 9). The previous octave, which had told of exchange, gives way to a sense of loss, of impasse and of the speaker's powerlessness:

So late in summer one forgets the spring,
  Forgets the summer with its opulence,
The callow birds that long have found a wing,
  The swallows that more lately got them hence:
Will anything like spring, will anything
  Like summer, rouse one day the slumbering sense?

(ll. 9–14)

The memory of the act of exchange leads to a rhetorical question that doubts the inevitability of the cycle of the seasons, the eventual substitution of autumn for spring.[30] Exchange between subject and beloved is entirely retrospective and intransigent. The final line suggests a fruitless anticipation that the 'slumbering sense' might awaken; the passive speaker's loss is heightened by the absence of the addressee, for the question is rhetorical.

As a figure for the relation between subject and beloved, the phrase '*cor mio*' does not work rhetorically as a metaphor, as a similarity of things not normally contiguous. Instead, there is a metonymical substitution of the attribute of the beloved for the beloved himself, of heart ('*cor*') for other. This substitution is a type of translation (or, in Julia Kristeva's terms, transposition) which dramatises less the assimilation of the subject with the other than a repression of the difference between them.[31] By the sonnet's sestet, however, the act of translation gives way to the acknowledgement of difference. Significantly, the structure of the sestet sets up an analogy (an expression of the same subject with a difference) between itself and the octave by the phrase 'So' (l. 9) that admits the inability to maintain the incorporation of subject and other, for the difference repressed in metonymy returns.[32] The poem suggests that a metonymical identity between subject and other can only be sustained in retrospect and memory. Such an intersubjective exchange is, however, the condition of the pre-œdipal child's relation to the mother, which in this poem is posited as the imaginary (if unsustainable) union of speaker and beloved. The use of analogy is here a rhetorical figure based upon the primal loss of the maternal, when the same subjects (to adapt Coleridge's expression) become inscribed with difference. In the poem, the sestet's analogical structure suggests that the memory of the union between the speaker and the beloved cannot repress the difference between them.

Absence of the beloved also predominates in the Italian sequence *Il rosseggiar dell'Oriente* (*The Reddening Dawn*), which is similarly concerned with a type of exchange between the subject and beloved utilising the phrase *'cor mio'*, but the exchange is here superseded by a looking forward rather than back in a proleptic desire for the afterlife. As in the sonnet 'Cor Mio', reciprocity is stressed and *'cor mio'* is the space that enables this, for it connotes both the subject and the beloved:

> Possibil non sarebbe
> Ch'io non t'amassi, o caro:
> Chi mai si scorderebbe
> Del proprio core?
> Se amaro il dolce fai,
> Dolce mi fai l'amaro;
> Se qualche amor mi dài,
> Ti do l'amore.
>
> (Poem 16)

[It would not be possible for me not to love you, oh darling: whoever would forget their own heart? If you make bitter the sweet, sweet you make the bitter; if you give me a little love, I give you love.[33]]

The sense of a secretive locale, the *cor mio* and the more amorphous concept of the afterlife, is especially emphatic in this sequence, for it is loaded with personal references, presumably to Charles Bagot Cayley whom the sequence is traditionally taken to address.[34] W.M. Rossetti names Cayley as the addressee of the sequence in the memoir to the *Poetical Works* of 1904 and suggests that, although his sister apparently rejected his proposal of marriage on religious grounds 'she loved the scholarly recluse to the last day of his life, 5 December 1883, and, to the last day of her own, his memory' (p. liii). He asserts that much of the relationship was very private, for 'Christina was extremely reticent in all matters in which her affections were deeply engaged'. The suggestion that the relationship has a wholly private and interior existence, especially after Cayley's death when it was located in her memory, is again repeated in his notes to the sequence with reference to the manuscript itself:

> For any quasi-explanation as to these singularly pathetic verses – 'Love's very vesture and elect disguise,' the inborn idiom of a pure

> and impassioned heart—I refer the reader to the Memoir. The verses were kept by Christina in the jealous seclusion of her writing-desk, and I suppose no human eye had looked upon them until I found them there after her death. (p. 439)

In *Il rosseggiar*, there is a constant emphasis upon reciprocity between the subject and the beloved within the secret space of the subject's heart. In poem 4 the speaker posits possible reunions independent of material time, and concludes:

> E perciò 'Fuggi' io dico al tempo, e omai
> 'Passa pur' dico al vanitoso mondo:
> Mentre mi sogno quel che dici e fai
> Ripeto in me 'Doman sarà giocondo,
> 'Doman sarem' – mai s'ami tu lo sai,
> E se non ami a che mostrarti il fondo?
>
> (Poem 4)

[And therefore to time I say 'flee', and now 'please pass by' I say to the vain world. While I dream what which you say and do, I say to myself again and again 'tomorrow will be joyful, tomorrow we will be . . .' – but if you love me you know, and if you don't love, why show you the depths of my heart?]

Exchange is located in anticipation, memory, and dreams; but, significantly, the reverie is broken off with an assertion that the beloved does not, or should not, know her thoughts, for the gesture of showing the heart to the beloved is deemed unnecessary if he loves her and superfluous if he does not. The interplay of subject and other is thus grounded in retrospect, expectation, and gesture.

The exchange is made possible by the separation of subject from beloved – in fact, the sequence's subtitle translates 'To my distant friend'.[35] His absence incites the desire for presence, as in poem 13, where the speaker looks out from her 'eastern window' in the direction where the beloved lives, and yearns for him. Unlike Barrett Browning's *Sonnets From the Portuguese*, which was an important influence upon Rossetti, the sequence does not seem to be based upon a linear narrative, for interspersed amongst poems that imply that the beloved is alive there are lyrics based upon his death. The first suggestion of this is in poem 5, where the speaker laments 'Dolce cor mio perduto e non perduto, / Dolce mia vita che mi lasci in morte' [my sweet heart lost and not lost, my sweet life that left me on dying]. The following poem seems placed before the beloved's death, when the speaker imagines meeting the beloved in his house; but the death of the beloved does not impede communion and exchange, for he is both 'lost and not lost' (poem 5). The physical separation through death of the other, however, signals another type of exchange in which the beloved is bargained for by the speaker, who urges God to allow them a union in the afterlife:

Che Ti darò Gesù Signor mio buono?
Ah quello ch'amo più, quello Ti dono:
Accettalo Signor Gesù mio Dio,
Il sol mio dolce amor, anzi il cor mio;
Accettalo per Te, siati prezioso;
Accettalo per me, salva il mio sposo.

(Poem 12)

[What shall I give You, Jesus my good Lord? Ah that which I love the most I will give You: accept it, Lord Jesus, my God, my only sweet love, indeed my heart; accept it for Yourself, may it be precious to you; accept it for me, save my groom.]

The gesturing towards the afterlife that allows glimpses of paradise is by virtue of the '*cor mio*'. In the secret space of the heart, a movement is signalled towards an intersubjective exchange and translation between subject and other. In the sonnet 'Cor Mio', the metonymical identity of subject and other could not repress the difference between them. Poem 12, however, sustains the translation through God, who acts rhetorically as a supplement to the binary pair subject/other. In poem 19, the speaker describes the transformative effect of the separation caused by death in Dantesque terms:

Cor mio a cui si volge l'altro mio core
  Qual calamita al polo, e non ti trova,
  La nascita della mia vita nuova
Con pianto fu, con grida e con dolore.

Ma l'aspro duolo fummi precursore
  Di speranza gentil che canta e cova
[..................................]
O tu che in Dio mi sei, ma dopo Iddio,
  Tutta la terra mia ed assai del cielo

(19)

[My heart towards which the other heart of mine turns like a magnet to the pole, and can't find you: the birth of my new life was with crying, with shouting and with pain. But the bitter grief was the precursor of a gracious hope that sings and broods [...] oh you who are in God for me, but after God, all of my world and much of my sky]

The doubleness of 'cor mio' and 'l'altro cor mio' suggests a mutual identification which is frustrated by separation; the 'new life', however, intimates a mystical communion that is now possible, if painful, because of the separation. The semantic twists – 'O tu che in Dio mi sei, ma dopo Iddio' – place, again painfully, the beloved as secondary to God. The very last poem in the sequence also suggests that there is hope for reunion in the afterlife through the speaker's mediation and negotiation with God: 'Tu che moristi per virtù d'amor, / Nel l'altro mondo donami quel cor / Che tanto amai' [You who died for love, in the other world give me that heart I loved so much].

The ability to glimpse the afterlife which sustains hope of a reunion occurs through the deployment of the phrase '*cor mio*', in which language is manipulated so that it exceeds its denotation as a platitude. As a cliché, '*cor mio*' includes and exceeds its own semantic limitations and, by virtue of its almost mystical reiteration, enables the afterlife to be connoted through its metonymical repression of difference between subject and (m)other. W. David Shaw discusses Rossetti's creation of 'elusive contextual definitions for the dictionary meaning of so apparently simple a word as "heart"'.[36] He suggests that the gesturing beyond accepted meanings is a 'crisis of representation,' an attempt 'to cross the divide that separates knowledge from belief' (p. 251). Her reserve and obliqueness are sceptical, self-protective, and yet rooted in her faith, for 'rather than saying less about God than she means to say, she prefers to say nothing' (p. 252). The '*cor mio*' signifies less a crisis of representation than the impossibility of representing the crisis; it gestures towards the afterlife which is *beyond* direct representation, for it is non-referential and can only be intimated in fragmentary visions. As such, it refers to the original, semiotic union of mother and child prior to the acquisition of language and prior to the child's entry into the Symbolic Order.

These brief mystical glimpses of the afterlife are themselves uncannily half-familiar. Paradise is 'the other life' (l. 1), 'the other world' (l. 21), 'up there' (l. 5),

> [......................] Con lui discerno
> Giorno che spunta da gelata sera,
> Lungo cielo al di là di breve inferno,
> Al di là dell'inverno primavera
>
> (Poem 5)

[With him I discern the day that breaks from the icy evening, the long heaven beyond the brief hell, beyond winter, spring]

In poem 10, the afterlife is both known and unknown as 'the day of love,' but it is an eternal day without moon or sun:

> ...venga poi, ma non con luna o sole,
> Giorno d'amor, giorno di gran delizia,
> Giorno che spunta non per tramontare.
>
> (Poem 10)

[then let the day of love come, but not with moon or sun, day of love, day of great delight, day which breaks never to set.]

The speaker in poem 13, 'Finestra mia orientale' (My eastern window) seems to give the land in which the lovers are imagined together Italian traits, which correspond *almost* to paradise:

> Fossiamo insieme in bel paese aprico!
>
> Fossiamo insieme!
> Che importerebbe

U'si facesse
  Il nostro nido?
Cielo sarebbe
  Quasi quel lido.

[If only we were together in the sunny land! If we were together! What would it matter where we had made our nest? It would almost be paradise, that shore.]

The south, Italy, is seen as the counterpart of the colder north in 'Italy, io ti saluto' and 'Enrica'. The latter, published in *Goblin Market, The Prince's Progress and Other Poems* (1875) maintains such a stereotype and finds it manifest in the character of an Italian visitor to England: 'She summer-like and we like snow' (Crump 1: 194).

The construction of the paradisal as both known and unknown marks, in Freudian terms, an uncanny moment. As the speaker in 'En Route' declares, Italy is 'Sister-land of Paradise', for the familiarity of Italy and the paradisal recalls the primal union with the maternal body in alternative feminine terms (here as sisterhood). The poetical transformation of Italy into a paradisal homeland thus reworks the memory of the separation from the maternal body, to recur to the maternal prior to the painful experience of loss. The exchange between subject and beloved that the phrase '*cor mio*' initiates represses the difference between them, allowing perfect earthly love to be envisioned in a re-membering of the semiotic plenitude of the maternal body.[37] The utopian love envisaged in 'Monna Innominata' – 'With separate "I" and "Thou" free love has done / For one is both and both are one in love' (Crump 2: 88) – is both anticipated and intimated rhetorically. But when, as in *Il rosseggiar,* the beloved is transposed and depicted as absent, the anticipation of a meeting in the afterlife heightens the pressure of memory on the Symbolic Order. Such retrospection combines with anticipation: effectively in Freudian terms a maternal trope, the conjugation of birth with death which intimates, for Kristeva, the maternal space of the *chora* (the Greek for receptacle, womb). The *chora* is the place prior to a knowledge of sexual difference where the drives of the preœdipal child gather and, after the entry into the Symbolic Order, allows a disruptive pressure to be exerted on language: 'the *chora* precedes and underlies figuration and thus secularisation, and is analogous only to vocal or kinetic rhythm'.[38] The afterlife, in such moments, is glimpsed in dreams and non-verbal language, a type of non-significatory practise that is associated with the semiotic and the maternal. The *'cor mio'* signals the analogous secret space of the grave where the sleeping soul dreams of Paradise. The pulsations of the *'core'*, suggesting the pulsations of the *chora* upon the Symbolic,[39] intimate a movement of retrospection as well as a longing for death that would release the subject from the Symbolic Order. Both constructs are spatial and amorphous, physical and spiritual, embedded in but also positioned beyond the significatory practise that they interrupt.

The special associations that Italy and the Italian language hold in the nineteenth-century construct the trope Italy, even when figured as a homeland, as partially or completely alien. For Christina Rossetti's poetry, the overdetermined concept of Italy aligns the feminine subject with the maternal in an act of translation from the paternal. This is exemplified by the addressee of 'Il rosseggiar dell'Oriente', Cayley, the real-life translator of Dante Alighieri, whose rhetorical function in the sequence enables a translation and exchange from earth to heaven and between speaker and beloved.[40] In fact, both the beloved and the maternal attempt to reclaim Italy from the place of the father to the space of the mother. In this way, Rossetti is a translator *par excellence*: from father to mother, subject to other, home to Italy.[41] Margaret Waller, introducing her translation of Kristeva's *Revolution in Poetic Language*, argues that the act of translation itself effaces the 'paternal' text:

> In representing what is textually 'other', the translation inevitably appropriates the 'alien' through the familiar. Indeed, inasmuch as it replaces the previous work, a translation is not only a transformation of that text but also its elimination: the homage paid is a covert form of parricide.[42]

For Rossetti, however, this elimination is not so clear: Italy is not wholly translated into the familiar, and, as well as bearing maternal connotations, Italy retains its uncanny otherness.

Rossetti's poetry thus imagines the paradisal through a revision of the primary separation from the maternal body. *'Il rosseggiar dell'Oriente'* reconfigures the relation between subject and other that is predicated on this revision, and which suggests a mode of figuration based, not on the repression of difference, but on the disruptive memory of the semiotic union between mother and child. The paradisal is a utopian homeland accessible through the Italian language as an alternative 'mother tongue', whose intimation suggests the possibilities of an alternative aesthetic that re-imagines the relation between the feminine and death, and which might provide us with a way of re-figuring not just maternity in Christina Rossetti's poetry, but our journey as readers, and indeed translators, into the strange homeland of Christina Rossetti and her poetics.

7
The Afterlife of Poetry: 'Goblin Market'

The consumptive signature

In the previous chapters we have been tracing Christina Rossetti as a product of the literary and biographical after-effect, together with something in between these effects which exists in the relationship between the critical reader and the signature. As a cultural artefact, our access to Christina Rossetti is always structured in this way, however dependent we might be on the illusion of an authentic literary, historical or biographical origin. This final chapter turns to address the critical consumption of Rossetti's most famous poem, 'Goblin Market', which affords a case study of the afterlife of her poetry and persona. Indeed, the poem presents itself meta-textually as a paradigm for reading its own reception history proleptically and as a commentary on the shaping of Christina Rossetti within the Victorian literary marketplace. The chapter begins by unfolding what I term the consumptive signature that is Christina Rossetti: a sign for authorship that is always already situated within the site of its own sexual, economic and pathological consumption. The chapter then focuses upon the reception history of 'Goblin Market' as curiously structured by the text's discursive doubleness. It is a history, furthermore, which illustrates a compelling dynamics between the agency of poem and critic. The chapter ends with a consideration of Jeanie as a figure for reading and the reading effect. By remembering Jeanie, we forge a new conception of the afterlife of poetry and its effects within the history of Christina Rossetti's consumption.

As a poem about the consumption of fruit, and a poem with a remarkable and unprecedented history of consumption in the critical marketplace, 'Goblin Market' is a consumptive text *par excellence*. The poem inscribes consumption as a multiple trope: at once pathological (tuberculosis, the implied disease caused by the fruit), moral (sexual fallenness), and economic (commodification). Ushered into the literary marketplace through the efforts of D.G. Rossetti, whose textual revisions to her early volumes we have already encountered, *Goblin Market and Other Poems* (1862) heralds the literary ambitions of the Pre-Raphaelite Brotherhood with which Christina Rossetti was associated but also excluded by virtue of her gender. Her uncanny doubling as both artist and model, producer and commodity of Pre-Raphaelitism, sets her up in a superlative position in the mid-nineteenth century marketplace as the consumptive signature *par excellence*, a fitting author for such a consumptive text in a Victorian ideology which maps the text directly onto the author as an experiential reflex.[1] Recent feminist analysis of capitalism makes clear that the consumptive feminine subject is also an object to be consumed in the marketplace. When Laura succumbs to the tempting goblin fruit, she is transformed in just this very way from purchaser to purchased, from subject to object. Lévi-Strauss famously demonstrates that women are objects to be exchanged within culture but, crucially, as Elisabeth Bronfen argues in her discussion of commodification, the distinction between woman as economic body exchanged, for example, within kinship structures from father to husband, and woman as semiotic trope, become blurred. 'Woman', in this cultural exchange, ends up being both a sign of exchange and a signifier for exchange itself.[2] That exchange, as Bronfen argues and as Laura also makes clear, is an exchange between life and death, which puts the agency of the woman, and the categories active and passive, in question: object or agent, producer or consumer, consumer or commodity?

We have already seen such issues played out in relation to the biographical representation of Christina Rossetti, but they also profoundly affected the profession of authorship at mid-century. Christina Rossetti was well aware of her position as a poet inescapably within the marketplace, despite Dante Gabriel Rossetti's attempt to chaperone her entry into commerce.[3] Christina Rossetti wryly suggests that her short story 'Nick' would sell better if it was prefaced by a flattering portrait of the author (*Letters* 1: 74). But, at a later date, on a more serious note, she denies that she would authorise the publication of her portrait (*Letters* 2: 115), indicating once again her duplicitous entry into commerce.[4] In an early letter to William Michael Rossetti (31 January 1851), she playfully, in an odd double of the personal and impersonal, suggests a strategy to secure the financial success of *The Germ*: publish her letters with a tantalising hint of their authorship by a 'Lady M——' at 'B-ck-m P-l-e' for 'an immediate sensation' (*Letters* 1: 37). And yet William Michael Rossetti tells how Christina, as well as Dante Gabriel, burned 'huge bundles of letters'.[5] Linda M. Shires argues that authors become commodified in a market which demands the consumption of their private lives: so much so, in fact, that there is 'a concomitant loss of substance'.[6] Subjectivity is hollowed out and, as the individual becomes disembodied, the trope of the author is emptied (p. 129). The case of Christina Rossetti suggests that, as the author loses his or her interiority in the literary marketplace, he or she becomes commodified and the status of the writer as producer is elided. Both author and text become a commodity: feminised, specularised, and put into circulation. Alexander Macmillan described the *Goblin Market* volume as a privileged object of consumption in the literary marketplace:

> My idea is to make an exceedingly pretty little volume, and to bring it out as a small Christmas book. This would give it every chance of coming right to the public. If the public prove a wise and discerning public and take a great fancy to it, we could soon give them an adequate supply.[7]

Christina Rossetti, cannily, describes *Speaking Likenesses* as 'merely a Christmas-trifle, would-be in the *Alice* style with an eye to the market' (*Letters* 2: 12).[8]

The figure of the female author in the modern literary marketplace has, perhaps, always been an empty trope. Catherine Gallagher's discussion of women writers from 1670 to 1820 argues that 'the literary marketplace [...] is often the setting for what might be called the authors' vanishing acts. It is a place where the writers appear mainly through their frequently quite spectacular displacements and disappearances in literary and economic exchanges'.[9] Gallagher does not mean either the disappearance of women novelists from the canon nor the premature death of the author, whose institutional demise was pronounced by Roland Barthes in this century. Rather, Gallagher's authorial nobodies are an effect of the process of economic exchange. Drawing on the first chapter of Marx's *Capital*, Gallagher describes the commodity as an oscillation between materiality and ideality: 'as long as it is in the marketplace – that is, as long as it is a commodity – the item's materiality is constantly on the brink of disappearing, being replaced by a mere notation of value, such as money' (p. xxiii). A text is a commodity, and yet a text's materiality exceeds that of the commodity because its value is less certain (as both exchange value and literary value). Gallagher argues that 'the recurrence of dematerialization and rematerialization, like that of dispossession and debt, might be attributed, then, to something that seems more abstract than either patriarchy or the marketplace: textuality itself' (p. xxiii). Furthermore, female authorship compounds the text's uncertain status: 'several of the women authors in this study repeatedly identify not only their texts but also their authorship with the vacillating materiality of the signifier' (p. xxiv).

Chapter 3 explicates how reminiscences and biographies empty out the figure of Christina Rossetti as always already posthumous. Christina Rossetti functions here as a sign not only for a certain conception of a woman poet but also, in a related gesture, for the textuality of her œuvre within the literary marketplace. With the nineteenth-century's humanistic collapse of literature into the artist's life (in particular for a female poet working within and against the sentimental tradition whose ideology posited art as a direct experiential reflex), the new focus upon the author as a commodity renders the position of the author more ambiguous than certain commentators make out.[10] The text itself, and textuality *per se*, is a sign that signifies the author, and thus collapses the producer with the production. This doubleness is rendered more problematic with the ambiguity of the so-called separate spheres of gendered activity: the sentimental author, and text-as-author, is a spectacle for public consumption, but also belongs to the private sphere of emotion and sentiment.[11] Thus, the poetic text in particular circulates as a commodity and as a sign not only for the author, but for transgressive femininity. While Chapter 3 argues that the empty and posthumous biographical trope Christina Rossetti inhabits accounts of her life and analyses of her poetry, here I wish to stress that the signature of the female poet as a sign in the literary marketplace operates in a similar way, corresponding to Marx's notion of commodity as fetish, collapsing the emptied trope of the female poet with the poetry itself, suppressing the material fact of production, while also attempting to contain the transgression.

To take an example from Paul Elmer More's review of W.M. Rossetti's 1904 edition of his sister's poetry:

> for page after page we are in the society of a spirit always refined and exquisite in sentiment, but without any guiding and restraining poetic impulse; she never drew to the shutters of her soul, but lay open to every wandering breath of heaven.[12]

As More continues to describe the qualities of Rossetti's poetry, he insists on her passive renunciation of earthly life along with the ethereal and spiritual nature of her thought. This otherworldliness More repeatedly defines as 'feminine': 'as pure and fine an expression of the feminine genius as the world has yet heard' (p. 816), 'the purely feminine spirit of her imagination' (p. 816), 'her feminine disposition' (p. 816), her 'feminine mind' (p. 818), 'feminine genius' (pp. 818, 819), and 'feminine heart' (p. 820). The article's litany of the 'feminine' discloses its value as a trope of passivity, ethereality and the non-material: in fact, 'utter womanliness' (p. 819). In this rhetorical move, the cultural construction of femininity collapses into the biological category female while denying that the feminine in its most perfect manifestation has any investment in a bodily existence. More comments: 'this womanly poet does not properly renounce at all, she passively allows the world to glide away from her' (p. 816). The non-materiality even extends to her poetic voice, which at its most feminine does not even speak at all: 'am I misguided in thinking that in this stillness, this silence more musical than any song, the feminine heart speaks with a simplicity and consummate purity?' (p. 820).[13]

But the point about this example is that even in her non-materiality, her passive renunciation, the poet-figure is given a pure vocality which insists upon its presence and source of poetic lyricism. The poet's materiality somehow still inheres. While More's review may be an extreme analysis of Rossetti's verse, as Chapter 3 explicates, it is not an unusual one. Although the origins of the poetic text are elided within the economics of the literary marketplace, the emptied figure of the poet, displaced as it is, continues to shadow her text in these critiques. She doesn't crumble away into nothingness, despite Rossetti's self-mocking description of her œuvre as 'remains' (*Letters* 1: 196) to Dante Gabriel who had urged her to publish another volume of poetry. Later these 'remains' are vocalised into 'posthumous groans' (*Letters* 1:348) when she rejects William James Stillman's suggestion, relayed through Dante Gabriel, that she widen her range to politics or philanthropy. We could say, indulging for a moment in our access to Christina Rossetti's historical personage, that her projection of her authorship manipulates the hollowed out feminine signature of her text.[14] The revisions and deletions executed by Dante Gabriel Rossetti on her manuscripts, and chronicled in Chapter 4, perform the diminishment and deletion of her position as a commodity. Her dependence on the gender ideology of feminine creativity, which underlies her pronouncements that she is a 'one string'd lyre' that she cannot publish, despite Dante Gabriel's urgings, before she is ready, afford her a measure of self-protection.[15] What she terms her 'poetics of conciseness', a term which Antony Harrison has unravelled,[16] mimics (just as her brother's revisions to her poetry did) the economic marketplace's disembodiment of authorship and textuality while it also, paradoxically, displaces her subjectivity safely outside of commerce. This displacement is the condition of the woman poet entering into the literary marketplace and becoming a consumptive subject. A letter to her family friend Adolf Heimann, which comments on his response to the *Goblin Market* volume, makes clear her coy playfulness with the ideological terms and conditions of her status as a published poet:

> On the subject of my little book I have not received kinder or dearer letter than the two which you and your wife have sent me. But some of my verses have grieved you: I recall titles and subjects, and suspect *At Home* and *Shut Out*, of being amongst these offenders. If *sad and melancholy*, I suggest that few people reach the age of 31 without sad and melancholy experiences: if *despondent*, I take shame and blame to myself, as they show I have been unmindful of the daily love and mercy lavished upon me. But remember, please, that these and the rest have been written during a period of some 14 years, and under many varying circumstances, health and spirits; that they are more-over not mainly the fruit of effort, but the record of sensation, fancy, and what not, much as these came and went. (*Letters* 1: 163–4)

Rossetti, in a characteristic double move, suggests that her poems are both a direct reflex of experience and emotions and also the 'record' of something that exceeds experience, 'sensation, fancy, and what not'. Poetic inspiration is represented here as beyond her control and therefore not her responsibility, and not really belonging to her.[17] The 'what not' playfully diminishes any claim she might have just made on her creative imagination and, with its negative, curiously figures that there both is and is not a record of anything in her poetry, which in any case is transient. This is a peculiar relationship between author and text. She is both medium and ghost, host and guest: the emptied trope of authorial identity inhabits and is inhabited by the poetry. The *oscillation* between silence and voice, active and passive, absence and presence, allows the signature Christina Rossetti to flirt coyly if dangerously with the literary economy in a way which both positions her as the superlative consumptive and also positions her outwith commod-ification.[18]

Critical Goblin Markets

The most important text in the commodification of Christina Rossetti is 'Goblin Market'. 'Come buy, come buy', cry the goblin merchant-men, and readers respond by tasting the poem's tempting fruits of interpretation, so much so, that the poem has attracted an overwhelming critical attention. Indeed, the poem's critical legacy establishes 'Goblin Market' as both paradigmatic of Rossetti's œuvre and also exceptional, both representative and eccentric. Most readings of the poem flag such an odd position by treating it in isolation from Rossetti's other work but also presuming that the poem has a metonymical relationship to the author's œuvre (hence the poem denoted by apostrophes as 'Goblin Market' is frequently translated into italics as the titular and emphatic *Goblin Market*).[19] Jerome McGann, for example, terms the poem a superlative 'masterpiece' and also typical and central.[20] The representative/exceptional double is structured in a similar way to the biographical personage of Christina Rossetti, whose figure represented both exemplary and eccentric womanliness, epitomised by the term coined by Katharine Tynan Hinkson, 'Santa Christina'. As readings of 'Goblin Market' continue to breed and proliferate, the poem has an intriguing afterlife in critical and literary economies.

The first recorded response to the poem is perhaps the most curious. D.G. Rossetti's efforts to find a publisher for his sister were rewarded when he secured the interest of Alexander Macmillan, who wrote to him of his decision to publish the book for the Christmas market (it eventually came out in the following spring), explaining the decision by offering the following anecdote:[21]

> I took the liberty of reading the *Goblin Market* aloud to a number of people belonging to a small working-man's society here. They seemed at first to wonder whether I was making fun of them; by degrees they got as still as death, and when I finished there was a tremendous burst of applause.[22]

This experiment to test the response to the poem is telling. The audience's reaction suggests their confusion over how the poem should be designated – as a fairy tale or moral story. The beginning of 'Goblin Market', suggestive as it is of fantasy, provokes puzzlement and perhaps resentment at Macmillan's seeming patronage; then, the emergence of moral overtones compete with the fairy tale to excite narrative tension which captivates the audience until, with the conclusion, they evidently show appreciation that the conventional status quo has been retained, that it triumphs, even, over the menacing goblins. This recorded audience response is paradigmatic of the history of critiques of 'Goblin Market' structured within the impossible contradiction produced by the poem's competing fairy tale and moral discourses.[23]

In his *Victorian Poets and the Politics of Culture*, Antony Harrison suggests that the reading was a form of market research for Macmillan, which he undertook before deciding to risk publishing the almost completely unknown Rossetti's poems in volume form. Harrison comments:

> The ideological dynamic of these lower-class men's response to this poem is instructive. Their initial feelings of affront, as assumed by Macmillan, are understandable: typically such men would have taken their evenings' intellectual endeavours seriously. Being read to in the first instance effectually reduced them to children, and having a fairy tale about girls read to them would appear to reinforce that insult. That this text takes the form of a poem of the sort normally aimed at a leisured middle- or upper-class audience would have increased their mistrust by underscoring the difference between the men's social position and those of the poem's author as well as its reader. Yet the socially constructed pleasure this particular text elicits triumphs over apparent obstacles to its ideological efficacy. Presumably, such pleasure would have derived not only from the (now famous) sensuousness and musicality of Rossetti's verse, the familiarity of the narrative form, and the intensity of familial relationships and events presented in the poem but also from an intuition by the men that this literary work had social value. (Why else applaud?)[24]

This astute commentary articulates the ambiguous double discourse of 'Goblin Market', fairy tale and moral, which elicits such a dazed and finally appreciative response from the working-class men's club. But Harrison's key argument, that this constitutes a test of the literary market for the publisher as yet undecided about a potentially risky venture on a poet whose output was hitherto modestly confined to a few poems in periodicals, tells us something more about the poem's relationship to its audience. In fact, Alexander Macmillan's reading performs the poem's discursive doubleness upon perhaps the most resistant group of potential purchasers in the literary marketplace, in class as well as gender terms. This performance is integral to the poem's position in criticism, for it performs its discursive indeterminacy upon the reader who is forced to partake in the poem's own act of interpretation, in the fruits of the poem's own reading. Critical responses to 'Goblin Market' are structured by the poem's duplicitous double discourse in such a way that interpretation becomes a product of the text.

James Ashcroft Noble is an early critic who signals the competing discourses within 'Goblin Market':

> The poem [. . .] which gave its name to her first volume, may be read and enjoyed merely as a charming fairy-fantasy, and as such it is delightful and satisfying; but behind the simple story of the two children and the goblin fruit-sellers is a little spiritual drama of love's vicarious redemption, in which the child redeemer goes into the wilderness to be tempted by the devil, that by her painful conquest she may succour and save the sister who has been vanquished and all but slain.[25]

Noble's retelling of the poem attempts to separate and reformulate the fairy and moral discourses and to give priority to the 'little spiritual drama' over (or in front of) the 'charming fairy-fantasy'. This critical sleight of hand is a commonplace in criticism of 'Goblin Market', for, in an attempt to represent the poem in terms of a stable and coherent narrative structure, one discourse is erased or elided. Another nineteenth-century critic, Edmund Gosse, prefers to term the poem 'purely fantastic'. He does, in passing, register an awareness of the moral tale, but his inability to integrate it with the fantasy which is, for him, 'Goblin Market', leaves him baffled: 'I confess that while I dimly perceive the underlying theme to be a didactic one, and nothing less than the sacrifice of self by a sister to recuperate a sister's virtue, I cannot follow the parable through to all its delicious episodes.' He concludes: 'one is satisfied with the beauty of the detail, without comprehending or wishing to comprehend every part of the execution' (p. 149). As Lorraine Janzen Kooistra summarises, 'the discourses of moral tale and fairy tale cannot co-habit peacefully in one narrative poem'.[26]

W.M. Rossetti's editorial comments on the poem are seminal to the history of the poem's reception:

> I have more than once heard Christina say that she did not mean anything profound by this fairy tale – it is not a moral apologue consistently carried out in detail. Still the incidents are such as to be at any rate suggestive, and different minds may be likely to read different messages into them. (*PW: CR* p. 459)[27]

The reported authorial intention has often represented an impasse in the history of responses to the poem, as critics attempt to reconcile Christina Rossetti's statement with spiritual or moral truths perceived in the narrative. Consequently, critics attempt to make meaning out of 'Goblin Market' by giving priority to one discourse and eliding the other. The author's reported denial of profundity and the implicit assertion that 'she did not mean anything' *at all* by the tale has thrown the gauntlet of interpretation, so that the poem in critique partly functions as an empty vessel to fill with stable meanings, a blank page on which to transfer critical desires. The figure of the poem as a repository for critical fantasies and a site of transference recalls the biographical representation of Christina Rossetti as bracketed subjectivity, displaced and emptied to make way for the meaning of her tropic construction. Indeed, the violence done to a poem about violence[28] is haunted by the trope of the poetess, devoid of a situated or concrete historicity, whose poetry, in the logic of nineteenth-century gendered theories of creativity, is a direct reflex of her experience and emotions. The poem 'Goblin Market' tempts us to continue reading within this scheme, to fill the poem with stable meaning and to position the author as a metonymy for the text, as well as the text as a metonymy for the author.

The process of animation and deanimation, of presence and absence, which categorises the trope Christina Rossetti and her texts, also marks the emergence of the market economy not only for Marx, as we have seen, but also for the ancient Greek commentators who first experienced coins and their circulation. Gyges, taken to be the founder of coinage, was a tyrant who was said by Herodotus and Plato to have the power to make visibles invisibles and vice versa. Marc Shell argues that we continue to be profoundly and sometimes unconsciously influenced by Greek thought and its economics. What Walter Benjamin asserts for photography in 'Art in the Age of Mechanical Reproduction' – that it abolishes the ontological difference between an origin and its representation – Shell asserts was initiated by ancient coinage.[29] Furthermore, within the market economy's power to exchange visibles for invisibles, and vice versa, coins collapse the distinction between passive and active, original and representation:

> Coins are themselves both artful reproductions and active participants in the sum total of the relations of production. They are things ontologically equal to each other as products of the same die, and money, which they symbolise, equalises *in potentia* all (other) things.[30]

Coins, then, are potent figures for the exchange which they are part of: as referent and sign for the process of exchange, they confuse product and consumption, origin and value.

Coins are crucial but problematical currency in 'Goblin Market'. The girls never manage to purchase anything with pennies. The goblin market is, however, no gift economy and the coins, rather than being devalued, are substituted for other types of currency.[31] The coins are part of a semiotic circulation of things within a familiar economy that collapses production and consumption, consumer and consumed. Laura is tempted by the goblin fruits but cannot offer money: '"Good folk, I have no coin; / To take were to purloin"' (ll. 116–17). The goblins suggest the 'gold upon your head' (l. 123) as alternative currency, and thus Laura is able to consume their wares. When Lizzie goes to market with a silver penny, the goblins refuse to enter into a financial transaction and, after assaulting her, contemptuously toss back the penny. On her way home to Laura she 'heard her penny jingle / Bouncing in her purse / Its bounce was music to her ear' (ll. 452–3). McGann declares these lines to be 'Rossetti's sign of true poetic power – a mere penny which jingles like the surface of the verse' (pp. 227–8). The jingle of the coin is the sign not so much for the power of the author but for the disturbing power of the poem and the continuing hold of the authorial signature. Indeed, the coin's semiotic ability to be substituted for something else in the goblin transactions figures the critical transactions which confuse agency and passivity, consumer and consumed, so that the discourse of the critic becomes caught up in the discursive duplicity of the poem. As Leighton asserts: 'curls and coins, pennies and purses, goblins and men, are figuratively interchangeable in a free market of meaning where one thing constantly shifts into another.'[32] In such an economy of exchange, poem and critical discourse and poet are situated within a metaphorical process of substitution which further distances the text from the source and origin of its production and places it irretrievably within a rhetoric of reproduction and also, of course, the proliferation of critical readings.

The substitution of coin for figurative currency to enable the fruit transaction to take place means that the text has been purloined – in the sense of both stolen and put at a distance – through academic reading and rereading, and which attempts to represent the meaning of 'Goblin Market' according to the particular critical discourse employed, but which also, in a double manœuvre, enters the critic irrevocably within the poem's interpretative game.[33] Thus, Alexander Macmillan's anecdote of his canny market research interweaves the reader's consumption of the text with the contrary claims of the text's competing discourses. In this respect, it is ironical that the most recent trend is to locate the poem within the Victorian ideology of the marketplace, bringing to the surface as a theme of the poem the rhetorical tricks it plays on the reader. This type of reading, however, is still determined by the poem's rhetoric.[34] Of course, to some extent to position 'Goblin Market' in a meta-critical fashion makes an obvious point: criticism is always structured by the specific discursive practises of the critic and also, inevitably, those practises the critic suppresses. But the excessive attention paid to 'Goblin Market' is an *effect* of the poem's representational strategy that denies any stable meaning within the poem.

Kooistra lists the proliferation of competing interpretations: '*Goblin Market* has been represented as central feminist text, as a lesbian manifesto, as an aesthetic manifesto, as a sexual allegory, as a Christian allegory, as a social indictment of Victorian culture, as a psychological case-study, and as a subversive treatment of the issues of language and form, including the form of fairy tale.'[35] All interpretations, however, are structured around positioning the poem either as a moral tale (revolving around Christianity, socio-cultural concerns, female sexuality, or aesthetics) or a fairy-tale (revolving around fantasy and the genre of the fairy tale). Mary Arseneau demonstrates the relation between 'Goblin Market' and Rossetti's religious beliefs without a consideration of the fairy-tale element.[36] Marion Shalkhauser proposes the poem as a re-telling of the biblical temptation/fall/redemption story. The article's concluding reference to the fairy-tale subsumes this discourse into the moral message:

> Though there are surely many other elements, particularly that of folk-lore, which contribute to the composition of the entire poem, 'Goblin Market' sets forth Christina Rossetti's beliefs in original sin and in the sacrificial nature of Christ's death through her creation of a Christian fairy tale in which a feminine Christ redeems a feminine mankind from a masculine Satan.[37]

Folk-lore is, in Shalkhauser's terminology, caught up in the Christian discourse and the conflict between moral and fairy tale is elided – the narrative becomes a Christian fairy tale.[38] Ellen Golub and Patricia Andrews give a psychological interpretation of the poem through a reading of the fantasy as, respectively, the conflict between the oral and anal stage and the latent neurotic perversion functioning behind the manifest moral allegory.[39] A further school sees 'Goblin Market' as a demonstration of Rossetti's concern with sensuality, reading the fairy-tale as equivalent to the sensuous which she must, for the benefit of her religious scruples, not be tempted by.[40] The sisterhood criticism, which suggests that Laura and Lizzie are the two sides to Rossetti's personality, the aesthetic and the ascetic, re-presents the poem as either an allegory of psychic re-integration,[41] 'a fantasy of feminine freedom, heroism, and self-sufficiency and a celebration of sisterly and maternal love',[42] or an allegory of repression.[43] The moral of Christian redemption is translated into psychic redemption or fall; in both cases, the critics mark their difference from the text, and also their place within its theatre of effects, by the elision of the fairy-tale.[44]

There has been only one critic who addresses the poem's history of its reception. Lorraine Janzen Kooistra's analysis of the illustrations to 'Goblin Market' suggests how each verbal/visual combination, not least D.G. Rossetti's first illustrations, re-presents the poem and reinterprets the text according to the illustrator's concerns. She figures illustrators as critics who attempt to dominate the text:

> Each successive critic's will to power is in evidence in his/her desire to suppress difference and to assert dominance in the powerful symbolic mode of writing, for criticism may be described as a wilful representation of the creative text according to a particular interpretative approach.[45]

Kooistra sees this as a result of the poem's thematic concern with representation: 'by tantalisingly exposing its own failure to tell the "real story", the poem entices other would-be story-tellers – both artists and critics – into its narrative game' (p. 307). In another article, Kooistra emphasises the dominance of the illustrations in receptions of the text, exemplified by Dante Gabriel Rossetti's frontispiece and title-page. These original illustrations, she argues, embody and produce the contradictory meanings of the poem. Dante Gabriel Rossetti's visual text 'substitutes sororal difference with feminine sameness, thereby displacing the moral story with sexual fantasy'.[46] In a more recent essay, she reifies the verbal, associating it with a subversive recuperation of femininity and of spectatorship while illustrations return the text to the status of a verbal icon.[47] The meta-history of 'Goblin Market', however, demonstrates that the text is always already part of the consumption which produced it, initially within the aesthetic of D.G. Rossetti's revisions. In other words, the text has no pure origin outside of or prior to its status as a consumptive text, further compounded by the loss of the manuscript version of the poem (only the copy-text has survived). As we have seen in Chapter 4, Dante Gabriel Rossetti's inability to control and reify meaning in his early pictures teaches us that the anxious doubling of poem and picture evades, rather than instigates, stable audience response. The illustrations' attempt to displace the poem's moral discourse does not fully determine the poem's meaning, for what interpretations (visual or otherwise) leave out returns like the repressed to haunt us and the rhetorical economy of the poem continues to infect our readings.[48]

How, then, does the poem's duplicitous doubled discourses effect the act of reading? How are we seduced by 'Goblin Market' and 'goblin-ridden' (l. 484)? Hillis Miller answers the charge that the deconstructive critic is a parasite on the obvious or univocal meaning of a text. He argues that both types of critic are simultaneously host and guest for, in a typical deconstructive move, both terms mutually contaminate the other. Recalling the Eucharist as a type of host that is at once both sacrifice and guest, Miller argues: 'if the host is both eater and eaten, he also contains in himself the double antithetical relation of host and guest, guest in the bifold sense of friendly and alien invader'.[49] In the battle for mastery between deconstruction and its opposition over the text, the text ends up figured as tertiary:

> The poem in itself, then, is neither the host nor the parasite but the food they both need, host in another sense, the third element in this particular triangle. [...] The poem, in my figure, is that ambiguous gift, food, host in the sense of victim, sacrifice. It is broken, divided, passed around, consumed by the critics canny and uncanny who are in that odd relation to one another of host and parasite. Any poem, however, is parasitical in its turn on earlier poems, or it contains earlier poems within itself as enclosed parasites, in another version of the perpetual reversal of parasite and host. If the poem is food and poison for the critics, it must in its turn have eaten. It must have been a cannibal consumer of earlier poems. (p. 225)

Miller's parasitic logic not only is blind to the implications of his effortless gendering of the parasite as feminine, as Barbara Johnson points out,[50] but also to the poem as a parasite not only upon its precursors but also within the critic's analysis. 'Goblin Market', written in the same year as that other text announcing the mutating proliferation of nature was published, *The Origin of Species*, offers its interpretative fruits as Eucharistic, as both sacrificial host and Host, food and master: 'Eat me, drink me, love me; / Laura, make much of me' (ll. 471–2). Like the relationship between host and guest that Miller traces, the goblin fruits are both poisonous and medicinal, both parasitical and nurturing. And they infect critical discourses, as those discourses invade the text, for the poem is a host to critics and also contaminates critical readings. 'Goblin Market' is both object and subject of criticism as it stages the scene of its (re)reading.

Shoshana Felman's analysis of responses to Henry James's novella *The Turn of the Screw* implicitly positions that text as paradigmatic of a certain textual influence upon the act of reading. She points out that the critical debate (is the governess mad or really seeing ghosts?) recirculates the lexical motifs of the text:

> The scene of the critical debate is thus a *repetition* of the scene dramatised in the text. The critical interpretation, in other words, not only elucidates the text but also reproduces it dramatically, unwittingly *participates in it*. Through its very reading, the text, so to speak, acts itself out. As a reading effect, this inadvertent 'acting out' is indeed uncanny: whichever way the reader turns, he can but be turned by the text, he can but *perform* it by *repeating* it.[51]

By plumbing for one interpretation of *The Turn of the Screw* over another, which we are forced to do by the text (is she or isn't she mad?), the critic is compelled to attempt to stabilise the story's ambivalent meaning in a way that paradoxically exposes what that reading represses: 'in precisely trying to *unify* the meaning of the text and to proclaim it as unambiguous, the critics only mark more forcefully its constitutive *division* and duplicity' (p. 114). Felman asks: 'could the critical debate itself be considered *ghost effect?*' (p. 98), for 'it is not so much the critic who comprehends the text, as the text which comprehends the critic' (p. 115). Revising the priority which Miller seems to give to the interpretative event, Felman offers criticism as a product, a 'ghost effect', of the text: what lies between visibility and invisibility, the legible and the illegible. Reading, in Felman's terms, is not just an issue of whether the governess actually sees the ghosts. Miller reminds us, however, that both guest and host have the same etymological root: *ghos-ti* (p. 220). The critical response to 'Goblin Market' has been infected by the play with analogy in such a way that the repression of difference haunts the poem's reception. Proliferating interpretations of 'Goblin Market' are not only produced by the text, but the discursive doubleness of the text continues to structure the debate. With this in mind, remembering Jeanie (often displaced by critics as a moral to be learnt by Lizzie) also entails remembering the ghost within 'Goblin Market' who is a figure for reading and for the reading effect.

Remembering Jeanie

'Goblin Market' is curiously severed from its origin of production. While critics have recently attempted to explain the poem with reference to a particular context – ranging from a shortage of fruit in London to Rossetti's involvement in Anglican Sisterhoods and the Highgate Penitentiary for Fallen Women[52] – the poem has so far defied an absolute explanation which would stabilise its indeterminacy. Rossetti's assurance that it has no hidden meaning compounds the contextlessness of the poem. Indeed, the poem itself dramatises a loss of origins. The poem's setting – the brook, the glen, the girls' cottage, Jeanie's grave – is oddly contextless. The fruits, unnaturally 'All ripe together / In summer weather' (ll. 15–16), are from an 'unknown orchard' (l. 135) and 'Men sell not such in any town' (l. 101): '"Who knows upon what soil they fed" / "Their hungry thirsty roots?"' (ll. 44–5). And who, and where, are the fathers of Laura and Lizzie's children? What little we know of the poem's production compounds its dissociation from its origin. As Chapter 4 discusses, Dante Gabriel Rossetti's 'revising hand' altered the original title 'A Peep at the Pixies' (a reference to their aunt, Eliza Bray) and, presumably, deleted the dedication to Maria, thus removing references to a female literary genealogy.

As we have seen, all commodities, according to Marx, are fetishised in their alienation from the means and mode of production. The voyeuristic 'peep' of the original title is revised in a process which names both the poem and the manner by which it enters the literary marketplace and becomes a commodity. As a commodity dissociated *par excellence* from its origin – from the author as a historical personage (a 'nobody'), from the material circumstances of its production – 'Goblin Market' has a superlative and representative position. Chapter 1 explicates the connection between focus and fetishisation, for both manufacture an illusory point of origin (the vanishing point in geometric perspective; the castrated woman). Not to focus is, paradoxically, to see. 'Goblin Market' also offers figures of focus and of vanishing. In the first encounter with the goblin men, Laura knows that to look at them is to be tempted: '"We must not look at goblin men, / We must not buy their fruits"' (ll. 42–3). It is Lizzie, however, that refuses to look (or 'peep', l. 49), which allows her to perceive their 'evil gifts' (l. 66): 'Lizzie covered up her eyes, /

Covered close lest they should look' (ll. 50–1). Laura, however, stays and gazes at the goblins and their tempting fruits: she 'stared but did not stir' (l. 105). After the first taste of the fruit, Laura craves more, but it is her sister who hears the goblin cries: '"I hear the fruit-call but I dare not look"' (l. 243). Laura has been initiated into a grotesque parody of the market place, in which focusing on a commodity – both literally and metaphorically here – does not correspond with seeing their illusory products. Once she has tasted the goblin wares they vanish from her sight. In order to procure the fruit for her ailing sister, Lizzie 'for the first time in her life / Began to listen and to look' (ll. 327–8). And the goblins, of course, as grotesque representatives of masculinity (constructed in the Freudian narrative of sexuality in terms of fetishisation) duly appear.

There is a figure, however, in 'Goblin Market', which consistently escapes our focus: Jeanie, who is the sisters' paradigm, their dread precursor. Three times she is recalled. First, after Laura tasted the goblin fruits and returns home, Lizzie upbraids her with the memory of the girl who transgressed:

> 'Dear, you should not stay so late,
> Twilight is not good for maidens;
> Should not loiter in the glen
> In the haunts of goblin men.
> Do you not remember Jeanie,
> How she met them in the moonlight,
> Took their gifts both choice and many,
> Ate their fruits and wore their flowers
> Plucked from bowers
> Where summer ripens at all hours?
> But ever in the noonlight
> She pined and pined away;
> Sought them by night and day,
> Found them no more but dwindled and grew grey;
> Then fell with the first snow,
> While to this day no grass will grow
> Where she lies low:
> I planted daisies there a year ago
> That never blow.
> You should not loiter so.'
>
> (ll.143–62)

Jeanie is a shadowy figure. In her pining and dwindling she becomes the vanishing point of the poem. The second reference to Jeanie occurs when Lizzie longs to help her sister, who is desperate for a second taste at the goblin fruit. Lizzie:

> Longed to buy fruit to comfort her,
> But feared to pay too dear.
> She thought of Jeanie in her grave,
> Who should have been a bride:
> But who for joys brides hope to have
> Fell sick and died
> In her gay prime
>
> (ll. 310–15)

Again Jeanie is associated with diminishment and depletion. The final reference comes at the point when Lizzie decides that she must confront the goblin men, in order to purchase the fruits that her sister is craving as the antidote to her consumptive disorder. Lizzie is 'mindful of Jeanie' (l. 364), in other words she both remembers her and takes care as a consequence. But the phrase 'mindful' also suggests how very large the precursor looms for Lizzie. It is clear from the poem that Jeanie is both a prostitute and a consumptive: she purchases and then consumes the goblin fruit and then is pathologically and morally consumed herself. Jeanie is a victim of the multiple meanings of consumption: tuberculosis, fallenness and commodification. But, as a result, Jeanie is also a compelling figure for the oscillation of the fallen woman's femininity across the boundaries of the separate spheres, and an oscillation that is dangerously transgressive, and also a figure for the authorial signature, rhetorically linked as woman poet to the fallen woman.[53]

'Goblin Market' dramatises these issues of influence, agency and transgression as it engages in the textual consumption of its literary other. Jeanie is related to D.G. Rossetti's 'Jenny', a bold and controversial interior monologue spoken by a client to his prostitute. The first version of D.G. Rossetti's poem pre-dates 'Goblin Market',[54] although he continued to revise it after his sister's volume was published.[55] In D.G. Rossetti's poem, Jenny is either asleep or on the point of sleep (significantly, her exact state of unconsciousness is difficult to determine), and the speaker establishes his interior monologue upon her absence and reassuring otherness, so that he can even read her thoughts: 'Ah Jenny, yes, we know your dreams'.[56] Despite this, however, the prostitute is also perceived to be the speaker's 'monstrous double', for his status as a writer is figured in the poem as analogous to Jenny's profession.[57] The speaker here feminises his position as a writer whose profession has transgressed the separate spheres. To counter his anxiety at the fact that he predicates his monologue on Jenny's precarious absence (for at any moment she might awaken), and that he associates with her his own profession as a writer, the speaker constructs Jenny as a phantasmagoric text that he proceeds to read. But, despite himself, the text of Jenny is only incompletely understood:

> You know not what a book you seem,
> Half-read by lightening in a dream!
> How should you know, my Jenny?
>
> (ll. 51–3)

The prostitute is represented as a text, but this is an explicit mis-representation, for she is only half-read. Later in the monologue, Jenny is also compared to a volume:

> What if to her all this were said?
> Why, as a volume seldom read
> Being open halfway shuts again,
> So might the pages of her brain
> Be parted at such words, and thence
> Close back upon the dusty sense.
>
> (ll. 159–64)

Although these lines dismiss Jenny's agency due to her unconsciousness, they also suggest that she is literally a 'shut book', and evades her client's attempt to control her autonomy. Her status as an object is only precariously dependent upon her unconscious: she may awaken at any moment and cut short the poetic act. Inevitably, the speaker of the poem recognises that Jenny exists beyond and independently of his perception of her and, indeed, this fact threatens his creativity, predicated as it is upon her absence. Jenny's threat is inscribed and held by virtue of a reflexive doubling within her figure: she is both an object and a sign for the feminine subject subsumed by the text. J.B. Bullen comments that the poem is unfinished, in the sense that it has 'an indeterminate air, an openness or lack of resolution'.[58] He interprets the poem as perpetually shifting its distinctions between the speaker and the prostitute. But Bullen also stresses that 'this is a poem not about the unreadibility of the other, but the unreadibility of the self' (p. 66). The other and the self, however, are not so securely separated. Although Anderson argues that the female is denied any autonomy and although Bullen claims the poem circulates primarily around male desire, 'Jenny' perpetually resists attributing unproblematical agency to either speaker or addressee. Both are implicated in the play of empowerment and disempowerment. Indeed, crucially, Jenny is incompletely appropriated as a cipher of male desire. The speaker, in fact, wonders what Jenny's thoughts are and, although he proceeds to transcribe them, ironically in the following lines she sleepily refuses the glass of wine that he offers. Jenny, despite the efforts of the speaker, resists being read.[59]

This poem, which sets up a prostitute as the ultimate literary commodity – the eroticised muse upon which the speaker constructs his identity – ends up illustrating that the other might also be a 'subject who knows', a text that can only be 'half read' and that resists the reader's will to power.[60] In 'Goblin Market', Jenny becomes Jeanie (in fact, Jeanie is even rhymed with 'many', so as to be pronounced Jenny, l. 147), whose seduction by the goblins has caused her physical demise.[61] Jeanie is the figure for the multiple meanings of consumption and for the oscillating position of woman in the marketplace as both commodity and consumer. But Jeanie also represents the elided history of literary production behind 'Goblin Market': that is, the text's commerce with D.G. Rossetti's poem 'Jenny', as well as his influence in the shaping of the poem and, indeed, his revisions to Christina Rossetti's first two volumes. Although Jeanie is firmly placed underground in her grave, she is also a wandering signifier who haunts 'Goblin Market' as Laura and Lizzie's precursor. It is ironic, if macabre, that the reclamation of D.G. Rossetti's bundle of papers from Lizzie Siddal's grave unearths the manuscript of 'Jenny' eaten through by grave worms.[62] The figure of Jeanie suggests the slippery thresholds of production and consumption, for, in fact, it could be said that the text's history of production is also the history of its consumption within D.G. Rossetti's aesthetics.[63]

In a perceptive essay, Catherine Maxwell has demonstrated how consumption in 'Goblin Market' is a not only a figure for woman's vulnerability in the male literary marketplace, but also suggests how the 'Goblin Market' itself consumes its male precursor texts.:

> While the poem itself literally and figuratively demonstrates how each new text consumes other texts, is ceaselessly chewing over and

> redistributing the language of other texts, it also intimates that male-authored writings require extra-careful digestion by a woman poet's intertext. The female poet's management of consumption suggests a scrupulous evaluation of what will best nourish her and how it can be made to satisy her needs.[64]

Maxwell suggests that, underneath the œdipal rivalry normally taken to characterise literary influence, 'is a more primitive and instinctual vocabulary of feeding and forbidden fruit' (p. 97). The doubleness underlying her account of consumption in the poem – the text as consumer and consumed within a poetic geneaology – also has implications for its continuing influence upon critical readers. The poem and its afterlife offer the figure of a double model for literary and critical influence based upon Julia Kristeva's concept of abjection that is the flipside of a more intersubjective *rapprochement* and that is also distinguished from the violence of the œdipal model of literary relations between poet and precursor. In the borderline state of abjection, the child (pre-subject) pulls away from total identification with the mother, and thus also from a total annihilation of agency and autonomy. But the adult subject also remembers and repeats this primary uncanny of identification with and resistance to the experience of undifferentiated sameness with the mother: 'I abject *myself* within the same motion through which "I" claim to establish *myself*.'[65] The dread of being overwhelmed by the other (or by the maternal body) has given rise to rituals of purification and 'foundations for instituting sexual difference and for establishing hierarchical social order', but the abject still returns to disturb the adult subject's sense of difference from the other.[66] In the model of literary influence suggested by D.G. Rossetti's relationship with his sister, the precursor is the other that threatens to consume the subject. Categories of subject and other are consequently destabilised, for, as Kristeva comments, the abject is: 'what does not respect borders, positions, rules. The in-between, the ambiguous, the composite' (p. 4). It is a division and a merging.[67] Jeanie's presence-in-absence represents the abject position; she has been seduced into becoming a commodity (or a 'nobody') by the goblin-market and through literary influence, for Jeanie figures as a metonymy for the textual precursor of 'Goblin Market', the poem 'Jenny', which in turn signifies the author who revises, or consumes, the *Goblin Market* volume. And yet Jeanie is also remembered and serves as a warning, and thus is given an agency as the precursor. Jeanie's namesake, Jenny, also resists wholly losing her agency and autonomy, and the memory of Jeanie/Jenny inspires Lizzie to overcome the threat of the goblins and their wares.[68] Thus, as the figure for literary influence, Jeanie suggests the horror and necessity of engaging with a textual other, which both establishes literary identity and also threatens to overwhelm it.[69] Jeanie as the abject signifies the unstable doubleness of the intertextual engagement.

Kristeva's formulation of the abject exposes the untenability of all boundaries – nature/nurture, semiotic/Symbolic, sense/nonsense – but, perhaps most significantly and metatextually, pure/impure. As Angela Leighton persuasively argues, the Victorian woman poet represents the fallen woman as transgressing the boundary between pure and impure, a 'willed confusion of fallen and unfallen'.[70] This blurring of fallen with unfallen counteracts the dominant ideology which brands fallen women as so impure as to be contagious, both morally and physiologically, in a process which culminated in the first Contagious Diseases Act of 1864.[71] Indeed, prostitutes came to be identified with contagion *per se*. W.S. Wiesenthal suggests that the 'mass anxiety' about infectious disease in nineteenth-century culture produces metaphorical 'anti-bodies' before the scientific understanding of immunisation. The threat of fatal bodily disease, he ingeniously argues, produces imaginary or psychical anti-bodies. He declares these anti-bodies to be ghosts, which provide a self-inoculation against death through apparitions.[72] Jeanie, who haunts 'Goblin Market' as both the dread/dead precursor and wandering signifier, also embodies in her consumptive deanimation a metaphorical concern with contagion. But she also signifies the way in which the poem's seductive discourses operate infectiously in the critical debate. As figure and meta-figure, Jeanie's fall prefigures our own seduction by the rhetoric of 'Goblin Market'.

Catherine Gallagher unravels the associations between female authorship and prostitution and comments that hostility towards prostitution is part of a more general alarm at a realm of exchange divorced from production: 'prostitution [...] is a metaphor for one of the ancient models of literary production: the unnatural multiplication of interchangeable signs'.[73] Furthermore, 'the activities of authoring, of procuring illegitimate income, of alienating one's self through prostitution seem particularly closely associated with one another in the Victorian period' (p. 43).[74] Even if authors attempt to dissociate themselves from commerce, Gallagher argues, they are nevertheless embroiled in language as a web of exchange: 'language itself, especially published writing, is [...] often identified with money as a alien, artificial, and entrapping system of circulation' (p. 44).[75] Indeed, in 'Goblin Market' exchange is a key trope that points to not only the infection of the marketplace but also to language itself. Leighton notes: 'in this market, everything may be goblinised into something else'.[76]

For Kristeva, abjection involves both a turn and a fall. It is a turn back to the archaic union with the mother and a falling away from meaning and identity. Similarly, the contagious rhetoric of 'Goblin Market' is marked by not only fallenness but turning, both in a moral and rhetorical sense. In her redemption, Laura undergoes and abject 'writhing' (l. 496) which culminates in her cure:

> She fell at last;
> Pleasure past and anguish past,
> Is it life or is it death?
>
> Life out of death.
>
> (ll. 521–4)

The redemption involves both a fall and, in the chiasmus which reverses 'life or death?', a moral and rhetorical turn. As 'the trope of crossing over', W. David Shaw terms Rossetti's use of the chiasmus 'heroic': 'it helps her to cross the divide between life and death, knowledge and ignorance, in an ironic double movement that is sanctioned ultimately by the perfect chiasmus of the Cross'.[77] In another poem taken to be spoken by a fallen woman, 'From Sunset to Star Rise' (Crump 1: 191), the Petrarchan structural turn marks a similar moment of redemption:

> Go from me, summer friends, and tarry not:
> I am no summer friend, but wintry cold,
> A silly sheep benighted from the fold,
> A sluggard with a thorn-choked garden plot.
> Take counsel, sever from my lot your lot,
> Dwell in your pleasant places, hoard your gold;
> Lest you with me should shiver on the wold,
> Athirst and hungering on a barren spot.
> For I have hedged me with a thorny hedge,
> I live alone, I look to die alone:
> Yet sometimes when a wind sighs through the sedge
> Ghosts of my buried years and friends come back,
> My heart goes sighing after swallows flown
> On sometime summer's unreturning track.

This poem doubles back on itself, but the turn, which conventionally occurs at the start of the sestet, is delayed until line 11.[78] This is not just a turn in the way that Shoshana Felman means when she describes being turned by the literary text. The language of the sonnet recalls 'Goblin Market': the gold, barren spot, and the 'unreturning' past. But the turn (of the seasons and of the sonnet) signals the speaker's redemption, for that familiar Victorian trope of the turn and the return, the swallow, marks the future return of the past. In his notes to the poem, William Michael Rossetti comments that, in the manuscript, Christina Rossetti has pencilled in the margin by the poem 'House of Charity', and he surmises that the poem is 'an utterance of one of these women, not of herself. Yet one hesitates to think so, for the sonnet has a tone which seems deeply personal'.[79] His absorption within the ideology of female creativity makes him wonder if any poetic 'utterance' by his sister could be anything other than a direct experiential reflex, thus inadvertently identifying fallenness with his sister. Rossetti sometimes gives her poems symbolic dates. The manuscript dates this poem 23 February 1865 and the entry for the spiritual reading diary *Time Flies* on that date has a pertinent commentary on the vigil of St Matthias who replaced Judas among the twelve Apostles. Rossetti argues that it is impossible to disentangle the memory of Judas from that of Matthias in this life: 'as impossible as for the tide not to stand connected in thought with the ebb, or light with darkness. So, too, hope and fear tremble responsively.'[80] In other words, opposites are mutually contaminating: Judas and Matthias, sinner and redeemed, fear and hope. 'From Sunset to Star Rise', located as it is in a period of darkness before the starlight illuminates, and thus just before the turn from darkness to partial light, the sonnet's delayed turn and its concluding hope of a re-turn transforms a fall into a redemption. Confronting the falling away of difference – octave/sestet, pure/impure, poet/poem, poem/reader – redeems in the same way as confronting abjection can redeem the subject from its double-bind.[81]

In fact, it has been argued that abjection is a condition of reading. Anna Smith's analysis of Kristeva's work on exile and estrangement suggests that critical reading is always 'reading strangely'.[82]

> [R]eading is actually a kind of affective transference or voyage that involves adopting the mutually interchangeable roles of analyst and analysand. Just as the power of the transference derives from the analyst's ability to sweep the analysand off her feet by the unexpectedness of the interpretation, the conviction of analytical discourse

> rests on a speech that is put together co-operatively. In this way critical reading confesses it is founded on a fundamental lack of absolute knowledge, not an original plenitude. And in confessing its weakness, it allows itself to be transformed by the speech of the other towards which it travels. Knowledge is founded paradoxically on estrangement, on a dazzling that confuses the boundaries between subject and object. In reading no-one knows who achieves mastery, for the reader discovers herself to be both narrator and narrattee, the traveller who reads and the traveller who is read. Therefore the space of the voyage of interpretation becomes double, indeterminate, unhomely. (pp. 73–4)

Smith continues that the uncanny space of reading is also a space of redemption from an exile from language and in language, a distinction which reading obscures: 'the reader can no longer stand solely in a place of transcendence exterior to the language of the text. Instead, she is drawn into its orbit and experiences its regenerative qualities, as it were, from within' (p. 74). In this way, the infection of the text becomes a process which moves and restores us, but not to an illusory wholeness. Further, it allows the tropic construction of Christina Rossetti to be contested, something which Tricia Lootens calls for at the end of *Lost Saints*: 'what we stand to lose in giving up our monumental saints, we may gain in our capacity to understand different kinds of literary love'.[83]

There are far-reaching implications here for literary tradition. Linda Williams argues that the conventional matrilineal conception of a female literary tradition implies an unmediated transmission of ideas, analogous to Irigaray's model of the relationship between mother and child so intra-personal as to exclude 'individual identity and power'.[84] The consequences for the tradition are profound, for literary interchange is posited as an 'immaculate connection' (p. 50). The result renders women's literary history as a family history; 'thus it seems, ironically, that the very force which some writers have drawn upon to signal the breakdown of patriarchal family relations – a feminine communication which disrupts normal epistemologies – has then been used to make coherent an alternative Great (Female) Tradition' (p. 53). Williams's response, however, is imagined as a violent break from the economy of gratitude, of debt to the mother, of utopian release.

Williams raises some crucial problems that cluster around the concept of literary mediation, not least concerning the positive plenitude of an undifferentiated relation between (literary) mothers and daughters. If, however, a dreadful abject underside to the model of literary influence were to be conceived, this might provide the beginnings of rethinking both female influence and histories *and* our critical reading – rejecting the mutually exclusive Bloomian model of patriarchal œdipal aggression and the feminist model of benign mother poets. The anxiety of agency involved in readership would both embrace and reject the (literary) abject mother – or her substitute literary precursor (of any sex) – and prepare for the possibility of what Williams describes as 'a position of release, where thinking takes place without a safety net' (p. 60). Only, she argues, a violent refusal to accept a debt of gratitude can achieve this. The model of abjection offers a way out of this impasse, acknowledging at once the necessity and horror of the literary precursor and the critical engagement. The violence of the encounter between the goblins and the girls in 'Goblin Market' suggests, allegorically, such a refusal, given the critical tendency to interpret the fruits as metaphors for literature.[85]

Conceiving literary influence and reading affects as abjection allows a recuperation of the otherness of Jenny/Jeanie without attributing an over-determined autonomy and agency. In addition, it acknowledges the doubleness and duplicity behind Christina Rossetti's relationship not only to her brother's 'suggestive wit and revising hand', but also to her literary sister and aunt whose dedication is symbolically deleted in the manuscript of 'Goblin Market'.[86] The suspension between the boundaries of pure and impure, which Kristeva argues is characteristic of abjection, is also the mark of Victorian women poets' representation of the fallen woman, as well as Hillis Miller's host/guest model of the critic and the text. And it is the mark of the critical reader's engagement with the poetic text and authorial signature. Abjection here discloses itself as both the underlying structure of textuality, literary influence, and the act of critical reading. It is a literary afterlife which is predicated on archaic maternal origins to which we are nevertheles denied direct access. In a double bind which recalls abjection as the ground and abyss of identity, the goblins' fruits uncannily represent both danger and restoration, and these are also the fruits of my reading.

Notes

Introduction: the Haunting of Christina Rossetti

1 Jean-Luc Nancy, 'Finite History', in David Carroll (ed.), *The States of 'Theory': History, Art, and Critical Discourses* (Stanford, California: Stanford University Press, 1990) p. 152.

2 Italian proverb recounted in Christina Rossetti, *Time Flies: a Reading Diary* (London: SPCK, 1885) p. 4.

3 Cited in Jan Marsh, *Christina Rossetti: a Literary Biography* (London: Jonathan Cape, 1994) pp. 567–8.

4 Note, however, that some woman poets had a problematical literary relation to Rossetti as precursor. For a discussion of Michael Field's elegy, which figures Rossetti as an unfit muse for future poets, see Susan Conley, '"Poet's Right": Elegy and the Woman Poet', in Angela Leighton (ed.), *Victorian Women Poets: a Critical Reader* (Oxford: Blackwell, 1996) pp. 235–44. Diane D'Amico's analysis of Rossetti's influence on Katharine Tynan and Sara Teasdale suggests that they figured her as, respectively, a saint and artefact. See 'Saintly Singer or Tanagra Figurine? Christina Rossetti Through the Eyes of Katharine Tynan and Sara Teasdale', *Victorian Poetry* 32 (1994) 387–407. Neither option embodies Christina Rossetti's historical personage. For a further discussion of Tynan and Rossetti, see Peter van de Kamp, 'Wrapped in a Dream: Katharine Tynan and Christina Rossetti', in Peter Liebregts and Wim Tigges (eds), *Beauty and the Beast: Christina Rossetti, Walter Pater, R.L. Stevenson and their Contemporaries* (Amsterdam: Rodopi, 1996) pp. 59–97.

5 Tricia Lootens, *Lost Saints: Silence, Gender, and Victorian Literary Canonization* (Charlottesville: University Press of Virginia, 1996).

6 Tomás Eloy Martínez, *Santa Evita*, trans. Helen Lane (London: Anchor, 1997) p. 68.

7 Jacqueline Rose, *The Haunting of Sylvia Plath* (London: Virago, 1991) p. 1.

8 Marjorie Garber, *Shakespeare's Ghost Writers: Literature as Uncanny Causality* (New York: Methuen, 1987) p. xiv.

9 Andrew Bennett, *Keats, Narrative and Audience: the Posthumous Life of Writing* (Cambridge: Cambridge University Press, 1994) pp. 10, 11.

10 See Holman Hunt's *Isabella and the Pot of Basil*, dated 1867 but finished between 1867 and 1868.

11 Jacques Derrida, 'Signature Event Context', trans. Alan Bass, in Peggy Kamuf (ed.), *A Derrida Reader: Between the Blinds* (New York: Harvester Wheatsheaf, 1991) p. 107. Garber also makes the connection between Keats's 'living hand' and Derrida's conception of the signature, but she overly deanimates the latter, equating the signature directly with the ghost (p. 21). Yopi Prins offers a similarly annihilistic reading of the signature of Sappho in the nineteenth-century, which sidesteps the continuing durability and tenacity of the myth of Sappho. See *Victorian Sappho* (Princeton, New Jersey: Princeton University Press, 1999).

12 The term muscular is D.G. Rossetti's suggestive but derisory epithet for women's poetry on social or political themes. See *PW: CR* pp. 460–1.
13 *Letters* 1: 348. For a discussion on the literary relationship between Rossetti and Barrett Browning, see Antony H. Harrison, 'In the Shadow of E.B.B.: Christina Rossetti and Ideological Estrangement', in his *Victorian Poets and Romantic Poems* (Charlottesville: University Press of Virginia, 1990), and also Marjorie Stone, 'Sisters in Art: Christina Rossetti and Elizabeth Barrett Browning', *Victorian Poetry* 32 (1994) 339–64. Tricia Lootens explores the reception histories of Rossetti and Barrett Browning as one of competitiveness for a place in the literary canon (Chapter 5).
14 Kathy Psomiades makes a similar point about feminist reading of nineteenth-century literature, but not specifically in relation to new historicism: 'because modern feminism has its roots in nineteenth-century constructions of gender, it is possible, and indeed more than likely, that in the course of recovery nineteenth-century ideologies may be replicated, rather than subjected to scrutiny.' See '"Material Witness": Feminism and Nineteenth-Century Studies', *Nineteenth-Century Contexts* 31.1 (1989) 13–18 (p. 14). For further comments on the continuation of nineteenth-century paradigms in contemporary critique, see her *Beauty's Body: Femininity and Representation in British Aestheticism* (Stanford, California: Stanford University Press, 1997) pp. 29–30.
15 Brook Thomas, *The New Historicism and Other Old-Fashioned Topics* (Princeton, New Jersey: Princeton University Press, 1991) pp. 193–4.
16 Ros Ballaster, 'New Hystericism: Aphra Behn's *Oroonoko*: The body, the text and the feminist critic', in Isobel Armstrong (ed.) *New Feminist Discourses: Critical Essays on Theories and Texts* (London: Routledge, 1992) p. 284.
17 Linda Marshall explains the poetry's concern with 'postmortem awareness', a specific form of self-deletion, as part of Rossetti's theological interest in Hades. Marshall comments: 'whether one sees the intermediate state [between death and Resurrection] as withdrawal of consciousness or the heightening of it, perhaps the same point is made: life is neither sweet nor good, and to die is the best criticism of it'. See 'What the Dead Are Doing Underground: Hades and Heaven in the Writings of Christina Rossetti', *Victorian Newsletter* (Fall 1987) 55–60 (p. 58). Marshall also reminds us that, despite her investment in the afterlife, she had an intractable sense of selfhood, as the biographical anecdote 'I am Christina Rossetti' illustrates. See Chapter 3 for a further discussion of this episode.
18 See his two chapters on Christina Rossetti in *The Beauty of Inflections: Literary Investigations in Historical Method and Theory* (Oxford: Clarendon Press, 1985).
19 Margaret Linley, 'Dying to Be A Poetess: The Conundrum of Christina Rossetti', in Mary Arseneau, Antony H. Harrison and Lorraine Janzen Kooistra (eds), *The Culture of Christina Rossetti: Female Poetics and Victorian Contexts* (Athens, Ohio: Ohio University Press, 1999), p. 292.
20 Jan Marsh (ed.), *Christina Rossetti: Poems and Prose* (London: Everyman, 1994) p. 251. For the text of *Maude*, I use David A. Kent and P.G. Stanwood (eds), *Selected Prose of Christina Rossetti* (New York: St. Martin's Press, 1998).
21 Angela Leighton, '"When I am dead, my dearest": The Secret of Christina Rossetti', *Modern Philology* 87 (1989) 373–88 (p. 374).
22 Arthur Benson, 'Christina Rossetti', *The National Review* (26 February 1895) 753–63 (p. 756).

23 See Isobel Armstrong, *Victorian Poetry: Poetry, Poetics and Politics* (London: Routledge, 1993) p. 339.

24 The 'subject-in-process/on trial', as Kelly Oliver shows, runs throughout Kristeva's writings, but perhaps most obviously in *Strangers to Ourselves*, trans. Leon Roudiez (New York: Columbia University Press, 1991). See Kelly Oliver, *Reading Kristeva: Unraveling the Double-bind* (Bloomington: Indiana University Press, 1993) p. 187 and *passim*. What is termed, with a mistaken homogeneity, French feminism, has much to say about the intersubjective *rapprochement* of mediating subjectivities. For an account more utopian than Kristeva's, see Luce Irigaray's witty revision of Plato in 'Sorcerer Love: a Reading of Plato, Symposium, "Diotima's Speech"' in *An Ethics of Sexual Difference*, trans. Carolyn Burke and Gillian C. Gill (London: The Athlone Press, 1993) p. 21. The project of Irigaray and Kristeva is to revise Lacanian intersubjectivity which insists upon the paranoia and alienation of the split subject. See Jacques Lacan, *The Four Fundamental Concepts of Psycho-Analysis*, trans. Alan Sheridan, ed. Jacques-Alain Miller (Harmondsworth: Penguin, 1979) Ch. 16.

25 Oliver p. 14. Toril Moi discusses Kristeva's 'difficult balancing act' in the introduction to her edition of *The Kristeva Reader* (Oxford: Basil Blackwell, 1986) p. 13.

26 One of the most perceptive commentators on the aesthetic, Kathy Alexis Psomiades, criticises Terry Eagleton's adoption of the figure of the mother in his account of Western aesthetics as the 'unhistorical other of history' (*Beauty's Body* pp. 19–21), and yet her analysis of two key texts, 'Goblin Market' and 'In an Artist's Studio', is predicated upon indeterminate figures that exceed legibility, commodification, and aestheticism, in a fashion similar to the position I am arguing for the maternal (pp. 53–4, 105). For an important account of Victorian motherhood which stresses the non-monolothic construction of the maternal in fiction, see Jill L. Matus, *Unstable Bodies: Victorian Representations of Sexuality and Maternity* (Manchester: Manchester University Press, 1995).

1 'A Bizarre Medium': the Return of the Dead and New Historicism

1 Mackenzie Bell, *Christina Rossetti: a Biographical and Critical Study*, second edition (London: Hurst and Brackett, 1898) p. 134.

2 See Christina Rossetti's 'The Lowest Room' (Crump 1: 200) and Kathleen Jones's biography, which is focused around this motif as the organising principle of Rossetti's life. See her *Learning Not to be First: the Life of Christina Rossetti* (Oxford: Oxford University Press, 1992).

3 In Chapters 9 and 10 of his *Ventures into Childhood: Victorians, Fairy Tales, and Femininity* (Chicago: University of Chicago Press, 1998), U.C. Knoepflmacher gives a full account of the literary relations between Dodgson and Rossetti.

4 The phrase describes, in William's memoir of his sister, how a photograph taken in 1856 proves, 'by the irrefutable evidence of the sun, that she was not very far from being beautiful'. He also approves of the authenticity of Dodgson's photographs taken at Cheyne Walk: 'in each of these Christina is

capitally characterised'. William is at pains in the memoir to position himself as the authority on his sister, and yet his distinction between some photographs as more authentic than others betray the very tenuous assumption of photography's veracity (*PW: CR* pp. lxiii, lxiv).

5 Bell p. 134.

6 In a letter to Dodgson dated 1878, Rossetti compounds the association of the autumnal photographic session with loss: 'thank you for wishing us "well & happy": at any rate we are many ways changed since a certain summer day in the Cheyne Walk garden. My dear good sister died more than a year ago' (*Letters* 2: 160).

7 Jennifer Green-Lewis, 'Landscape, Loss, and Sexuality: Three Recent Books on Victorian Photography', *Victorian Studies* 39.3 (Spring 1996) 391–404 (p. 393). The books reviewed are: Carol Mavor, *Pleasures Taken: Performances of Sexuality and Loss in Victorian Photographs* (Durham: Duke University Press, 1995); John Taylor, *A Dream of England: Landscape, Photography and the Tourist's Imagination* (Manchester: Manchester University Press, 1994); Ellen Handy (ed.), *Pictorial Effect/Naturalistic Vision: the Photographs and Theories of Henry Peach Robinson and Peter Henry Emerson* (Norfolk, VA: The Chrysler Museum, 1994).

8 Lindsay Smith, 'The Politics of Focus: Feminism and Photographic Theory', in Isobel Armstrong (ed.), *New Feminist Discourses: Critical Essays on Theories and Texts* (London: Routledge, 1992) p. 256. This essay is included, in a revised form, in *The Politics of Focus: Women, Children and Nineteenth-Century Photography* (Manchester: Manchester University Press, 1998), Chapter 1.

9 In practice, Smith continues, nineteenth-century photography problematises geometrical perspective, and she offers the examples of combination prints and of Cameron's soft focus photography to illustrate her point (see especially pp. 242–7). It is thus peculiar that Dodgson should be set up as the exception.

10 Sigmund Freud, 'Fetishism' (1927), *SE* 21: 157.

11 Roland Barthes, *Camera Lucida,* trans. Richard Howard (London: Vintage, 1993) p. 9.

12 Jane Gallop, *Thinking Through the Body* (New York: Columbia University Press, 1988) pp. 156, 157.

13 Note that here I continue to follow Richard Howard's translation, whereas Gallop gives her own translation.

14 Although Gallop does not spell out the eroticism as heterosexual, she makes it clear that her approach to the punctum is not only semi-autobiographical, but that it is also predicated upon her heterosexual desire. See the photograph reproduced on p. 161, which wittily links the *punctum* with the male model's (just off-frame) phallus. The photograph is subtitled, *pace* Barthes, 'Minnette Lehmann, JANE GALLOP, ENDOWED WITH AN UNLOCATABLE PUNCTUM, IS SOMEONE I WANT TO MEET.'

15 Liliane Weissberg, 'Circulating Images: Notes on the Photographic Exchange', in Jean-Michel Rabaté, *Writing the Image After Roland Barthes* (Philadelphia: University of Pennsylvania Press, 1997) p. 113.

16 Diana Knight, 'Roland Barthes, or The Woman Without a Shadow', in Rabaté p. 140.

17 Derek Attridge makes a similar point in 'Roland Barthes's Obtuse, Sharp Meaning', in Rabaté pp. 82–3. He argues that the *punctum* is always incommunicable. The other essays in this collection give some flavour of the differing interpretations that the absence of the photograph incites.

18 *Camera Lucida* p. 21. See also Mavor p. 54, who talks of the pull of the umbilical scar but without exploring the anti-fetish.

19 Jerome McGann represents one of the two schools of new historicism in nineteenth-century studies. His analyses are characterised by an interest in recovering the materiality of literary production and reception. McGann insists that the 'concrete particulars' of literature can and must be unearthed, that its referentiality can be retrieved. See his Introduction to *Historical Studies and Literary Criticism*, ed. Jerome McGann (Madison, Wisconsin: University of Wisconsin Press, 1985) pp. 7–11. See also his study *A Critique of Modern Textual Criticism* (Chicago: Chicago University Press, 1983). The other school, dominated by the Renaissance critic Stephen Greenblatt, and influenced by Foucaldian concepts of history, is addressed in the following chapter.

20 Jerome J. McGann, *The Beauty of Inflections: Literary Investigations in Historical Method and Theory* (Oxford: Clarendon Press, 1985) p. 216.

21 *Letters* 2: 289. The second quotation refers to 'The Key-Note' (Crump 2: 59), another poem of seasonal and personal loss. In the next sentence, humorously, she punctures this self-image: 'if only my figure would shrink somewhat! for a fat poetess is incongruous, especially when seated by the grave of buried hope'. For a further discussion of Rossetti's body, see Chapter 3.

22 Séan Burke, *The Death and Return of the Author: Criticism and Subjectivity in Barthes, Foucault and Derrida*, second edition (Edinburgh: Edinburgh University Press, 1998 [1992]) p. 6.

23 Julia Kristeva, 'Stabat Mater', in Toril Moi (ed.), *The Kristeva Reader* (Oxford: Blackwell, 1986) p. 162. 'Flash' and 'photos' appear in the original French version. See *Histoires d'amour* (n.p.: Denoel, 1983) p. 296.

24 Kelly Oliver, *Reading Kristeva: Unraveling the Double-bind* (Bloomington: Indiana University Press, 1993) p. 53.

25 Anna Smith, *Julia Kristeva: Readings of Exile and Estrangement* (Houndmills, Basingstoke: Macmillan, 1996) pp. 138–9.

26 See Oliver p. 183.

27 Kristeva, 'Stabat Mater' p. 185.

2 Speaking with the Dead: Recovering Lost Voices

1 Hélène Cixous, 'Sorties', in Hélène Cixous and Catherine Clément, *The Newly Born Woman*, trans. Betsy Wing (London: I.B. Tauris, 1996) p. 94.

2 Christina Rossetti, *Time Flies: a Reading Diary* (London: SPCK, 1885) p. 30.

3 See, for example, Stephen Heath's review essay 'Female Tones and Timbres', *Women: a Cultural Review*, 7.3 (Winter 1996) 309–16.

4 One of the most recent accounts of the process by which voices are silenced is the excellent study by Tricia Lootens, *Lost Saints: Silence, Gender, and Victorian Literary Canonization* (Charlottesville: University Press of Virginia, 1996).

Lootens is, however, implicitly supportive of new historicist recovery of the silenced voices and never puts the voice itself in question.

5 Stephen Greenblatt, *Shakespearean Negotiations: the Circulation of Social Energy in Renaissance England* (Oxford: Clarendon Press, 1988) p.1. Greenblatt has frequently protested against those who represent him as the central figure and founding father of new historicism. His deployment of the voice in the project of recovery is, however, paradigmatic of new historicism's critical praxis.

6 Stephen Greenblatt, *Renaissance Self-Fashioning: From More to Shakespeare* (Chicago: University of Chicago Press, 1980) pp. 255–7.

7 Perhaps it isn't too farfetched to note here that there is an increasing new historicist interest in death as a subject of enquiry as the methodology turns in upon itself. For example, see Esther Schor, *Bearing the Dead: the British Culture of Mourning from the Enlightenment to Victoria* (Princeton, NJ: Princeton University Press, 1994). The interest in death represents an uncanny turn, by which new historicism, in critical praxis, becomes its own ghost, a shadow of its former self. See also Edward Pechter's opening comments to 'The New Historicism and Its Discontents: Politicising Renaissance Drama': 'A specter is haunting criticism – the specter of a new historicism.' See *PMLA* 102.3 (May 1987): 292–303.

8 Nick Cox, 'Specters of Greenblatt', paper delivered to the Northern Renaissance Seminar Group at Sheffield Hallam University, 9 November 1996.

9 This critical failure is often cited on another level of methodology in the relation between new and old historicism. For example see Frank Lentricchia, 'Foucault's Legacy: a New Historicism?', in H. Aram Veeser (ed.), *The New Historicism* (New York: Routledge, 1989) pp. 231–42, and Brook Thomas, *The New Historicism and Other Old-Fashioned Topics* (Princeton, New Jersey: Princeton University Press, 1991).

10 Mladen Dolar, 'The Object Voice', in Renata Salecl and Slavoj Žižek (eds), *Gaze and Voice as Love Objects* (Durham: Duke University Press, 1996) p. 15.

11 Slavoj Žižek, '"I Hear You with My Eyes"; or, The Invisible Master', *Gaze and Voice* p. 92.

12 Joel Fineman argues that the anecdote in new historicist criticism is, in psychoanalytical terms, both hole and rim. See 'The History of the Anecdote: Fiction and Fiction', in Veeser p. 61. If Fineman is right, the anecdote may be recuperated in new historicism as the inscription of the voice's presence and absence: it allows spectrality to be motivated so that history is not necessarily always represented as monolithic.

Most of the objections to the use of the anecdote argue that it does, in fact, represent power as a monolithic entity. Kiernan Ryan, for example, objects to the anecdote's assumption of a pervasive and inescapable cultural logic; see his *New Historicism and Cultural Materialism: a Reader* (London: Arnold, 1996) p. xvii. Frank Lentricchia argues that anecdotes undermine the new historicist project by assuming direct access to history (p. 234). Carolyn Porter suggests that anecdotes exemplify the relationship between text and context as one of specious analogy, which only works if analogy translates into homology and succeeds in its repression of difference between text and context. See 'Are We Being Historical Yet?', in David Carroll (ed.), *The States of 'Theory': History, Art, and Critical Discourses* (Stanford, California: Stanford

University Press, 1990) pp. 42–3. How, then, to deploy the anecdote in praxis as a representation of the excess of symbolisation? New historicism has to confront the fact that, not only does it have no access to the real (as its poststructuralist origins suggest), but its purchase on representation is predicated upon its other, upon representation's remainder. See Chapter 3 for a further discussion of the anecdote in relation to biographies of Christina Rossetti.

13 Jeremy Hawthorn, *Cunning Passages: New Historicism, Cultural Materialism and Marxism in the Contemporary Literary Debate* (London: Arnold, 1996) p. 5.

14 Greenblatt, *Shakespearean Negotiations* p. 95.

15 Thomas Docherty, *Alterities: Criticism, History, Representation* (Oxford: Clarendon Press, 1996) p. 206.

16 Tilly Olsen, *Silences* (London: Virago, 1980).

17 Joanna Russ, *How to Suppress Women's Writing* (Austin: University of Texas Press, 1983). See also Elaine Hedges and Shelley Fisher Fishkin (eds), *Listening to Silences: New Essays in Feminist Criticism* (Oxford: Oxford University Press, 1994) especially pp. 3–5 which chart the influence to feminists of Olsen's *Silences*.

18 See, for example, Ros Ballaster, 'New Hystericism: Aphra Behn's *Oroonoko*: The Body, the Text, and the Feminist Critic', in Isobel Armstrong (ed.), *New Feminist Discourses: Critical Essays on Theories and Texts* (London: Routledge, 1992) pp. 283–95.

19 Toril Moi, *Sexual/Textual Politics: Feminist Literary Theory* (London: Routledge, 1988) p. 59.

20 Interestingly, in the opening of *Shakespearean Negotiations*, Greenblatt figures the projection the other way round, as the dead voices speaking 'through' the critic. This gives a peculiar agency to the text independent of the critic which has the effect of heightening the text's status as a source of plenitude and originary meaning.

21 Elizabeth Harvey, *Ventriloquized Voices: Feminist Theory and English Renaissance Texts* (London: Routledge, 1992) p. 6.

22 Diana Fuss, *Essentially Speaking: Feminism, Nature and Difference* (London: Routledge, 1989). Fuss unsettles the binary essentialism/constructionism to argue that one term depends upon the other. In other words, essentialism is the unspoken, repressed basis of constructionist accounts, and vice versa. Her study is an important contribution to the re-evaluation of essentialism in feminist theory. See also Naomi Schor, 'This Essentialism Which Is Not One: Coming to Grips with Irigaray', in Carolyn Burke, Naomi Schor and Margaret Whitford (eds), *Engaging With Irigaray: Feminist Philosophy and Modern European Thought* (New York: Columbia, 1994) pp. 57–78.

23 James Ashcroft Noble, *Impressions and Memories* (London: Dent, 1895) p. 56.

24 Alice Meynell, 'Christina Rossetti', *New Review* (12 February 1895) 201–6 (p. 203).

25 William Sharp, 'Some Reminiscences of Christina Rossetti', *Atlantic Monthly* LXXV (June 1895) 736–49 (p. 737).

26 Yopi Prins, *Victorian Sappho* (Princeton, New Jersey: Princeton University Press, 1999) p. 16 and *passim*.

27 Isobel Armstrong, *Victorian Poetry: Poetry, Poetics and Politics* (London: Routledge, 1993) Chapter 12, esp. pp. 326, 339, 346.

28 Elisabeth Bronfen, *Over Her Dead Body: Death, Femininity, and the Aesthetic* (Manchester: Manchester University Press, 1992) pp. 168–78.
29 Roger C. Lewis and Mark Samuels Lasner (eds), *Poems and Drawings of Elizabeth Siddal* (Wolfville, NS: Wombat Press, 1978).
30 Maggie Berg, 'A Neglected Voice: Elizabeth Siddal', *Dalhousie Review* 60 (1980–81) 151–6 (p. 151). Compare Constance W. Hassett's attempt to read Siddal's poetry as literary and intertextual, not as a biographical index, in 'Elizabeth Siddal's Poetry: a Problem and Some Suggestions', *Victorian Poetry* 35 (1997) 443–70.
31 Jan Marsh, *Elizabeth Siddal 1829–1862: Pre-Raphaelite Artist* (Sheffield: The Ruskin Gallery, 1991).
32 Jan Marsh, *The Legend of Elizabeth Siddal* (London: Quartet, 1989).
33 Isobel Armstrong and Joseph Bristow (eds), with Cath Sharrock, *Nineteenth-Century Women Poets* (Oxford: Clarendon Press, 1996) and Angela Leighton and Margaret Reynolds (eds), *Victorian Women Poets: an Anthology* (Oxford: Blackwell, 1995).
34 Armstrong and Bristow's account of Siddal also insist on the privacy of her poetry, re-circulating the aesthetic which positions women's creativity as interior and personal: 'Siddal's poetry remained a private affair, unlike her pictorial work. No one in her immediate circle seemed to know of these writings during her lifetime' (p. 514).
35 In Leighton's study, an analysis of each poet's work is prefaced by a biographical essay. In the introduction, she defends her rationale. Firstly, the woman writer is important to recover because, citing Rosi Braidotti: 'one cannot deconstruct a subjectivity one has never been fully granted'. But this assumes that subjectivity *per se* can be fully present to itself rather than a fantasy of origin. Leighton, however, vigorously insists on the necessity of recovering the author's background and context without suggesting that such a project may be inherently problematic and in the end re-inscribes the ideology that silenced and marginalised these poets in the first place. Secondly, Leighton denies that recovering biographical details subscribes to a form of authorial intentionalism and, to emphasise this, she separates the biographical account from the literary analysis. But the relation between context and analysis, biography and poetry, is rather confusingly sketched: 'the two parts are not necessarily either causally related or obviously compatible, but neither are they, therefore, totally unrelated and different'. This has it both ways, as the gap between the two parts in fact intertwines them ambivalently: literary analysis bears an uncanny and enigmatic relation to the biographical narrative. See Angela Leighton, *Victorian Women Poets: Writing Against the Heart* (Hemel Hempstead: Harvester Wheatsheaf, 1992) p. 4.
36 See Deborah Cherry and Griselda Pollock, 'Woman as Sign in Pre-Raphaelite Literature: a Study of the Representation of Elizabeth Siddall', *Art History* 7.1 (March 1984) 206–27. Pollock reprints a version of the essay in her *Vision and Difference: Femininity, Feminism and Histories of Art* (London: Routledge, 1988). References in this chapter will be to the earlier version of the article. Cherry and Pollock's work acknowledges its debt to Elizabeth Cowie's groundbreaking work on the semiotics of 'Woman'. See Elizabeth Cowie, 'Woman as Sign', *m/f* 1.1 (1978) 49–63. A further important related review article by Cherry and

Pollock is 'Patriarchal Power and the Pre-Raphaelites', *Art History* 7.4 (December 1984) 480–95.

37 Cherry and Pollock insist on using the family spelling of the surname, Siddall, in order to differentiate it from the Pre-Raphaelite invention Siddal. While this obviously avoids confusion, the differentiation, as they themselves admit, is rather hard to make out. I have avoided their practice as a potential reinscription of a historical persona as origin, to whom we can have no meaningful direct access divorced from the fictive 'Siddal'.

38 Hélène Cixous p. 92.

39 For a discussion of *écriture feminine* as a writing of the other, see Susan Sellers, *Hélène Cixous* (London: Routledge, 1996).

40 For an account of this tradition see Isobel Armstrong, *Victorian Poetry: Poetry, Poetics, Politics* (London: Routledge, 1993) and Leighton, *Victorian Women Poets: Writing Against the Heart.*

3 Christina Rossetti in Effect: Reading Biographies

1 William Sharp, 'Some Reminiscences of Christina Rossetti', *Atlantic Monthly* 75 (June 1895) 736–49 (p. 749).

2 Georgina Battiscombe, *Christina Rossetti: a Divided Life* (London: Constable, 1981) p. 13. Valerie Ross suggests that the outside/inside distinction is a feature of the genre within academy: 'being about the unruly "inside" that must be kept "outside" of institutional discourse, biography, I argue, facilitates and provokes the construction, consolidation, and reinforcement of professional identity and authority', 'Too Close to Home: Repressing Biography, Instituting Authority', in *Contesting the Subject: Essays in the Postmodern Theory and Practice of Biography and Biographical Criticism*, ed. William H. Epstein (West Lafayette: Purdue University Press, 1991) pp. 135–65 (p. 138).

3 The first biography of Rossetti, by Mackenzie Bell, draws explicitly on the authority of William Michael Rossetti throughout. Indeed, it could be argued that William Michael controls the posthumous representations of his sister directly, through his 'Memoir' and other writings on his family, and indirectly, through his dealings with Bell's biography. In his edition of his sister's *Poetical Works*, however, William Michael is anxious to counter the reviewers' complaints that he had too much control over Bell's biography (pp. ix–xi).

4 Edward Boyle, *Biographical and Critical Essays, 1790–1890* (London: Oxford University Press, 1936; repr. Freeport, New York: Books for Libraries, 1968) p. 196.

5 Tricia Lootens, who examines the canonisation of Victorian women poets from the perspective of religion, also argues that Rossetti's sanctification requires her removal from history. The discussion of Rossetti's construction focuses on the 1890s and is useful for the link forged between canonisation and the poetry's neglect, as it removes 'the worldliness necessary to make it live', its historical contingency. See *Lost Saints: Silence, Gender, and Victorian Literary Canonization* (Charlottesville: University Press of Virginia, 1996) pp. 160, 182.

6 Virginia Woolf, *The Common Reader: Second Series* (London: The Hogarth Press, 1932) p. 237.

7 Ellen A. Proctor, *A Brief Memoir of Christina G. Rossetti* (London: SPCK, 1895; repr. 1978) pp. 44–5.

8 Mackenzie Bell, *Christina Rossetti: a Biographical and Critical Study* (London: Hurst and Blackett, 1898). In the preface to his edition of Rossetti's collected poems, W.M. Rossetti admits supplying Bell with much of his information but denies censoring him, except in a few instances (*PW: CR* pp. ix–xi).

9 See Chapter 2 for a discussion of the groundbreaking work on the representation of Pre-Raphaelite artists in literary biography undertaken by Deborah Cherry and Griselda Pollock. In 'Patriarchal Power and the Pre-Raphaelites', *Art History* 7.4 (December 1984) 480–95, they expose the reminiscences of the Brotherhood as historically and culturally determined and not simply a window to the past. Similarly, in 'Woman as Sign in Pre-Raphaelite Literature: a Study of the Representation of Elizabeth Siddall', *Art History* 7.1 (June 1984) 206–27, representations of 'Elizabeth Siddal' are separated from the historical personage Elizabeth Siddall (see Chapter 2 for a discussion of this essay). Both articles also point to the circulation of similar material in biographical texts. The latest biography of Rossetti by Jan Marsh admirably attempts to reconstruct and recover Christina Rossetti as an historical personage and is the most meticulously researched biography to date. See Jan Marsh, *Christina Rossetti: a Literary Biography* (London: Jonathan Cape, 1994). Nevertheless, all biographies cannot escape confusing historical personage with representation – the unavoidable mark of the genre.

10 Marsh, *Christina Rossetti: a Literary Biography* p. 8.

11 *PW: CR* pp. xlix–l; Bell p. 11.

12 Katharine Tynan Hinkson, 'Santa Christina', *The Bookman* (London) LXLI (Jan. 1912) 185–90 (p. 187).

13 Kathleen Jones, *Learning Not to be First: the Life of Christina Rossetti* (Oxford: Oxford University Press, 1992) p. 224.

14 Jones p. 206.

15 The Pre-Raphaelite circle displayed a general tendency to destroy or control personal material. Christina Rossetti had a habit of destroying letters addressed to her upon receipt. She also requested that her letters to her long-term intimate friend Charles Cayley be destroyed at his death. See Lona Mosk Packer, *Christina Rossetti* (Berkeley: University of California Press, 1963) p. 362. At D.G. Rossetti's death, she helped W.M. Rossetti select letters that were suitable for publication (ibid., pp. 354–6). All the Rossettis, but Christina perhaps more than any, were acutely aware of their literary persona; certainly the dearth of historical information about her life is a result of the deliberate construction of her mythical and idealised image. 'Christina Rossetti complicates but never disentangles herself from attendant men's angelic dream of her' (Nina Auerbach, *Woman and the Demon: the Life of a Victorian Myth* (Cambridge, MA: Harvard University Press, 1982) pp. 115–16).

16 James A. Kohl, 'A Medical Comment on Christina Rossetti', *Notes and Queries* 213 (Nov. 1968) 423–4 (p. 424). Felicita Jurlaro's biography is motivated by the same concerns. She explains the organisation of her book thus: 'to discover the "Universale", i.e., the significance and genius of the Rossettis, the "particolare" is introduced [...] with short additional sections entitled, "Quei piccoli particolari...!!! or...anecdotes and homely sketches." The aim is to

examine and analyse the simple events of everyday life', *Christina Georgina Rossetti: the True Story* (London: Excalibur, 1991). Rossetti's Anglo-Italian heritage is also perceived here to be the key to her identity. Jurlaro quotes from Olivia Rossetti Agresti, Rossetti's niece, who provides much of the 'authoritative' anecdotal information (and hence the 'true story'): 'Christina Rossetti! The name is musical and the thoughts it arouses in all familiar with her poetry are quite other than those of a Bloomsbury Square [and her] dowdy mid-Victorian dress. [...] The fire was there, the passionate heart was there [...] the deep and tender family affections so characteristic of her Italian ancestry were there, but all under strict control, all mastered and repressed by the puritanical conventional strain inherited from the quarter of English blood that came to her from the Pierces' (p. 75).

17 Elisabeth Bronfen, *Over Her Dead Body: Death, Femininity, and the Aesthetic* (Manchester: Manchester University Press, 1992) p. 228. Bronfen is drawing here on Barthes's *Mythologies*, which explores the semiotics of myth as an exchange between presence and absence which empties myth of history and turns it into nature in a process of deanimation. See Roland Barthes, *Mythologies*, selected and trans. by Annette Lavers (London: Paladin, 1973) pp. 127, 140. Bronfen reformulates Barthes: 'reversing his argument that myth turns meaning into a speaking corpse, I will suggest that speaking corpses produce mythic meaning' (p. 228).

18 Compare Lootens, who argues that Rossetti's construction as a poetess required a dissolution, a denial of the poetic power's source while, for Elizabeth Barrett Browning, the process was one of displacement (p. 159).

19 William Michael Rossetti defines his sister as 'replete with the spirit of self-postponement', *PW: CR* p. lxvii.

20 *PW: CR* p. l.

21 Kohl, 'A Medical Comment' p. 423.

22 Marsh, *CR: Literary Biography* p. 55.

23 Mary Poovey points out that hysterics were seen to pose a threat to the doctor's authority because they crossed the border between somatic and psychological diseases. See *Uneven Developments: the Ideological Work of Gender in Mid-Victorian England* (Chicago: The University of Chicago Press, 1988) pp. 45–7. There was therefore an anxiety attached to diagnosing and curing the hysteric, which perhaps also accounts for the elliptical biographical narrative of Rossetti's disorder in early accounts of her life. Marsh, in her biography, also suspects hysteria or depression (p. 51). Later on in her study, Marsh returns to the teenage breakdown and explores the possibility of paternal incest as the key to her poor health. This theory has been contentiously received, as Jan Marsh recounted in a paper to the English Department at the University of Dundee on 20 January 1999. For the purposes of this chapter, Marsh's theory is interesting firstly because it corresponds to the biographical tendency to explain Rossetti's poetry with reference to a traumatic life event, also evinced by Lona Mosk Packer's claim, which structures her biography, that Rossetti was in love with William Bell Scott. Secondly, Marsh's biography curiously (and sensitively) defers naming the cause of her subject's trauma in adolescence until just under half way through the study, suggesting the tentative way hysteria is treated by Rossetti's early biographers. Indeed, Marsh suggests that sexual abuse is the underlying cause of Rossetti's

hysterical episodes (pp. 260–2). Although Marsh, as well as Kathleen Jones, concur in their diagnosis of hysteria, the point is not whether Rossetti can be definitively diagnosed as a hysteric, but that the diagnosis in the biographies has a particular and telling discursive effect.

24 See Elaine Showalter, *The Female Malady: Women, Madness, and English Culture, 1830–1980* (London: Virago, 1987), Chapter 6 and also, for an overview of the history of hysteria, the Introduction to *In Dora's Case: Freud-Hysteria-Feminism*, Charles Bernheimer and Claire Kahane (eds) (London: Virago, 1985).

25 *SE* vols. 2 and 7.

26 She later so confessed in letters to Swinburne and W.M. Rossetti. See Packer, *Christina Rossetti* p. 21.

27 Packer, *Christina Rossetti* pp. 397–8, and Jones p. 223.

28 David A. Kent condemns biographical attempts to understand Rossetti's distress before her death as a symptom, not of spiritual anguish (and religious hysteria) but of extreme physical pain. He blames William Michael's representation of his sister's health for the tendency to see her death as a religious crisis, because it overemphasises her melancholy and despondency. While Kent's comments are interesting, his attempt to recuperate the meaning of Rossetti's distress as physiological and not religious re-states Rossetti's stoic faith in a way that reasserts the narrative of her saintliness, rather than her historical reality. See 'Christina Rossetti's Dying', *Journal of Pre-Raphaelite Studies* 5 (Fall 1996) 83–97.

29 Bell p. 51.

30 Dorothy Margaret Stuart, *Christina Rossetti* (London: Macmillan, 1930) pp. 79–80. The lines quoted are from 'From Sunset to Star Rise' (Crump 1: 192).

31 Packer p. 222

32 Battiscombe p. 126.

33 Jones p. 139.

34 The actual window of her bedroom at Penkill Castle does indeed resemble a picture frame. On the cover of a Penkill Foundation newsletter, *The Order of the Owl* 3.1 (1987), is a photograph of a woman dressed as Rossetti sitting at the window. The frame of the window has a triple stone border, the middle section resembling lattice work; it uncannily suggests a painted portrait of Rossetti (the photograph itself makes this point by "picturing" a Rossetti double looking out of the window). For a general survey of representations of women at windows, see Elaine Shefer, 'The Woman at the Window in Victorian Art and Christina Rossetti as the Subject of Millais's *Mariana*', *Journal of Pre-Raphaelite and Aesthetic Studies* 4.1 (1983) 14–25.

35 *PW: CR* p. lxiv.

36 Compare Chapter 4, which demonstrates how D.G. Rossetti's revisions to his sister's poetry replace the feminine subject with a locale and gives priority to the experiential over the imagination.

37 Edmund Gosse, *Critical Kit-Kats* (London: Heinemann, 1896) p. 139.

38 Cited in Bell p. 331.

39 Lynne Pearce, *Woman/Image/Text: Readings in Pre-Raphaelite Art and Literature* (Hemel Hempstead: Harvester Wheatsheaf, 1991) p. 38.

40 See Elizabeth Grosz's entry under voyeurism/the gaze in *Feminism and Psychoanalysis. a Critical Dictionary*, Elizabeth Wright (ed.) (Oxford: Blackwell,

1992) pp. 448–9, in which Lacan's stress on the primacy of the subject's possibility of being seen is distinguished from Sartre's notion of the reciprocal gaze. See also Jacques Lacan *The Four Fundamental Concepts of Psychoanalysis*, trans. by Alan Sheridan (London: Hogarth Press, 1977) pp. 182–3.

41 Andrew Belsey and Catherine Belsey, 'Christina Rossetti: Sister to the Brotherhood', *Textual Practice* 2.1 (1988) 30–50 (p. 45).

42 See Bronfen pp. 225–8.

43 Lootens describes the pattern of Rossetti's canonisation as a struggle with the 'ultimate untenability' of her representation as lady, poet, and saint (p. 158). The tensions in the formulation are, however, more complex, for the biographical trope Christina Rossetti is both historical and ahistorical, both representational and exceptional, both feminine and exceeding gender. Lootens also sees Rossetti's death and her spinsterhood as problems for the early accounts of her life and poetry, where in fact they the apotheosis of her tropic identity. Lootens is optimistic that the process of canonisation can be contested: by the poets themselves (although exactly how is not spelt out), and, she argues, the fractures in the 'papier-mâché' (p. 159) constructions of poetic sainthood which make them predisposed to crumble away. And yet the constructions, and the ideology of femininity and creativity behind them, are especially durable, as seen in Lootens' insistence that there is a recoverable historical personage beneath.

44 Christina Rossetti's reply to her brother is both meek and ironical: 'Well, Gabriel, I don't know, I'm sure, you yourself always dress very simply' (Battiscombe p. 18).

45 Bell pp. 52–3; Jones p. 54.

46 *PW: CR* p. xlvii, and Marsh, *Christina Rossetti: a Literary Biography* p. 72.

47 Letitia Elizabeth Landon was also, Glennis Stephenson argues, decontextualised by her critics in their contribution to the construction of L.E.L. See 'Letitia Elizabeth Landon and the Victorian Improvisatrice: The Construction of L.E.L.', *Victorian Poetry* 30 (1992) 1–17 (p. 14).

48 Barthes, *Mythologies* p. 53.

49 Many feminist critiques are concerned with the dominant Victorian representational system's denotation of the feminine as private, in opposition to the masculine as public. Most pertinent here is Kathy Alexis Psomiades, *Beauty's Body: Femininity and Representation in British Aestheticism* (Stanford: Stanford University Press, 1997), Chapter 1. At issue here is the removal of the feminine from capitalist production; in representations of 'Rossetti' as a biographical subject this removal extends to an effacement of social and historical contexts that produced such representations. Cora Kaplan, *Sea Changes: Essays on Culture and Feminism* (London: Verso, 1986), argues that Rossetti's lyrics witness to a female psyche deliberately defiant of the social in order to forefront the psychological (Chapter 5). I would argue that, rather than an *intentional* attempt to erase contexts, the poetry (together with its author and reception) is largely predicated by the aesthetic which equated female poetry with the feminine subject position constituted within the realm of privacy, domesticity, and the a-contextual.

50 Rossetti herself feared such an interpretation of her poetry. In one of her earliest extant letters, for example, she worried that her poetry would be construed as 'love personals' (*Letters* 1: 16). But she also had a certain

conflicted investment in biographical readings. She contributed to the *Imperial Dictionary of Universal Biography* (Marsh, *Christina Rossetti: a Literary Biography* p. 189), which included an entry on Petrarch which claimed Laura as 'my own ancestress, as family documents prove' (ibid., p. 212), which, as Marsh notes, must be a symbolic rather than factual ancestry. She was keen to embark on biographies of Adelaide Proctor, Elizabeth Barrett and Ann Radcliffe for the Eminent Women series, although all projects had to be aborted (ibid., pp. 495–6). See also her biographical readings in the article 'Dante. The Poet Illustrated out of the Poem', in *The Century* (February 1884) 566–73. Her semi-autobiographical novella *Maude* contains a similar ambivalence about biographical reading, which it both mocks in the case of Maude's melancholy verses, and also invites in the case of Rossetti as author. See the introduction for a discussion of *Maude* in this context.

51 D.G. Rossetti refers to Barrett Browning derogatively with masculine imagery: 'modern vicious style', 'falsetto muscularity' (quoted in *PW: CR* p. 460).

52 For example, see W.M. Rossetti, *PW: CR* p. lxvii.

53 Bell p. 155.

54 Bell p. 62, and Woolf p. 238.

55 For a fuller explanation of this, with its implications from women's poetry, see Margaret Homans, *Bearing the Word: Language and Female Experience in Nineteenth-Century Women's Writing* (Chicago: The University of Chicago Press, 1986) Chapter 1.

56 As an appendix to the collection of his sister's letters, W.M. Rossetti gives extracts from his diary from 1871–95, which frequently mentions her illnesses and chronicles her last days (*FL: CR* pp. 207–22). He acknowledges in the preface that many of the entries deal with such matters but mentions that many more have been omitted (p. xii).

57 William H. Epstein describes this as a phenomenon of the genre: 'traditional biographical narrative habitually re-enacts the scene of an abduction because, in order to discursively repair the biologically irreparable fracture (the alterity, the otherness, the discontinuity) between any two human individuals (reified generically as biographer and biological subject), biography recesses the broken parts and causes the gaping of a wound'. Thus, the attempt to heal the gap between the biographer and subject exposes the gap and undermines the biographical project. See '(Post) Modern Lives: Abducting the Biographical Subject', in Epstein's *Contesting the Subject* pp. 217–36 (p. 218).

58 *SE* 2: 270–1.

59 D.G. Rossetti advised the change in a letter to his sister, 28 January 1861 (*DGR: FL* 2: 164). The poem is an apt choice for Bell, for it speaks from the position of the posthumous subject as it describes the return after death of the speaker's spirit to her house (Crump 1: 28).

60 Epstein, '(Post) Modern Lives' p. 224.

61 Recent biographical criticism has confronted the problematics of (specifically women's) representation in the genre and has made some tentative suggestions for experimental writing. See Sharon O'Brien, 'Feminist Theory and Literary Biography', in Epstein's *Contesting the Subject* pp. 123–33. To date, there has been very little critical enquiry into biographical representations of Rossetti; the only exception to this is Janet Gray's analysis of the problematics

of narrating an anecdote. See 'The Sewing Contest: Christina Rossetti and the Other Women', *a/b: Auto/Biographical Studies* 8.2 (1993) 233–57.

62 Since Packer's biography in 1963, there were no biographies for almost two decades, until four biographies appeared in the space of thirteen years: Battiscombe (1981); Jones (1992); Frances Thomas, *Christina Rossetti: a Biography* (London (?): Self Publishing Association, 1992; repr. Virago, 1994); and Marsh (1994).

63 Rossetti as an unknowable biographical subject is also suggested by her first biographer who claims that only a close personal knowledge of his subject discloses the essence of her personality and also how autobiographical her writing is (p. 4). Thus, Bell, in a curious double move, both authorises himself as a friend of Rossetti, but also withholds her from the reader who has not the advantage of knowing her personally.

64 *PW: CR* p. lxv.

65 *PW: CR* p. lxiii.

66 Thomas's biography is the first to reproduce the photograph.

67 Intriguingly, Bell cites Christina Rossetti's rather brutal reference to the photograph in a letter to Mrs Patchett Martin dated 4 January 1892 as a 'stern transcript' (p. 53). In *The Face of the Deep*, Rossetti refers to photography as analogous to the Book of Works, for death will make visible was what thought to be hidden and yet has been recorded secretly and accurately: 'it is as if all along one had walked in a world of invisible cameras charged with instantaneous plates' (p. 91). Here, the veracity of photography has its apotheosis in death, much like the feminine subject in biographical discourse.

4 Defining the Feminine Subject: Fraternal Revisions I

1 *Goblin Market and Other Poems* (London: Macmillan, 1862), *The Prince's Progress and Other Poems* (London: Macmillan, 1866).

2 Quoted in Antony H. Harrison, *Christina Rossetti in Context* (Brighton: The Harvester Press, 1988) p. 10.

3 The editorial role of W.M. Rossetti is also clarified by Crump's edition, and analysed by Gwynneth Hatton's 'An Edition of the Unpublished Poems of Christina Rossetti, with a critical introduction and interpretative notes to all the posthumous poems', St Hilda's College, Oxford, BLitt. thesis, 1955. Most significantly, Hatton lists W.M. Rossetti's editorial errors, which include the silent addition of his own titles and cancellation of stanzas (pp. xxxvii–xlviii). The extent to which he concealed revisions – although his notes do occasionally refer to certain manuscript changes – is suggested by his comment in the memoir that prefaces his edition: 'her habits of composition were entirely of the casual and spontaneous kind. [. . .] It came to her (I take it) very easily, without her meditating a possible subject, and without her making any great difference in the first from the latest form of the verses which embodied it; but some difference, with a view to right and fine detail of execution, she did of course make when needful. [. . .] What she wrote was pretty well known in the family as soon as her impeccably neat manuscript of it appeared in one of her little notebooks; but she did not show it about as an achievement, and still less had she, in the course of her work, invited any hint, counsel,

or co-operation', *PW: CR* pp. lxviii–lxix. Compare George W. Bethune: 'the prominent fault of female poetical writers is an unwillingness to apply the pruning-knife and the pumice-stone. They write from impulse, and rapidly as they think. [...] As the line first came to the brain, so it was written; as it was written so it was printed', Preface to *British Female Poets* (1848), quoted in the Critical Introduction to *Aurora Leigh*, Margaret Reynolds (ed.) (Athens: Ohio University Press, 1992) n. 20, p. 56. In the preface to his edition of Walt Whitman's poems, W.M. Rossetti is explicit about his editorial practises in this instance, and defends his revisions (rearrangement and categorisation of poems, addition of titles, suppression of 'offensive' poems) for literary and moral reasons. See *Poems by Walt Whitman* (London: Chatto and Windus, 1895) pp. 16–19. The silent revisions to his sister's poems maintain the posthumous biographical trope of the poet, described in Chapter 3 and revisited in later chapters.

4 David G. Riede argues that D.G. Rossetti's revisions to a volume of his own poetry, the *Poems* of 1870, systematically removes any indication of religious faith. See David Reide, 'Erasing the Art-Catholic: Rossetti's *Poems*, 1870', *Journal of Pre-Raphaelite Studies* 1.2 (1981) 50–70 (p. 50).

5 See 'A Superscription' (one message written on top of another) from *The House of Life* (*CW: DGR* 1: 225):

> Unto thine eyes the glass where that is seen
> Which had Life's form and Love's, but by my spell
> Is now a shaken shadow intolerable,
> Of ultimate things unuttered the frail screen.
>
> (ll. 5–8)

6 The most sustained analysis of Rossetti's affinity with Pre-Raphaelite aesthetics is in Harrison, *Christina Rossetti in Context*, Chapter 3.

7 *PW: CR* pp. lxviii–lxix. See Chapter 7 for a discussion of Christina Rossetti's complicity with and subversion of this ideology of creativity.

8 Alice Meynell, 'Christina Rossetti', *New Review* (12 February 1895) 201–6 (p. 202)

9 Paul Elmer More, 'Christina Rossetti', *Atlantic Monthly* 94 (December 1904) 815–21 (p. 818).

10 Edward Boyle, *Biographical and Critical Essays, 1790–1890* (London: Oxford University Press, 1936; repr. Freeport, New York: Books for Libraries Press, 1986) p. 201.

11 Tricia Lootens, *Lost Saints: Silence, Gender, and Victorian Literary Canonization* (Charlottesville: University Press of Virginia, 1996) p. 165.

12 See William Sharp, 'Some Reminiscences of Christina Rossetti', *Atlantic Monthly* LXXV (June 1895) 736–49 (p. 741).

13 Andrew Belsey and Catherine Belsey, 'Christina Rossetti: Sister to the Brotherhood', *Textual Practice* 2.1 (1988) 30–50 (p. 31).

14 *CW: DGR* 1: 216, ll. 6, 7–8.

15 Surtees 1: 116–17, and 2, plate 293.

16 J. Hillis Miller, 'The Mirror's Secret: Dante Gabriel Rossetti's Double Work of Art', *Victorian Poetry* 29 (1991) 333–65 (p. 333).

17 Christina Rossetti's awareness of the dangerous implications (for the soul and the poetic subject) of the mirror is suggested in her short story 'Folio Q'. As W.M. Rossetti relates: 'it dealt with some supernatural matter – I think, a man whose doom it was not to get reflected in a looking-glass [...] but unfortunately it turned out to raise – or *seem* as if it were meant to raise – some dangerous moral question; and, on having her attention directed to this, my sister, who had been unconscious of any such matter, destroyed the MS. on the spot' (*DGR: FL* 2: 162).
18 For a further discussion of 'Jenny' see Chapter 7.
19 *New Poems*, W.M. Rossetti (ed.) (London: Macmillan, 1896).
20 W. David Shaw, *Victorians and Mystery: Crises of Representation* (Ithaca: Cornell University Press, 1990) p. 255.
21 As Shaw notes pp. 256–8.
22 W.M. Rossetti notes that: 'the "enormous improvement" which Dante Gabriel effected in L.E.L. consisted in making lines 1 and 3 of each stanza rhyme – which they do not in the original MS', *Rossetti Papers 1862 to 1870*, William Michael Rossetti (ed.) (London: Sands, 1903) p. 97. As discussed below, this is another instance where the manuscript revision regularises the verse form.
23 'My life's life' is similar in its reflexivity to what Rossetti elsewhere calls her 'I am I', the manifestation of her 'Poet Mind' (*Letters* 1: 232, 233).
24 Angela Leighton, *Victorian Women Poets: Writing Against the Heart* (Hemel Hempstead: Harvester, 1992) p. 3.
25 Jerome McGann, 'Christina Rossetti's poems: a new edition and a revaluation', *Victorian Studies* 23 (1980) 247; quoted by Leighton p. 154. McGann's article is reprinted in *The Beauty of Inflections*.
26 For example, Jones p. 46. Packer argues that the poem suggests an illicit love for the married William Bell Scott, rather than Collinson. See *Christina Rossetti* (Berkeley: University of California Press, 1963) p. 54.
27 *PW: CR* p. 481.
28 Christina Rossetti, in a letter to D.G. Rossetti dated ?4 April 1865, concedes his change: '*By the Sea*, has superseded *A Yawn*; for which however I retain a sneaking kindness' (*Letters* 1: 243). In its transformation to a nature poem from an expression of ennui, the original loses three stanzas, which suggests once again the 'revising hand' of D.G. Rossetti. The poem was first published in *Goblin Market, The Prince's Progress and Other Poems* (London: Macmillan, 1875).
29 The title change is suggested by D.G. Rossetti in a letter to Christina Rossetti dated 28 January 1861 (*DGR: FL* 2:164).
30 D.G. Rossetti to Christina Rossetti, 8 November 1853 (*DGR: FL* 2:119–20).
31 Elisabeth Bronfen, *Over her Dead Body: Death, Femininity, and the Aesthetic* (Manchester: Manchester University Press, 1992) p. 174.
32 The correspondence is published variously in *The Rossetti Papers*, Lona Mosk Packer (ed.), *The Rossetti–Macmillan Letters* (Berkeley: University of California Press, 1963) pp. 37–56; *DGR: FL*, and Janet Camp Troxell (ed.), *The Three Rossettis: Unpublished Papers to and from Dante Gabriel, Christina and William* (Cambridge, Mass.: Harvard University Press, 1939). Christina Rossetti's letters are, of course, now collected in Harrison's authoritative edition. In their biographies of Christina Rossetti, Lona Mosk Packer, Chapter 10, and

Jan Marsh, *Christina Rossetti: a Literary Biography* (London: Jonathan Cape, 1994), Chapter 24, give the fullest account of D.G. Rossetti's interventions.

33 Christina Rossetti's favourite (*Rossetti Papers* p. 84).

34 D.G. Rossetti evidently disapproved of an allusion to Barrett Browning's 'My Heart and I', which she disputed. If he persists, she writes, in seeing the likeness: 'I could easily turn my own *heart* into *wish*, and save the little piece for which I have a kindness' (*Letters* 1: 228).

35 *Rossetti Papers* pp. 98–9; *Letters* 1: 234 ('Squad finally rejected for vol. 2, though I keep my commercial eye upon it for Magazine pot-boilers').

36 *Letters* 1: 235.

37 See Gail Lynn Goldberg, 'Dante Gabriel Rossetti's "Revising Hand": His Illustrations for Christina Rossetti's Poems', *Victorian Poetry* 20 (1982) 145–59. Goldberg's analysis assumes a harmonic correspondence between illustrations and text, an integration of different perspectives: 'the conflation and conversion of poem into picture may be regarded as a change in medium but not meaning' (p. 158).

38 As in the case of the title change to 'Cousin Kate' from 'Up and Down' (Crump 1: 239), and in 'From House to Home' where, apparently to obscure the reference to Tennyson's 'The Palace of Art', 'palace' is changed to 'mansion' on l. 13 (Crump 1: 263). W.M. Rossetti gives a note pencilled by D.G. Rossetti on the manuscript notebook: 'this is so good it cannot be omitted; but could not something be done to make it less like *Palace of Art*?' (*PW: CR* p. 461). Crump makes no reference to this note. Evidently, D.G. Rossetti also thought that stanza 11 of 'A Royal Princess' echoed Keats, but Christina Rossetti refused to omit it (*Letters* 1: 242).

39 *PW: CR* pp. 483, 158. Crump does not mention this note in her variorum edition.

40 Marsh, *Christina Rossetti: a Literary Biography* p. 297.

41 *Letters* 1: 242. See William Michael Rossetti's note to the poem, which compounds his brother's revisions by insisting the poem has nothing to do with Landon and everything to do with the author's own emotions. He puzzles over the new title in particular, preferring the original 'Spring' indeed, he suggests, with his usual view of his sister's self-reflexive creativity, that the new title is a 'cloud' behind which his sister wished to retire (*PW: CR* pp. 482–3).

42 *Ruskin: Rossetti: Pre-Raphaelitism: Papers 1854 to 1862*, W.M. Rossetti (ed.) (London: George Allen, 1899) pp. 258–9.

43 As well as consulting her brother during the composition and compilation of *The Prince's Progress*, the manuscript was sent to Macmillan through him and there is some evidence that he may have also revised proofs: 'may I hope that you will again look at my proofs as they go through the press? if so, you had better have them before they come to me: and then I think I shall send them home for lynx-eyed research after errors, before letting them go to press'. Letter to D.G. Rossetti, 3 March 1865 (*Letters* 1: 229).

44 *Letters* 1: 225, 239, 243, 244.

45 *PW: CR* p. 461.

46 *PW: CR* pp. 460–1. Compare W.M. Rossetti's systematic attempt to change Christina Rossetti's indentation into a regular pattern, as he had done in *New Poems*. In the 1904 edition he claims this task was contemplated and then

rejected as impossible, owing to his sister's irregular line lengths (*PW: CR* p. viii). A comparison is also relevant with the textual history of Emily Dickinson's poetry. Thomas Wentworth Higginson, whom Dickinson first approached with a sample of her work in 1862, found the irregular rhyme and spasmodic metric beat, her 'lack' of form and unusual figural language rendered the poetry unpublishable. Later, after Dickinson's death, a selection was prepared for publication, but as Thomas H. Johnson describes in the introduction to his edition which attempts to restore the poetry to its original form: 'Higginson was apprehensive about the willingness of the public to accept the poems as they stood. Therefore in preparing copy for the printer he undertook to smooth rhymes, regularise the metre, delete provincialisms, and substitute "sensible" metaphors. Thus "folks" become "those", "heft" became "weight", and occasionally line arrangement was altered' (*Emily Dickinson: the Complete Works*, Thomas H. Johnson (ed.) (London: Faber, 1970; repr. 1975), p. ix).

47 *Letters* 1: 234.

48 *PW: CR* p. 461.

49 D.G. Rossetti persuaded his sister in vain to omit this poem from *The Prince's Progress*, after it had been revised and published in *Macmillan's Magazine* in March 1863 (*Letters* 1: 243).

50 W.M. Rossetti explains his version as the salvaging of previously unpublished stanzas: 'in the notebook this composition numbers twelve stanzas; two of them, under the title *The Bourne*, were eventually published ('Underneath the growing grass', etc.). The remaining ten were not unworthy to pair with those two, but I thought it best to use only five of them' (*PW: CR* pp. 470–1).

51 Harrison's discussion of 'The Bourne' comments upon the poem's play with physical form and the spiritual. Artistic autonomy is, however, ascribed to Christina Rossetti and no account is taken of D.G. Rossetti's influence in the revisions (*Christina Rossetti in Context* pp. 9–10).

52 Shaw, *Victorians and Mystery* p. 266.

53 Harrison, *Christina Rossetti in Context* pp. 10–11, and Chapter 2. See also Chapter 7 of this study for a further discussion of the 'poetics of conciseness'.

54 She threatens, in a letter to D.G. Rossetti dated 23 December 1864, 'amongst your ousted I recognise sundry of my own favourites, which perhaps I may adroitly re-insert *when* publishing day comes round: especially I am inclined to show fight for at least one *terza-rima*, in honour of our Italian element' (*Letters* 1: 209). She also twice forcefully, if playfully, pleads for her autonomy using the phrase 'I am I': 'only don't make vast changes as "I am I"' (*Letters* 1: 232) and, of his alterations to 'The Prince's Progress', '"I am I" is so strong with me that I again may modify details' (*Letters* 1: 233).

55 *Letters* 1: 234.

56 Sharon Smulders argues that Rossetti's revisions for her final volume of poetry deletes personal pronouns, particularly in poems dealing with gender issues: 'they are purged of the gender specific in order to address concerns of "Man's universal mind"'. Sharon M. Smulders, 'Women's Enfranchisement in Christina Rossetti's Poetry', *Texas Studies in Literature and Language* 34.4 (Winter 1992) 568–88 (p. 578).

57 For example, see W.M. Rossetti's reading of 'The Lowest Room' above. Glennis Stephenson notes that Letitia Elizabeth Landon also combines submission

to and subversion of contemporary notions of the feminine in her own construction of 'L.E.L.' See 'Letitia Elizabeth Landon and the Victorian Improvisatrice: the Construction of L.E.L.', *Victorian Poetry* 30 (1992): 1–17 (p. 3).

5 Spectres and Spectators: Fraternal Revisions II

1 Edmund Gosse, *Critical Kit-Kats* (London: Heineman, 1896) pp. 146, 147–8.
2 Derrida terms the 're-mark' a sign of belonging, what he terms 'the law of the law of genre', which is also 'a principle of contamination' because 'this supplementary and distinctive trait, a mark of belonging or inclusion, does not properly pertain to any genre or class'. See 'The Law of Genre', in *Acts of Literature*, Derrick Attridge (ed.) (New York: Routledge, 1992) pp. 227–30.
3 Jan Marsh, *Christina Rossetti: Poems and Prose* (London: Everyman, 1994) p. 460.
4 Ibid., p. 461.
5 Arthur Christopher Benson, 'Christina Rossetti', *The National Review* (26 February 1895) pp. 753–63 (p. 753).
6 William Sharp, 'Some Reminiscences of Christina Rossetti', *Atlantic Monthly* LXXV (June 1895) 136–49 (pp. 737–8). For a further discussion of the use of nature in nineteenth-century reviews of women poets, see the Introduction (Part Two) to Paula Day's 'Nature and Gender in Victorian Women's Writing: Emily Brontë, Charlotte Brontë, Elizabeth Barrett Browning, Christina Rossetti', PhD, The University of Lancaster, 1990.
7 Jerome Bump, 'Christina Rossetti and the Pre-Raphaelite Brotherhood', in *The Achievement of Christina Rossetti*, David A. Kent (ed.) (Ithaca: Cornell University Press, 1987) pp. 322–45.
8 See the Summary to Sharon Smulders, 'Christina Rossetti: Response and Responsibility', DPhil., University of Sussex, 1987.
9 Julia Kristeva, 'Stabat Mater', in Toril Moi (ed.), *The Kristeva Reader* (Oxford: Blackwell, 1986) n. 5, p. 186.
10 The later picture is almost a copy, but portrays Mrs. Adam Heaton, whilst the former depicts Lizzie Siddal. See Surtees 1: 75, 81. D.G. Rossetti painted a further *Regina Cordium* in 1866, unrelated to the earlier pictures except by title (Surtees 1: 111).
11 Jan Marsh's introduction to 'The Lost Titian' explains the references to the Brotherhood. *Christina Rossetti: Poems and Prose*, p. 305. 'The Lost Titian' may specifically refer to D.G. Rossetti's short story, 'Hand and Soul' (*CW: DGR* 1: 383–98).
12 Miss Love sat as a model for the hair of the Virgin in *The Annunciation*, and the face was painted over many times (Surtees 1: 13). W.M. Rossetti comments that the version of the painting exhibited in 1850 has a more pronounced likeness of Christina Rossetti than it does now (*PW: CR* p. lxii).
13 For example, Timothy Hilton notes that: 'stylistically, *The Girlhood of Mary Virgin* is composed with a kind of simple-minded originality, in which it is difficult to distinguish the parts played by calculation and by sheer lack of ability', *The Pre-Raphaelites* (London: Thames and Hudson, 1970; repr. 1987) p. 40.

14 Dolores Rosenblum fruitfully reads the Rossetti canon in terms of the model/artist double. See *Christina Rossetti: the Poetry of Endurance* (Carbondale: Southern Illinois University Press, 1986). David D. Nolta explores crossings over between the depictions of Christina Rossetti and self-perception in her poetry, in 'Whispering Likenesses: Images of Christina Rossetti, 1847–1853', *The Journal of Pre-Raphaelite and Aesthetic Studies* 2.1 (Spring 1989) 49–55.

15 William Bell Scott reports that Rossetti: 'was painting in oils with water-colour brushes, as thinly as in water-colour, on canvas which he had primed with white till the surface was smooth as cardboard, and every tint remained transparent', quoted in the Tate Gallery Catalogue, *The Pre-Raphaelites* (London: Tate Gallery and Alan Lane, 1984) p. 64.

16 Lynne Pearce shows how D.G. Rossetti made changes to the first sonnet which: 'reinforce Mary's domestic *obedience*.' See *Woman/Image/Text: Readings in Pre-Raphaelite Art and Literature* (Hemel Hempstead: Harvester Wheatsheaf, 1988) p. 44.

17 For a description of the changes to both these early paintings, see Surtees 1: 10–11, 12–14; and the Tate Gallery Catalogue, *The Pre-Raphaelites* pp. 65, 73.

18 D. G. Rossetti to Ford Madox Brown, 1 January and 14 January 1853. *Pre-Raphaelite Diaries and Letters*, W. M. Rossetti (ed.) (London: Hurst and Blackett, 1900) p. 29. For an example of a contemporary complaint about the technical deficiencies, see the review quoted in *DGR: FL* 1: 162. Later, in 1874, D.G. Rossetti commented to Ford Madox Brown of *The Annunciation*: 'in some of the highest respects I have hardly done anything else so good. [. . .] Of course it is very faulty in mechanical respects, but nothing can be done to it to any purpose except a very little stippling of surface here and there', *The Letters of Dante Gabriel Rossetti*, Oswald Doughty and John Robert Wahl (eds), 5 vols. (Oxford: Clarendon Press, 1967) 3: 1283.

19 Surtees 1: 13.

20 See also W.M. Rossetti's comment in *The Pre-Raphaelite Journal* entry for 23–29 January 1853: 'Gabriel finished and sent off the Annunciation picture. It has now lost its familiar name of *The Ancilla*, – the mottoes having been altered from Latin to English, to guard against the imputation of "popery"', *The P.R.B. Journal: William Michael Rossetti's Diary of the Pre-Raphaelite Brotherhood 1849–1853: Together With Other Pre-Raphaelite Documents*, William E. Fredeman (ed.) (Oxford: Clarendon Press, 1975) p. 99. I have been unable to find evidence of the exact phrases used.

21 Linda H. Peterson suggests that the main point of departure from biblical tradition is the depiction of the Virgin sewing, not reading; thus, D.G. Rossetti revises the convention of the Virgin as a faithful reader of scriptures. See '"Restoring the Book": The Typological Hermeneutics of Christina Rossetti and the PRB', *Victorian Poetry* 32 (1994) 209–32 (pp. 210–11). John Ruskin, in 'The Three Colours of pre-Raphaelitism' (1878) also notes the divergences from Biblical tradition: 'Rossetti's "Annunciation" differs from every previous conception of the scene known to me, in representing the angel as waking the Virgin from sleep to give her his message. The Messenger himself also differs from angels as they are commonly represented, in not depending, for recognition of his supernatural character, on the insertion of bird's wings at his shoulders', *The Works of John Ruskin*, E.T. Cook and Alexander Wedderburn (eds), 39 vols. (London: George Allen, 1903–1912) vol. 34 (1908), 149.

22 Pearce argues that this: 'is dictated by separateness of colour, by sharpness of line. [...] The extreme stillness and rigidity of *The Girlhood* is usually explained simply in terms of the early Pre-Raphaelite penchant for medieval two-dimensionality, but the sonnets betray a deeper fundamentalism in which the concept of "purity" is especially resonant' (pp. 37–8).

23 Laura L. Doan, 'Narrative and Transformative Iconography in D.G. Rossetti's Earliest Paintings', *Soundings* 17.4 (1988) 471–83 (p. 477).

24 See Mary Ann Caws, *The Art of Interference: Stressed Readings in Verbal and Visual Texts* (Cambridge: Polity Press, 1989): 'one of the odder elements of the Pre-Raphaelites' version of the relations between the visual and the verbal is a drastically visible undoing of the evidence of relations themselves' (p. 285). Caws argues that this is a frequent occurrence in Pre-Raphaelite art. Contrast the reading of Catherine Golden, who sees the verbal/visual combination as complementary, leading to a totality of meaning. See 'Dante Gabriel Rossetti's Two-Sided Art', *Victorian Poetry* 26 (1988) 395–402.

25 The Tate Gallery Catalogue, *The Pre-Raphaelites*, argues that the narrowness of *The Annunciation* may be partially explained by D.G. Rossetti's plan to add another picture on the Virgin's death and thus make a diptych, in which both pictures together would have made a perfect square. The plan was not executed (p. 73). The organisation of space is also explained here as symbolic of the spiritual and of time: 'the vertical division of space, made by the left side of the blue hanging and the edge of the bed, falls almost on the Golden section. The dove, symbolising the Holy Spirit, and the lily, with the bud still to break, move across this division and are the instruments of conception. The division of space is also one of time, for Rossetti saw the Virgin, when she conceived Christ: "Faith's present, partly what had been / From what began with her, and is for aye"' (p. 73). The correspondence between space and time is reminiscent of Blake's gendering of these terms in his notebook commentary on one of his paintings, *A Vision of the Last Judgement* (now lost): 'Time & Space are Real Beings[,] a Male & a Female[.] Time is a Man[,] Space is a Woman[,] & her Masculine Portion is Death', *The Complete Poetry and Prose of William Blake*, David V. Erdman (ed.) (New York: Doubleday, 1988) p. 563. This connection with Blake perhaps explains D.G. Rossetti's interest in painting the Virgin's death.

26 Compare the Renaissance tradition of including in Annunciation paintings a portion of the outside scene to heighten the effect of perspective; thus, interior and exterior are organised to suggest a stable and unitary point of view. See, for example, the Annunciation paintings by Sandro Botticelli (c.1490), and Fillipo Lippi (1406). Compare Leonardo da Vinci's *Annunciation* (1470), which employs his *sfumato* technique whereby the landscape dissolves into the far distance, further heightening the sense of perspective. This is to be distinguished from D.G. Rossetti's paintings where the entire depiction of the exterior space is indistinct. Although D.G. Rossetti is obviously drawing on a tradition of Annunciation pictures, as well as the Nazarenes, his particular handling of perspective and the interior/exterior distinction should be read, I argue, with reference to the problematics of his verbal/visual aesthetics.

27 Hilton gives D.G. Rossetti's problems with perspective as the reason for the following features of the painting: 'all the figures crowd up to the

picture plane, with St. Joachim looming disconcertingly close to us, the floorboards on the left shoot away to a different vanishing point from those on the right, and an unintegrated landscape peeps from behind a strong device of verticals and horizontals, the trellis-work forming a cross behind St. Ann' (p. 40).

28 E.H. Gombrich, *Art and Illusion: a Study in the Psychology of Pictorial Representation* (Oxford: Phaidon 1960; repr. 1986) p. 210.

29 *DGR: FL* 1: 121–2. Compare William Holman Hunt, *Pre-Raphaelitism and the Pre-Raphaelite Brotherhood*, 2 vols. (London: Macmillan, 1905) 1: 118.

30 Barbara Garlick, 'The Frozen Fountain: Christina Rossetti, the Virgin Model, and Youthful Pre-Raphaelitism', in *Virginal Sexuality and Textuality in Victorian Literature*, Lloyd Davies (ed.) (New York: State University of New York Press, 1993) pp. 105–27 (p. 109).

31 *CW: DGR* 1: 510. This is given in the section 'Sentences and Notes', selected from D.G. Rossetti's notebooks by his brother, who gives no date.

32 Toril Moi, *Sexual/Textual Politics* (London and New York: Routledge, 1990) p. 136. Paraphrase of Luce Irigaray, *Speculum of the Other Woman*, trans. by Gillian C. Gill (Ithaca: Cornell University Press, 1985) pp. 165–6.

33 Elisabeth Bronfen, *Over Her Dead Body: Death, Femininity, and the Aesthetic* (Manchester: Manchester University Press, 1992) pp. 209–10.

34 Leigh Gilmore, *Autobiographics: a Feminist Theory of Women's Self-Representation* (Ithaca: Cornell University Press, 1994) p. 11.

35 I use the phrase 'Woman' within quotation marks because, although my discussion of the position of the feminine within the aesthetic has a specificity, the term implies a stable and monolithic category. Judith Butler has shown the problematics of this phrase for feminist critiques. See *Gender Trouble: Feminism and the Subversion of Identity* (New York: Routledge, 1990) pp. 3–7.

36 Ruskin suggests the imprecise (or un-feminine) physicality of the Virgin in his comment that, in *The Annunciation*, she is: 'in severe fore-shortening [. . .] and the disturbed coverlid is thrown into confused angular folds, which admit no suggestion whatever of girlish grace,' *The Works of John Ruskin* 34: 149.

37 See Marina Warner, *Monuments and Maidens: the Allegory of the Female Form* (London: Picador, 1987) Ch. 11. For the historical development of the representation of the Virgin Mary, see Warner's *Alone of All Her Sex: the Myth and the Cult of the Virgin Mary* (London: Weidenfield, 1976) p. 256.

38 *PW: CR* p. lxviii. The place of Rossetti as a female poet in the nineteenth century is also described in these terms: pure and spiritual, but also spontaneous. Within this cultural construct, moral purity is a condition of artistic production. The phrase 'a fountain sealed' recurs in her poetry; see, for example, 'The heart knoweth its own bitterness': 'I must bear to wait / A fountain sealed thro' heat and cold' (Crump 3: 266). Other reminiscences reiterate the trope of the sealed fountain, or the sequestered virgin; see, for example Gosse pp. 158, 161.

39 See, for example, Hinkson.

40 Quoted in Jan Marsh, *Pre-Raphaelite Women: Images of Femininity in Pre-Raphaelite Art* (London: Weidenfield and Nicolson, 1987) p. 31.

41 Quoted in Garlick, 'The Frozen Fountain' pp. 113–14.

42 Surtees 1: 14.

43 Eve is both of Adam and deviant from him, and so she is the first to signify the feminine as the loss of the literal in language. Thus from her derives the creation of metaphor and the associated break between signifier and signified. See Stephen J. Nichols, Jr., 'Solomon's Wife: Deceit, Desire, and the Genealogy of Romance', in *Space, Time, Image, Sign*, James A.W. Heffernan (ed.) (New York: Peter Lang, 1987) pp. 19–37 (p. 23).
44 Compare Garlick's remark that flattened perspective deanimates the female figure, cited above.
45 This phrase is from Julia Kristeva's discussion of the Virgin Mary in 'Stabat Mater', reprinted in *The Kristeva Reader*, Toril Moi (ed.) (Oxford: Blackwell, 1986) p. 170.
46 Doan p. 481.
47 This is the nineteenth-century construction of female creativity, as a reflex of the experiential and visual. Peterson offers an interesting demonstration of how Christina Rossetti re-instates women as readers of Scripture and thus restores the Book which her brother had replaced with the domestic act of embroidery. There is no mention, however, of her brother's revision of the Virgin's hagiography from the perspective of conventional attitudes to female poetic creativity.
48 Stephen Heath, 'Difference', *Screen* 19.3 (Autumn 1978) p. 53.
49 Anna Smith, *Julia Kristeva: Readings of Exile and Estrangement* (Houndmills, Basingstoke: Macmillan, 1996) p. 139.
50 Julia Kristeva, 'Stabat Mater' p. 176.
51 J.B. Bullen, *The Pre-Raphaelite Body: Fear and Desire in Painting, Poetry, and Criticism* (Oxford: Clarendon Press, 1998) pp. 126–7.
52 *PW: CR* p. 480.
53 It is thus ironic that the sonnet has achieved the status of a reinscription of the legend, when it actually interrogates and questions the aesthetics which have framed Siddal as a sign of femininity rather than actual personage. See Chapter 2.
54 Bronfen p. 228.
55 Roland Barthes, *Camera Lucida* (London: Vintage, 1993) p. 115.
56 The date of composition of Christina Rossetti's poem is unknown. It was published in the *Magazine of Art*, XIII (September, 1890) 385 (Crump 3: 380). D.G. Rossetti's sequence was written 1847 to 1881.
57 *CW: DGR*. 1: 176.
58 See Alison Chapman, 'Uncanny Epiphanies in the Nineteenth-Century Sonnet Tradition', in Wim Tigges (ed.), *Moments of Moment: Aspects of the Literary Epiphany* (Amsterdam: Rodopi, 1999) pp. 115–35.
59 *CW: DG* 1: 201–2
60 Here, as elsewhere in the chapter, I take 'genre' in its widest possible meaning as a difference in type within a specific art form and also as an actual category of art form. The etymology of genre is linked to that of gender: both derive from the French 'genre' meaning kind, natural, and type.
61 See Sonnet XCVII, 'A Superscription', *CW: DGR* 1: 225.
62 Angela Leighton, *Victorian Women Poets: Writing Against the Heart* (Hemel Hempstead: Harvester, 1992) p. 151. Leighton is referring to Christina Rossetti's poem 'What Sappho would have said had her leap cured instead of killing her' (Crump 3: 166–8).

63 Yopi Prins, *Victorian Sappho* (Princeton, New Jersey: Princeton University Press, 1999) pp. 207, 208.

64 Compare 'The Queen of Hearts' (Crump 1: 132) which has two active subjects, the speaker and the addressee (the figurative Queen of Hearts), in contrast to D.G. Rossetti's two early *Regina Cordium* pictures, in which the female figure is not an active agent. Significantly, during their discussions for the preparation of the *Princes Progress* volume, D.G. Rossetti seems to have objected to the poem, then entitled 'Flora'. Christina Rossetti writes to him: '*Flora* (if that is the "next" you allude to) surely cannot give deep umbrage' (*CR: FL* p. 55). Griselda Pollock gives an interesting interpretation of the 1860 and 1866 versions of *Regina Cordium* in *Vision and Difference: Femininity, Feminism and Histories of Art* (London: Routledge, 1988) pp. 131–5.

65 The culmination of Rossetti's tentative and provisional intimation of feminine active subjectivity can be seen in Margaret Macdonald Mackintosh's *O Ye That Walk in Willow Wood* (1903–4), a painted gesso, originally designed for the Room de Lux in The Willow Tea Rooms and now in the Kelvingrove Art Gallery and Museum, Glasgow. See *Glasgow Girls: Women in Art and Design 1880–1920*, Jude Burkhauser (ed.) (Edinburgh: Canongate, 1990; repr. 1994) p. 39. Three female figures are represented within oval and vertical lines of coloured glass beads, as well as roses (signifying the feminine), that both reveal and conceal the figures. Only the faces of the figures are fully delineated and distinct, and the bodies seem to merge into one another within the fluidity of the lines of beads. Two figures have side profiles and the middle facing out of the gesso, directly engaging the view of the spectator and holding a rose to her face, suggesting an active subject within conventions of the feminine aesthetic.

66 The date of composition is unknown. The poem was published in *The Argosy*, XV (January, 1873) 31, and later in *Goblin Market, The Prince's Progress and Other Poems* (1875). Other poems play on the word 'love-lies-bleeding'. 'Balm in Gilead', published in *Verses* (1893), exploits parabolically the name of this plant and of 'heartsease' (the wild pansy): 'Heartsease I found, where Love-lies-bleeding' (Crump 2. 317). In *Sing-Song* (1872), another poem exploits the symbolic value of 'heartsease':

> Heartsease in my garden bed,
> With sweetwilliam white and red,
> Honeysuckle on my wall: –
> Heartsease blossoms in my heart
> When sweet William comes to call,
> But it withers when we part,
> And the honey-trumpets fall.
>
> (Crump 2: 26)

67 Originally in a sonnet form and published in 1842.

> You call it, 'Love lies bleeding,' – so you may,
> Though the red Flower, not prostrate, only droops,
> As we have seen it here from day to day,

> From month to month, life passing not away:
> A flower how rich in sadness!
>
> (ll. 1–5)

(*Poems*, ed. by John O. Hayden, 2 vols. (Harmondsworth: Penguin, 1977) 2: 776).

68 Compare Nichols's concept of the female image as transgrediential, palimpsestic – as if femininity operates through textual layering. Here, subjectivity seems to be present as a 'trace' or 'residue' of this operation (p. 23).

69 According to W.M. Rossetti: 'in a copy of her collected *Poems*, 1875, there is also the following note: "perhaps 'Love-in-Idleness' would be a better title, with an eye to the next one" – *i.e.* to *Love lies Bleeding*', *PW: CR* p. 487.

70 Graham Ovenden, *Pre-Raphaelite Photography* (London: Academy Press, 1972) p. 13.

71 William Michael Rossetti (ed.), *Rossetti Papers, 1862–1870* (London: Sands, 1903) p. 4.

72 Christina Rossetti to W.M. Rossetti, 4 June 1866, mentions that Cameron showed the Rossetti sisters and their mother her portfolio and then presented five photographs to them. Maria and Christina Rossetti returned the visit, whereupon they saw various literary personages. 'I am asked down to Freshwater Bay, and promised to see Tennyson if I go; but the plan is altogether uncertain, and I am too shy to contemplate it with anything like unmixed pleasure.' W.M. Rossetti's note prefacing the letter suggests that she never visited Cameron's Isle of Wight house, nor did she ever meet Tennyson (*Rossetti Papers* p. 202; *Letters* 1: 274). Jan Marsh mentions that the portfolio consisted of photographs of D.G. Rossetti's paintings. See *Christina Rossetti: a Literary Biography* (London: Jonathan Cape, 1994) p. 350.

73 Colin Ford reproduces a photograph of the lid of a negative box of Cameron's, on the inside of which is listed in her handwriting portraits which seem to date from 1865 to 1866, including a profile of Christina Rossetti. See Colin Ford (ed.), *The Cameron Collection: an Album of Photographs by Julia Margaret Cameron Presented to Sir John Herschel* (London: Van Nostrand Reinhold in association with The National Portrait Gallery, 1975) p. 15.

74 Such as *In the Garden*, a representation of Arthur Hughes's *April Love*, and *The Parting of Sir Lancelot and Queen Guinevere*, suggesting the earlier D.G. Rossetti painting *The Wedding of St. George and Princess Sabra* (Ovenden pp. 42–3, 50–1).

75 Such as Tennyson's 'The Gardener's Daughter', depicted in a photograph of the same title (Ford pp. 89, 133).

76 Most famously, of Tennyson (Ford pp. 26, 29, 95–7, 99, 107).

77 John Berger, *Ways of Seeing* (London: BBC and Penguin, 1972) p. 18.

78 Lindsay Smith, 'The Politics of Focus: Feminism and Photographic Theory', in Isobel Armstrong (ed.), *New Feminist Discourses: Critical Essays on Theories and Texts* (London: Routledge, 1992) p. 243.

79 From *The Photographic News*, 1864, quoted in Ford p. 18.

80 Ford p. 17.

81 Lindsay Smith, 'The Politics of Focus' pp. 249–50.

82 Elizabeth Wright (ed.), *Feminism and Psychoanalysis: a Critical Dictionary* (Oxford: Blackwell, 1992) p. 426.

6 Father's Place, Mother's Space: Italy and the Paradisal

1 Edmund Gosse, *Critical Kit-Kats* (London: Heineman, 1896) p. 139.

2 Hilary Fraser argues that the metaphorical colonisation of Italy in this period is part of a wider concern to reappropriate the past. See *The Victorians and Renaissance Italy* (Oxford: Blackwell, 1992) p. 4.

3 Angela Leighton and Margaret Reynolds (eds), *Victorian Women Poets: an Anthology* (Oxford: Blackwell, 1995) pp. xxxv–xxxvi.

4 Leighton p. 522.

5 Leighton pp. 610–11.

6 Rossetti only made one brief visit to Italy, between 22 May and 26 June 1865, with her mother and William Michael Rossetti. The trip encompassed Paris, Langres, Luzern and an Alpine journey via St. Gotthard into Italy. Once there, they visited Lake Como, Verona and Milan. See Jan Marsh, *Christina Rossetti: a Literary Biography* (London: Jonathan Cape, 1994) pp. 334–40. Dolores Rosenblum notes the importance of Italy as a metaphor for identity, the mother country and the afterlife, but assumes the relation is stable and unproblematic. See *Christina Rossetti: the Poetry of Endurance* (Carbondale: Sourthern Illinois University Press, 1986) pp. 49–50. See also Sandra M. Gilbert, 'From *Patria* to *Matria*: Elizabeth Barrett Browning's *Risorgimento*', *PMLA* 99 (1984) 194–209.

7 Freud, 'Three Essays on the Theory of Sexuality' (1905), *SE* 7: 123–245.

8 Paradise for Christina Rossetti, Linda Marshall argues, connotes Hades (as the intermediate state between death and the resurrection), not Heaven or the New Jerusalem. See 'What the Dead Are Doing Underground: Hades and Heaven in the Writings of Christina Rossetti', *Victorian Newsletter* (Fall 1987) 55–60.

9 Marsh, *Christina Rossetti: a Literary Biography* p. 18.

10 *PW: CR* p. lv.

11 Mackenzie Bell, *Christina Rossetti: a Biographical and Critical Study* (London: Hurst and Blackett, 1898) p. 21.

12 '[As] masculinity and femininity were defined in relation to their different fields of activity – the public and the private – gender identities became organised around the ideology of separate spheres', Lynda Nead, *Myths of Sexuality: Representations of Women in Victorian Britain* (Oxford: Basil Blackwell, 1988) pp. 32–3. Nina Auerbach sees Rossetti's spinsterhood as the springboard for her own self-recreation: 'The quiet sister's devout, family-bounded existence contained its own divine potential for violent metamorphoses.' See *Woman and the Demon: the Life of a Victorian Myth* (Cambridge, MA: Harvard University Press, 1982) p. 117.

13 Deborah Gorham, *The Victorian Girl and the Feminine Ideal* (London: Croon Hill, 1982) p. 7.

14 *Letters* 2: 158.

15 *Letters* 2: 40.

16 For an analysis of the implications of Rossetti's maternal conception of Christ, see Sharon Smulders, 'Woman's Enfranchisement in Christina Rossetti's Poetry', *Texas Studies in Literature and Language* 34.4 (Winter 1992) 568–88. Perhaps the gendering of Christ as both male and female may also be related to Holman Hunt's use of Christina Rossetti's as a model for the face of Christ in the painting *Light of the World* (1853).

17 *FL: CR* p. xiii.

18 Christina Rossetti, *Time Flies: a Reading Diary* (London: SPCK, 1885), p. 33.

19 Bronfen p. 324.

20 The desire for the maternal should be distinguished from an inability of the subject metaphorically to separate from the mother, which is a psychic necessity. See Elisabeth Bronfen, *Over Her Dead Body: Death, Femininity, and the Aesthetic* (Manchester: Manchester University Press, 1992) p. 135. In 'And the one doesn't stir without the other', *Signs* 7.1 (1981) 60–7, Luce Irigaray identifies the daughter's perception of the mother as one of two categories, the phallic or castrated mother. For the Victorians the identification of the daughter with the mother, and the daughter's struggle to forge a separate identity, is complicated by the tendency to conflate, in legal, social and cultural discourses, femininity and maternity. See Lila Hanft which relates these issues to *Sing-Song* in 'The Politics of Maternal Ambivalence in Christina Rossetti's *Sing-Song*', *Victorian Literature and Culture* 19 (1991) 213–32.

21 *PW: CR* p. 485.

22 Freud, 'The Uncanny' (1919), *SE* 17: 217–56.

23 'I was a flint – deaf and silent. [...] You draw nearer and break that mass which is my rocky heart. [...] See how it is torn, its fragments at last setting your heavens alight [...] by dying I live again', *Henry Vaughan: the Complete Poems* Alan Rudrum (ed.) (Harmondsworth: Penguin, 1976; repr. 1983) pp. 137–8.

24 Linda Marshall's article eloquently describes Rossetti's belief in Hades (p. 55).

25 In a letter to Lucy Rossetti, her sister-in-law, on 20 March 1892, she suggests not a double identity, but a partial one: 'perhaps it is enough to be half an Italian, but certainly it is enough to be a Rossetti, to render Dante a fascinating centre of thought' (*FL: CR*, p. 184).

26 The poems in which this phrase is used are: 'Lisetta all'Amante' (Crump 3: 133), *Il rosseggiar dell'Oriente* (Crump 3: 301ff), 'Cor mio, cor mio' (Crump 3: 336), 'Cor mio' (Crump 3: 346). See also 'Amore e Dovere' (Crump 3: 91).

27 In the preface to his edition of her poetical works, W.M. Rossetti quotes an unnamed Italian critic who disparages Rossetti's Italian verse: 'they not only do not add anything to her fame as a poet, but rather detract from it, so formless and inept do they seem to me. It might almost be thought that the writer of those verses did not, as we know she did, speak from early childhood her paternal language'. W.M. Rossetti declares such a criticism harsh and cites another unnamed literary Italian who values the poems as 'not undeserving of commendation, and [they] assimilate to native work more nearly than those of Dante Gabriel Rossetti' (*PW: CR* pp. vi–vii).

28 See also 'Cor mio, cor mio,' 'Cor del mio core' [heart of my heart] (Crump 3: 336).

29 Terence Holt suggests that '*Goblin Market* attempts to imagine a position for women outside systems of power, but its language, which cannot escape from gender, undoes the attempt: the autonomy is an illusion.' See '"Men sell not such in any town": Exchange in *Goblin Market*', *Victorian Poetry* 28 (1990) 51–67 (p. 51). The separation of Lizzie and Laura from the economics typified by the goblins is unstable; they emerge as embroiled in exchange but their position in this system does not seem to be clearly marked.

30 This octave is used for sonnet 18 of 'Later Life: a Double Sonnet of Sonnets,' published in *A Pageant and Other Poems* (Crump 2: 146), another type of substitution.

31 Kristeva defines transposition as 'the passage from one signifying system to another [which] demands a new articulation of the thetic'. See Toril Moi (ed.), *The Kristeva Reader* (Blackwell: Oxford, 1986) p. 111. The thetic is, significantly, the breaching of the semiotic *chora*, when the subject takes up an identity and position in the Symbolic Order.

32 S.T. Coleridge, in 'Aids to Reflection', terms analogy tautologous: 'expressing the *same* subject but with a difference'. In comparison, he formulates metaphors as 'always *alle*gorical (i.e. expressing a *different* subject but with a resemblance)'. See H.J. Jackson (ed.), *The Oxford Authors: S.T. Coleridge* (Oxford: Oxford University Press, 1985) p. 672. Of course, my deployment of this definition alters the sense of 'subject' from subject matter to speaking subject.

33 This conditional and provisional reciprocity is also to be found in 'Lisetta all'Amante': 'Se a te fedel son io, / Sarai fedele a me?' [If I am faithful to you, will you be faithful to me?] (Crump 3: 133). I am indebted to Bob Cummings and Jean Ellis D'Allessandro for checking my translation of *Il Rosseggiar dell'Oriente*.

34 Harrison notes that the afterlife is often depicted as amorphous in Rossetti's poetry. See *Christina Rossetti in Context* (Brighton: Harvester, 1988) p. 157. For an exploration of Rossetti's literary relationship to Charles Bagot Cayley, and in particular to his translations, see Kamilla Denham and Sarah Smith, 'Christina Rossetti's Copy of C.B. Cayley's *Divine Comedy*', *Victorian Poetry* 32 (1994) 315–38.

35 'All' Amico Lontano.' Crump's edition gives the last word as 'Contano', from Rossetti's manuscript. I use William Michael Rossetti's text which gives 'Lontano', assuming an error in the manuscript or in Crump's transcription (Crump 3: 480).

36 W. David Shaw, *Victorians and Mystery: Crises of Representation* (Ithaca: Cornell University Press, 1990) p. 258.

37 See also 'Monna Innominata', where this is a dominant concern: 'So shall we stand / As happy equals in the flowering land / Of love, that knows not a dividing sea' (Crump 2: 89). Later in this sonnet sequence the speaker employs the conventional Petrarchan conceit of giving the beloved up to another love if it makes him happy (Crump 2: 92). In the second sonnet of 'By way of Remembrance', the speaker promises to rejoice if the beloved dies before her and finds another 'to share / Your gladness, glowing as a virgin bride' (Crump 3: 313). Throughout Rossetti's œuvre, union with the beloved in the afterlife is not anticipated as a certainty.

38 Moi p. 94. The *chora* is controversial in feminist theory: see Judith Butler, *Gender Trouble: Feminism and the Subversion of Identity* (New York: Routledge, 1990) and Kelly Oliver, *Reading Kristeva: Unraveling the Double-bind* (Bloomington: Indiana University Press, 1993) for two different interpretations.

39 Despite the similarity of the two words, they denote separate concepts. Both are related semantically, however, to enclosed bodily space, the womb (as the etymological root of *chora*) and the heart. See *The Kristeva Reader* pp. 93–8.

40 Denham and Smith comment on Rossetti's annotations of Cayley's translation of Dante as part of a wider Pre-Raphaelite concern with translations: 'while the major themes of the Pre-Raphaelite poets include the translation of *eros* into *agape*, of Italian medieval art into English Victorian art, and while Rossetti herself certainly expressed these with power in her poetry, the annotations in her copy of Cayley's Dante point to a humbler engagement with translations, from the glorious words of her idolised Dante into the awkward efforts of her beloved friend' (pp. 329–30).

41 Rosenblum notes that Rossetti's poems on Italy: 'show how profoundly she is a *translator*: of the language of patriarchal tradition, of the language of scripture and into the language of scripture, of English into Italian into English again' (p. 51). Rossetti was interested in acts of translation, assisting the projects of W.M. Rossetti and Cayley, as well as translating *Sing-Song* into Italian.

42 Julia Kristeva, *Revolution in Poetic Language* trans. by Margaret Waller (New York: Columbia University Press, 1984) p. vii. Compare Barbara Johnson's comments on J. Hillis Miller's 'The Critic as Host', that the parasite is feminine and parricidal, a daughter. See *A World of Difference* (Baltimore: The Johns Hopkins University Press, 1987) p. 36. See also J. Hillis Miller, 'The Critic as Host', *Deconstruction and Criticism* (New York: Seabury, 1979) pp. 217–53. Johnson's and Hillis Miller's arguments are discussed in Chapter 7.

7 The Afterlife of Poetry: 'Goblin Market'

1 A number of recent articles have addressed the relationship between 'Goblin Market' and economic consumption. See Elizabeth Campbell, 'Of Mothers and Merchants: Female Economics in Christina Rossetti's "Goblin Market"', *Victorian Studies* (Spring 1990) 393–410; Mary Wilson Carpenter, '"Eat me, drink me, love me": The Consumable Female Body in Christina Rossetti's *Goblin Market*', *Victorian Poetry* 29 (1991) 415–34; Elizabeth K. Helsinger, 'Consumer Power and the Utopia of Desire: Christina Rossetti's "Goblin Market"', *ELH* 58.4 (Winter 1991) 903–33; and Terence Holt, '"Men sell not such in any town": Exchange in *Goblin Market*', *Victorian Poetry* 28 (1990) 51–67. My argument is indebted to this recent commentary on Rossetti and the market place; none of the critics, however, suggest that the poem is a consumptive (meta)text *per se*.

2 Elisabeth Bronfen, *Over Her Dead Body: Death, Femininity, and the Aesthetic* (Manchester: Manchester University Press, 1992) p. 226.

3 She implies in 1865 that her brother chaperones her into the marketplace when thanking him for his much delayed illustrations for 'The Prince's Progress': 'your protecting woodcuts help me face my small public' (*Letters* 1: 246). As Marsh points out, however, while D.G. Rossetti was soliciting Ruskin and then Thackeray as sponsors for his sister's first projected volume of verses, Christina was simultaneously approaching Macmillan through David Masson. See *Christina Rossetti: a Literary Biography* (London: Jonathan Cape, 1994) p. 268.

4 Barbara Onslow explores the relationship between women writers and the portrait in 'Deceiving Images, Revealing Images: The Portrait in Victorian Women's Writing,' *Victorian Poetry* 33 (1995) 450–75.

5 *DGR: FL* 1: 342.
6 Linda M. Shires, 'Literary Careers, Death, and the Body Politics of David Copperfield'. In John Schad (ed.), *Dickens Refigured: Bodies, Desires, and Other Histories* (Manchester: Manchester University Press, 1998) p. 123.
7 Oswald Doughty and John Robert Wahl (eds), *The Letters of Dante Gabriel Rossetti*, 5 vols. (Oxford: Clarendon Press, 1967) 2: 422.
8 *Speaking Likenesses*, as U.C. Knoepflmacher eloquently argues, is a sustained critique of 'the *Alice* style' the first example of which was inspired by Dodgson's reading of 'Goblin Market.' See U.C. Knoepflmacher, *Ventures into Childhood: Victorians, Fairy Tales, and Femininity* (Chicago: University of Chicago Press, 1998) Chapters 9 and 10. For interesting comments on Rossetti's posthumous marketability, see Edmund Gosse's essay, which notes that her privately printed first *Verses* has enormous commercial value, and yet which also condemns women poets who write for the profit. He excludes Rossetti from this charge and, in fact, it seems that Rossetti is only allowed a legitimate market value upon her death. *Critical Kit-Kats* (London: Heinemann, 1896) pp. 141, 136–8.
9 Catherine Gallagher, *Nobody's Story: the Vanishing Acts of Women Writers in the Marketplace, 1670–1820* (Oxford: Clarendon Press, 1994).
10 See, for example, Linda M. Shires, 'The Author as Spectacle and Commodity: Elizabeth Barrett Browning and Thomas Hardy', in *Victorian Literature and the Victorian Visual Imagination*, Carol T. Christ and John O. Jordan (eds) (Berkeley: University of California Press, 1995) pp. 198–212.
11 For a discussion of the slipperiness of the separate spheres, see my 'Phantasies of Matriarchy in Non-Canonical Children's Literature by Women', in Nicola Diane Thompson (ed.), *Victorian Women Novelists and the Woman Question* (Cambridge: Cambridge University Press, 1999) pp. 60–79.
12 Paul Elmer More, 'Christina Rossetti', *Atlantic Monthly* 94 (December 1904) 815–21 (p. 815).
13 Such a monotonous music compares unfavourably with Rossetti's own description of her musical ideal. In *Time Flies*, she comments 'a heaven of music seems rather a heaven of endless progression, of inexhaustible variety, than a heaven of monotony.' See *Time Flies: a Reading Diary* (London: SPCK, 1885) p. 29.
14 Compare Angela Leighton on the contradiction of Rossetti's absorption in the myth of the woman poet as 'fitfully inspired' and her calculating self-invention and self-mythologising. Angela Leighton, *Victorian Women Poets: Writing Against the Heart* (Hemel Hempstead: Harvester, 1992) p. 119.
15 Her insistence that she cannot write to order and that to do so would be writing against the grain of her creativity, is made repeatedly. While this removes her poetry from commerce it also reasserts the Victorian gendered ideology of women's writing as expressive and spontaneous. See *Letters* 1: 172, 174, 189, 196, 244, 288, 348, and *Letters* 2: 7. Her sudden decision that she does have enough material after all for a second poetry volume she explains explicitly as a concern to give pleasure to her mother while she has the opportunity (*Letters* 1: 223). Implicitly, a 'green tinge' and her 'envy and humiliation' which were occasioned by the eighth edition of her rival Jean Ingelow's volume may also have precipitated a change of heart (*Letters* 1: 208–9). Her admiration and jealousy for Ingelow's success in the literary

marketplace punctuate discussions and arguments with Dante Gabriel Rossetti about the contents of what would become *The Prince's Progress and Other Poems* (1866).

16 Antony H. Harrison, *Christina Rossetti in Context* (Brighton: Harvester, 1988) p. 10. The letter, dated 1888, is in the Troxell Collection of the Princeton University Library. Although Harrison discusses conciseness as a positive poetic strategy – leading to, for example, 'tautness and directness of expression' and a 'deceptive simplicity of poetic surfaces', 'dramatic intensity', 'deliberate ambiguity', 'open-ended symbolic modes' – conciseness is also a conventionally feminine trait of women's poetry. Gosse, for example, declares: 'it is no new theory that women, in order to succeed on poetry, must be brief, personal, and concentrated' (p. 136), implicitly reducing the market value of such poetry and undermining the commercial audacity of women who write too much. 'The multiplication of books of verse [...] should, one would fancy, tend to make our poets more exiguous, more concise, and more grimly taut. [...] Women who write, in particular, [are] pursued by that commercial fervour which is so curious a feature of our new literary life, and which sits so inelegantly on a female figure' (p. 137). Other reviewers praised the self-limitation of Rossetti's poetry. The anonymous critic in *The Saturday Review*, for example, declares that she is so artistically restrained and so very narrowly bound, that she deserves to be a poet rather than a poetess. In other words, by apparently conforming so superlatively to the feminine style, Rossetti exceeds her gender (5 January 1895, pp. 5–6). See Chapter 4 for a tangential discussion of manuscript revisions and conciseness.

17 Concurrently, though, Rossetti acutely felt the ethical responsibilities of publishing, with its associated moral influence. See Marsh, *Christina Rossetti: a Literary Biography* pp. 479–80.

18 See Kathy Alexis Psomiades, *Beauty's Body: Femininity and Representation in British Aestheticism* (Stanford: Stanford University Press, 1997) for a discussion of the aesthetic's relation to the economic in these terms. Like Linley, Psomiades points to an intertwining in Rossetti of commodification and the poem as an anti-commodity. Psomiades argues that 'Goblin Market' resists commodification and aestheticism in the last 25 lines, which inscribe a second poem, Laura's, which cannot be read (p. 53). The ambivalent inclusion and withdrawal of Rossetti's direct relationship as an author to her poetry may be read in relation to the Anglo-Catholic doctrine of reserve. See David J. DeLaura, 'Newman and the Victorian Cult of Style', *Victorian Newsletter* 51 (Spring 1977) 6–10.

19 The notable exception is Isobel Armstrong's reading of 'Goblin Market' within her breathtaking and exhilarating discussion of Victorian women poets' ambivalent responses to expressive theory. See *Victorian Poetry: Poetry, Poetics and Politics* (London: Routledge, 1993) Ch. 12. See also Steven Connor, '"Speaking Likenesses": Language and Repetition in Christina Rossetti's *Goblin Market*', *Victorian Poetry* 22 (1984) 439–48; and Helena Michie, '"There Is No Friend Like a Sister": Sisterhood as Sexual Difference', *ELH* 56.2 (Summer 1989) 401–21.

20 Jerome J. McGann, *The Beauty of Inflections: Literary Investigations in Historical Method and Theory* (Oxford: Clarendon Press, 1985) p. 220.

21 Christina Rossetti herself was astutely aware of manipulating the market. See Campbell for a discussion of this in relation to *Goblin Market.* Her correspondence with publishers shows an active concern with marketing her volumes. *Sing-Song,* for example, was also targeted for the Christmas market in 1871. Rossetti initially approached Dante Gabriel's publisher F.S. Ellis for this volume, and she offered it to them as 'a marketable proposition' (Jan Marsh, *Christina Rossetti: Poems and Prose* (London: Dent, 1994) p. 440). Kegan Paul proposed an edition of *Goblin Market* for Christmas, which never transpired (*CR: FL* pp. 190–1).

22 Quoted in Lona Mosk Packer, *Christina Rossetti* (Berkeley: University of California Press, 1963) p. 158.

23 The Macmillan anecdote is paradigmatic for a number of contemporary commentators on 'Goblin Market'. For Kathleen Mayberry, for example, it reaffirms her impression that the poem has childlike qualities that suggest that the poem was written for children. See her *Christina Rossetti and the Poetry of Discovery* (Baton Rouge: Louisiana State University Press, 1989) p. 89. Lorraine Janzen Kooistra reminds us, however, that the poem was marketed for children only in the twentieth-century. See 'Modern Markets for *Goblin Market*', *Victorian Poetry* 32 (1994) 249–77 (pp. 254–5).

24 Antony H. Harrison, *Victorian Poets and the Politics of Culture: Discourse and Ideology* (Charlottesville: University Press of Virginia, 1998) p. 12.

25 James Ashcroft Noble, 'The Burden of Christina Rossetti', *Impressions and Memories* (London: Dent, 1895) pp. 58–9.

26 Lorraine Janzen Kooistra, 'The Representation of Violence/The Violence of Representation: Housman's Illustrations to Rossetti's *Goblin Market*', *English Studies in Canada* 19.3 (September 1993) 305–28 (p. 306).

27 This is repeated almost word for word in Mackenzie Bell, *Christina Rossetti: a Biographical and Critical Study* (London: Hurst and Blackett, 1989) p. 207.

28 This phrase is borrowed from Kooistra's work on the influence of illustrations upon the critical reception of 'Goblin Market'. I am greatly indebted to her insightful work.

29 Walter Benjamin, 'The Work of Art in the Age of Mechanical Reproduction', in *Illuminations*, trans. Harry Zohn (London: Fontana, 1992).

30 Marc Shell, *The Economy of Literature* (Baltimore: The Johns Hopkins University Press, 1978) p. 86. The invention of paper and electronic money disrupts the semiology of exchange. See Marc Shell, *Money, Language, and Thought: Literary and Philosophical Economies from the Medieval to the Modern Era* (Berkeley: University of California Press, 1982). For a different interpretation of the literary economy, see Lee Erickson, *The Economy of Literary Form: English Literature and the Industrialization of Publishing, 1800–1850* (Baltimore: The Johns Hopkins University Press, 1996) and William G. Rowland Jr., *Literature and the Marketplace: Romantic Writers and Their Audiences in Great Britain and the United States* (Lincoln: University of Nebraska Press, 1996).

31 The best discussion of gift economies is found in Judith Still, *Feminine Economies: Thinking Against the Market in the Enlightenment and the Late Twentieth Century* (Manchester: Manchester University Press, 1997). Still's analysis of the difficulty of thinking about gifts divorced from circulation and obligation provides a useful gloss on Lizzie's gift of fruit to her sister, a gift bound up

with the goblin market economy which assaulted Lizzie with the fruit in the first place. See Still pp. 13–16.

32 Leighton, *Victorian Women Poets: Writing Against the Heart* p. 137.

33 For more on 'purloining' as a story of signification within the Symbolic Order, see Lacan's rereading of Poe's 'The Purloined Letter', in 'Seminar on "The Purloined Letter"', trans. J. Mehlman, *Yale French Studies* 48: 38–72.

34 Elizabeth Helsinger turns around the usual reading of the poem in order to validate her emphasis upon market relations rather than the Christian moral discourse:

> Much of the criticism of 'Goblin Market' treats its story of buying and selling, like its rhymes and goblins, as the figurative dress for a narrative of spiritual temptation, fall, and redemption. But what happens if instead we read the figure as the subject: buying and selling, or more specifically, the relation of women to those markets of the nursery tales?

By thus reversing the traditionally accepted terms of the poem, Helsinger reads 'Goblin Market' as a critique of patriarchal economic consumption, the secular moral of the tale (p. 903). But even this ingenious metatextual approach to the poem, reading the figure of the marketplace as its subject, is predicated upon the elision of the poem as a spiritual tale. See also Campbell, Carpenter and Holt. More recent anti-commodity readings of 'Goblin Market' end up reifying the poem as a stable origin of meanings separate from the economic marketplace to which it is in opposition. See, Psomiades, *Beauty's Body*; Kooistra; Richard Menke in Mary Arseneau, Antony H. Harrison and Lorraine Janzen Kooistra (eds), *The Culture of Christina Rossetti: Female Poetics and Victorian Contexts* (Ohio, Athens: Ohio University Press, 1999) pp. 105–36.

35 Kooistra, 'Violence of Representation' p. 305.

36 See Mary Arseneau, 'Incarnation and Interpretation: Christina Rossetti, the Oxford Movement, and *Goblin Market*', *Victorian Poetry* 31 (1993) 79–93.

37 Marion Shalkhauser, 'The Feminine Christ', *Victorian Newsletter* 10 (1956) 19–20 (p. 20).

38 In fact, folklore may be seen as central to the conception of the poem. 'Goblin Market' was originally entitled 'A Peep at the Goblins', until D.G. Rossetti suggested the title change. In a copy of the volume, Christina Rossetti explains the original title, which was 'in imitation of my cousin Mrs. Bray's "A Peep at the Pixies"' (Crump 1: 234). Anna Eliza Bray's *A Peep at the Pixies; or, Legends of the West* (London: Grant and Griffith, 1854) was based upon legends of Dartmoor and North Cornwall. Jan Marsh demonstrates the debt of 'Goblin Market' to folklore in 'Christina Rossetti's Poetic Vocation: The Importance of *Goblin Market*', *Victorian Poetry* 32 (1994) 233–48.

39 Ellen Golub, 'Untying Goblin Apron Strings: a Psychoanalytic Reading of "Goblin Market"', *Literature and Psychology* 25 (1975) 158–65; Patricia R. Andrews, 'Latent Meaning in "Goblin Market"', *Journal of Evolutionary Psychology* 5.3–4 (1984) 171–4.

40 Lynda Palazzo, 'Christina Rossetti's "Goblin Market": the Sensual Imagination', *Unisa English Studies* 26.2 (September 1988) 15–20; Alan P. Barr, 'Sen-

suality Survived: Christina Rossetti's "Goblin Market"', *English Miscellany: a Symposium of History, Literature and the Arts* 28–9 (1979–80) 267–82.

41 Winston Weathers, 'Christina Rossetti: The Sisterhood of Self', *Victorian Poetry* 3 (1965) 81–9.

42 Dorothy Mermin, 'Heroic Sisterhood in *Goblin Market*', *Victorian Poetry* 21 (1983) 107–18 (p. 108).

43 'That "Goblin Market" is not just an observation of the lives of other women but an accurate account of the aesthetics Rossetti worked out for herself helps finally to explain why, although Keats can imagine asserting himself from beyond the grave, Rossetti, banqueting on bitterness, must bury herself alive in a coffin of renunciation.' See Sandra Gilbert and Susan Gubar, *The Madwoman in the Attic: the Woman Writer and the Nineteenth-Century Literary Imagination* (New Haven: Yale University Press, 1979) pp. 574–5.

44 '[Housman] does what all critics do when they re-present stories: he follows out the implications of his own mastering discourse, even though this means the suppression of the text's difference from his own critical representation' (Kooistra, 'The Representation of Violence' pp. 311–12).

45 Kooistra, 'The Violence of Representation' p. 305.

46 Kooistra, 'Modern Markets' p. 253. Note that Kooistra also sees the reception of the poem as a matter of the critic projecting his or her cultural perceptions onto the Victorian period, rather than the Victorian ideology continuing to haunt us.

47 Lorraine Janzen Kooistra, 'Visualising the Fantastic Subject: *Goblin Market* and the Gaze', in Arseneau *et al.*, *The Culture of Christina Rossetti*, pp. 137–69.

48 Deborah Ann Thompson makes a similar point in relation to the poem's concern with the metaphoricity of eating: 'Gilbert and Gubar and Rosenblum reflect the tendency of critics of "Goblin Market" to re-enact the dialectical mechanisms of the poem by taking the side of either Laura or Lizzie, either bulimic excess or anorexic renunciation.' See 'Anorexia as a Lived Trope: Christina Rossetti's "Goblin Market"', *Mosaic: a Journal for the Interdisciplinary Study of Literature* 24 (1991) 89–106 (p. 94).

49 J. Hillis Miller, 'The Critic as Host', in Harold Bloom *et al.* (eds), *Deconstruction and Criticism* (London: Routledge and Kegan Paul, 1979) p. 220.

50 Barbara Johnson, *A World of Difference* (Baltimore: The Johns Hopkins University Press, 1987) p. 35.

51 Shoshana Felman, 'Turning the Screw of Interpretation', *Yale French Studies* 55–6: 94–207 (p. 101, Felman's italics).

52 See, respectively, Menke, and D.M.R. Bentley, 'The Meretricious and the Meritorious in *Goblin Market*: a Conjecture and an Analysis', in David A. Kent (ed.), *The Achievement of Christina Rossetti* (Ithaca: Cornell University Press, 1987) pp. 57–81.

53 See Helsinger pp. 903–33; Angela Leighton, '"Because Men Made the Laws"'.

54 *DGR: FL* 1: 166. Amanda Anderson comments that the tendency to give voice to fallen women in nineteenth-century literature and culture gives the fallen an autonomy and agency they did not possess. See *Tainted Souls and Painted Faces: the Rhetoric of Fallenness in Victorian Culture* (Ithaca: Cornell University Press, 1993). See also Elsie B. Michie's comment that reclamations of the prostitute reify and essentialise working-class life, in her *Outside the*

Pale: Cultural Exclusion, Gender Difference, and the Victorian Woman Writer (Ithaca: Cornell University Press, 1993) p. 139.

55 This fact makes it impossible to determine to what extent each poem influences the other, but my point is precisely that literary influence is non-monolithic, slippery and circuitous.

56 *CW: DGR*, 1. 93, l. 367.

57 Amanda S. Anderson, 'D. G. Rossetti's "Jenny": Agency, Intersubjectivity, and the Prostitute', *Genders* 4 (Spring 1989) pp. 103–21 (p. 110). A version of this chapter is given in *Tainted Souls and Painted Faces.*

58 J.B. Bullen, *The Pre-Raphaelite Body: Fear and Desire in Painting, Poetry, and Criticism* (Oxford: Clarendon Press, 1998) p. 74.

59 Anderson, in contrast, stresses the intersubjective mode of the monologue as part of the problematic agency of the nineteenth-century prostitute: 'the form of the poem, which constitutes an insistence on a continuous intersubjective context, thus displays the way in which the presence or fact of another consciousness not only produces moves to stabilise or foreclose but also continually thwarts such moves' ('D.G. Rossetti's "Jenny"' p. 119). In contrast, I lay emphasis on the abjection in the speaker's acknowledgement of Jenny's threatening otherness which constitutes both a poetic muse (and therefore a point of identification) *and* a block to poetic creativity. In 'Jenny', the speaker constructs the prostitute as both a 'monstrous double' and the figure for difference *per se*. But the muse/'monstrous double' and the other are not a securely opposed. This oscillation between terms is recalled by Jenny's counterpart, Jeanie.

60 For more on the 'subject presumed to know', the condition of transference, see Jacques Lacan, *The Four Fundamental Concepts of Psychoanalysis* (London: Hogarth Press, 1977) p. 253.

61 Jerome McGann, in fact, repeatedly names the 'Jeanie' of 'Goblin Market' as 'Jenny' (*Beauty of Inflections* pp. 222–3).

62 D.G. Rossetti laments to Ford Madox Brown about the condition of the exhumed manuscript: 'they are in a disappointing state. The things I have already seem mostly perfect, and there is a great hole right through the leaves of Jenny, which was the thing I most wanted'. See W.M. Rossetti, *Rossetti Papers 1862 to 1870* (London: Sands, 1903) p. 472.

63 Interestingly, his major revisions to the first two volumes include substantial deletions of the poems – a type of textual diminishment associated with the trope consumption.

64 Catherine Maxwell, 'Tasting the "Fruit Forbidden": Gender, Intertextuality, and Christina Rossetti's *Goblin Market*', in Arseneau *et al.*, *The Culture of Christina Rossetti* pp. 75–102 (p. 97).

65 Julia Kristeva, *Powers of Horror: an Essay on Abjection* trans. Leon S. Roudiez (New York: Columbia University Press, 1982) p. 3.

66 Diane Chisholm in *Feminism and Psychoanalysis: a Critical Dictionary*, Elizabeth Wright (ed.) (Oxford: Blackwell, 1992) p. 439.

67 Elizabeth Grosz, 'The Body of Signification', in *Abjection, Melancholia and Love: the Work of Julia Kristeva*, John Fletcher and Andrew Benjamin (eds) (London: Routledge, 1990) pp. 80–103 (p. 92).

68 Significantly, in 'Jenny' there is no scene of seduction: a relationship based around the trope of consumption is described that isn't sexually or economic-

ally consummated. Although the speaker leaves golden coins on the sleeping Jenny's hair, as Anderson notes the poem reveals and resists her commodification (D.G. Rossetti's "Jenny"' p. 107).

69 I argue elsewhere that the epistolary relationship between Elizabeth Barrett and Robert Browning positions Browning as the literary abject mother who engenders the *Sonnets from the Portuguese*. See 'Mesmerism and Agency in the Courtship of Elizabeth Barrett and Robert Browning', *Victorian Literature and Culture* (1998) 303–19 (p. 315).

70 Angela Leighton is specifically discussing 'Goblin Market' here, but her comment equally applies to other poets mentioned in her argument: Elizabeth Barrett Browning, Augusta Webster, Amy Levy, and Charlotte Mew. See '"Because men made the laws": the Fallen Woman and the Woman Poet', in Angela Leighton (ed.), *Victorian Women Poets: a Critical Reader* (Oxford: Blackwell, 1996) p. 226. Diane D'Amico points out that Rossetti's Magdalen figures are not explicitly prostitutes but repentant sinners. D'Amico, like Leighton, emphasises the interweaving of fallen and unfallen, shame and redemption, in Rossetti's treatment of sexual fallenness. See Diane D'Amico, 'Eve, Mary, and Mary Magdalen: Christina Rossetti's Feminine Triptych' in David Kent (ed.), *The Achievement of Christina Rossetti* (Ithaca: Cornell University Press, 1987) pp. 186, 191. Martha Vicinus points out that the Anglican sisterhoods afford a coexistence of the 'pure' Sister and 'impure' penitent and, moreover, the very ground of these distinctions suggest their inter-relation: 'Reform was through punishment, through an almost exaggerated rejection of the prostitutes' past behaviour, as if the reformers were afraid of its roots in the unacknowledged fantasies of the pure women who cared for them. Unconsciously the prostitute and sister may have shared more than they ever knew.' See *Independent Women: Work and Community for Single Women 1850–1920* (London: Virago, 1985) pp. 78–9.

71 The best account of these acts and the campaign for their repeal is found in Judith Walkowitz, *Prostitution and Victorian Society: Women, Class and the State* (Cambridge: Cambridge University Press, 1980) part 2. Bullen associates prostitution with abjection (pp. 53–5), although he insists on designating the fallen woman in Victorian culture as unproblematically defiled in relation to the purity of her obverse, the virginal woman.

72 C.S. Wiesenthal, 'Anti-Bodies of Disease and Defense: Spirit-Body Relations in Nineteenth-Century Culture and Fiction', *Victorian Literature and Culture* 22 (1994) 187–220.

73 Catherine Gallagher, 'George Eliot and *Daniel Deronda*: The Prostitute and the Jewish Question', in Ruth Bernard Yeazell (ed.), *Sex, Politics, and Science in the Nineteenth-Century Novel* (Baltimore: Johns Hopkins University Press, 1986) p. 41.

74 Gallagher also points out that changes in copyright law made authorship and commerce even more intimately related ('George Eliot and *Daniel Deronda*' p. 43). Mary Poovey traces the strain in the relationship: 'because it was conceptualised simultaneously as superior to the capitalist economy and as hopelessly embroiled within it, literary work was the work par excellence that denied and exemplified the alienation written into capitalist work'. See *Uneven Developments: the Ideological Work of Gender in Mid-Victorian England* (Chicago: University of Chicago Press, 1988) p. 106. Rossetti's letters illustrate

her business sense, her awareness of copyright, and also her concern to have a relationship that is at once personal and professional with Alexander Macmillan. See Lona Mosk Packer (ed.), *The Rossetti–Macmillan Letters* (Berkeley: University of California Press, 1963).

75 For a discussion of the corruption of female sexuality and language, see also Jacqueline Rose, 'George Eliot and the Spectacle of the Woman', in *Sexuality in the Field of Vision* (London: Verso, [1986] 1996), especially p. 115.

76 *Writing Against the Heart* p. 137.

77 W. David Shaw, *Victorian and Mystery: Crises of Representation* (Ithaca: Cornell University Press, 1990) p. 252. Compare John Schad: 'Rossetti's writing is forever turning back on itself.' See *Victorians in Theory: From Derrida to Browning* (Manchester: Manchester University Press, 1999) p. 31.

78 For a further discussion of the sonnet's turn and abjection, see Alison Chapman 'Uncanny Epiphanies in the Nineteenth-Century Sonnet Tradition', in Wim Tigges (ed.), *Moments of Moment: Aspects of the Literary Epiphany* (Amsterdam: Rodopi, 1999) and 'Mesmerism and Agency in the Courtship of Elizabeth Barrett and Robert Browning', *Victorian Literature and Culture* (1998) 313–19.

79 *PW: CR* p. 485. Diane D'Amico, however, suggests that the sin committed by the speaker in this sonnet is not necessarily sexual, for the House of Charity may have been a home for the destitute and not Highgate Penitentiary. See 'Christina Rossetti's "From Sunset to Star Rise": a New Reading', *Victorian Poetry* 27 (1989) 95–100.

80 Christina Rossetti, *Time Flies: a Reading Diary* (London: SPCK, 1885) p. 38.

81 For more on the double-bind of identity, caught between the semiotic and Symbolic, see Kelly Oliver, *Reading Kristeva: Unraveling the Double-bind* (Bloomington: Indiana University Press, 1993). Margaret Linley's discussion of *Maude* argues that the fragile and moribund category of the poetess was reformulated by Christina Rossetti through the discourse of resurrection and redemption. See 'Dying to be a Poetess: the Conundrum of Christina Rossetti', in Arseneau *et al.*, *The Culture of Christina Rossetti* pp. 285–314 (p. 288).

82 Anna Smith, *Julia Kristeva: Readings of Exile and Estrangement* (Houndmills, Basingstoke: Macmillan, 1996) p. 71.

83 Tricia Lootens, *Lost Saints: Silence, Gender, and Victorian Literary Canonization* (Charlottesville: University Press of Virginia, 1996) p. 184,

84 Linda Williams, 'Happy Families? Feminist Reproduction and Matrilineal Thought', in *New Feminist Discourses: Essays on Theories and Texts*, Isobel Armstrong (ed.) (London and New York: Routledge, 1992) pp. 48–64 (p. 49).

85 See, for example, Maxwell, and compare Jerome McGann: 'one can and ought to say that "Goblin Market" is *about* poetry' (*The Beauty of Inflections* p. 229). Kristeva's most famous example of abjection is the infant's revulsion and desire for mother's milk, later translating into the adult's ambivalent relationship to nourishment. Laura's experience of the goblin fruit represents a similar ambivalence.

86 In a copy of *Goblin Market* (1883), Christina Rossetti acknowledges her brother's influence, including his substitution of the original title which was a reference to her aunt Eliza Bray's *A Peep at the Pixies*. It is not known who deleted the inscription on the manuscript of 'Goblin Market', 'To M.F.R', Rossetti's sister (Crump 1: 234).

Bibliography

Anderson, Amanda S. 'D.G. Rossetti's "Jenny": Agency, Intersubjectivity, and the Prostitute'. *Genders* 4 (Spring 1989) 103–21.

Anderson Amanda S. *Tainted Souls and Painted Faces: the Rhetoric of Fallenness in Victorian Culture*. Ithaca: Cornell University Press, 1993.

Andrews, Patricia R. 'Latent Meaning in "Goblin Market"'. *Journal of Evolutionary Psychology* 5.3–4 (1984) 171–4.

Armstrong, Isobel. (Ed.) *New Feminist Discourses: Critical Essays on Theories and Texts*. London: Routledge, 1992.

Armstrong, Isobel, and Joseph Bristow. (Eds) With Cath Sharrock. *Nineteenth-Century Women Poets*. Oxford: Clarendon Press, 1996.

Armstrong, Isobel. *Victorian Poetry: Poetry, Poetics and Politics*. London: Routledge, 1993.

Arseneau, Mary, Antony H. Harrison and Lorraine Janzen Kooistra. (Eds) *The Culture of Christina Rossetti: Female Poetics and Victorian Contexts*. Athens, Ohio: Ohio University Press, 1999.

Arseneau, Mary. 'Incarnation and Interpretation: Christina Rossetti, the Oxford Movement, and *Goblin Market*'. *Victorian Poetry* 31 (1993) 79–93.

Attridge, Derek. 'Roland Barthes's Obtuse, Sharp Meaning'. In Rabaté, *Writing the Image*.

Auerbach, Nina. *Woman and the Demon: the Life of a Victorian Myth*. Cambridge, MA: Harvard University Press, 1982.

Ballaster, Ros. 'New Hystericism: Aphra Behn's *Oroonoko*: The body, the text and the feminist critic', in Armstrong, *New Feminist Discourses*.

Barr, Alan P. 'Sensuality Survived: Christina Rossetti's "Goblin Market"'. *English Miscellany: a Symposium of History, Literature and the Arts* 28–9 (1979–80) 267–82.

Barthes, Roland. *Camera Lucida*. Trans. Richard Howard. London: Vintage, 1993.

Barthes, Roland. *Mythologies*. Selected and trans. by Annette Lavers. London: Paladin, 1973.

Battiscombe, Georgina. *Christina Rossetti: a Divided Life*. London: Constable, 1981.

Bell, Mackenzie. *Christina Rossetti: a Biographical and Critical Study*. Second edition. London: Hurst and Brackett, 1898.

Belsey, Andrew and Catherine Belsey. 'Christina Rossetti: Sister to the Brotherhood'. *Textual Practice* 2.1 (1988) 30–50.

Benjamin, Walter. 'The Work of Art in the Age of Mechanical Reproduction'. In *Illuminations*. Trans. Harry Zohn. London: Fontana, 1992.

Bennett, Andrew. *Keats, Narrative and Audience: the Posthumous Life of Writing*. Cambridge: Cambridge University Press, 1994.

Benson, Arthur. 'Christina Rossetti'. *The National Review* (26 February 1895) 753–63.

Bentley, D.M.R. 'The Meretricious and the Meritorious in *Goblin Market*: A Conjecture and an Analysis'. In Kent, *The Achievement of Christina Rossetti*.

Berg, Maggie. 'A Neglected Voice: Elizabeth Siddal'. *Dalhousie Review* 60 (1980–81) 151–6.

Berger, John. *Ways of Seeing*. London: BBC and Penguin, 1972.

Bernheimer, Charles, and Claire Kahane. (Eds) *In Dora's Case: Freud-Hysteria-Feminism*. London: Virago, 1985.

Blake, William. *The Complete Poetry and Prose of William Blake*. Ed. by David V. Erdman. New York: Doubleday, 1988.

Bloom, Harold, *et al*. (Eds) *Deconstruction and Criticism*. London: Routledge and Kegan Paul, 1979.

Boyle, Edward. *Biographical and Critical Essays, 1790–1890*. London: Oxford University Press, 1936; repr. Freeport, New York: Books for Libraries, 1968.

Bray, Anna Eliza. *A Peep at the Pixies; or, Legends of the West*. London: Grant and Griffith, 1854.

Bronfen, Elisabeth. *Over Her Dead Body: Death, Femininity, and the Aesthetic*. Manchester: Manchester University Press, 1992.

Browning, Elizabeth Barrett. *Aurora Leigh*. Ed. by Margaret Reynolds. Athens: Ohio University Press, 1992.

Bullen, J.B. *The Pre-Raphaelite Body: Fear and Desire in Painting, Poetry, and Criticism*. Oxford: Clarendon Press, 1998.

Bump, Jerome. 'Christina Rossetti and the Pre-Raphaelite Brotherhood'. In Kent, *The Achievement of Christina Rossetti*.

Burke, Carolyn, Naomi Schor and Margaret Whitford. (Eds) *Engaging With Irigaray: Feminist Philosophy and Modern European Thought*. New York: Columbia, 1994.

Burke, Séan. *The Death and Return of the Author: Criticism and Subjectivity in Barthes, Foucault and Derrida*. Second edition. Edinburgh: Edinburgh University Press, 1998 [1992].

Burkhauser, Jude. (Ed.) *Glasgow Girls: Women in Art and Design 1880–1920*. Edinburgh: Canongate, 1990; repr. 1994.

Butler, Judith. *Gender Trouble: Feminism and the Subversion of Identity*. New York: Routledge, 1990.

Campbell, Elizabeth. 'Of Mothers and Merchants: Female Economics in Christina Rossetti's "Goblin Market"'. *Victorian Studies* (Spring 1990) 393–410.

Carpenter, Mary Wilson. '"Eat me, drink me, love me": The Consumable Female Body in Christina Rossetti's *Goblin Market*'. *Victorian Poetry* 29 (1991) 415–34.

Carroll, David. (Ed.) *The States of 'Theory': History, Art, and Critical Discourses*. Stanford, California: Stanford University Press, 1990.

Caws, Mary Ann. *The Art of Interference: Stressed Readings in Verbal and Visual Texts*. Cambridge: Polity Press, 1989.

Chapman, Alison. 'Mesmerism and Agency in the Courtship of Elizabeth Barrett and Robert Browning'. *Victorian Literature and Culture* (1998) 303–19.

Chapman, Alison. 'Phantasies of Matriarchy in Non-Canonical Children's Literature by Women'. In Thompson, *Victorian Women Novelists*, pp. 60–79.

Chapman, Alison. 'Uncanny Epiphanies in the Nineteenth-Century Sonnet Tradition'. In Tigges, *Moments of Moment*, pp. 114–35.

Cherry, Deborah, and Griselda Pollock. 'Patriarchal Power and the Pre-Raphaelites'. *Art History* 7.4 (December 1984) 480–95.

Cherry, Deborah, and Griselda Pollock. 'Woman as Sign in Pre-Raphaelite Literature: A Study of the Representation of Elizabeth Siddall'. *Art History* 7.1 (March 1984) 206–27.

Christ, Carol T., and John O. Jordan. (Eds) *Victorian Literature and the Victorian Visual Imagination*. Berkeley: University of California Press, 1995

Cixous, Hélène, and Catherine Clément. *The Newly Born Woman*. Trans. Betsy Wing. London: I.B. Tauris, 1996.

Coleridge, S.T. *The Oxford Authors: S.T. Coleridge*. Ed. by H.J. Jackson. Oxford: Oxford University Press, 1985.

Conley, Susan. '"Poet's Right": Elegy and the Woman Poet'. In Leighton, *Victorian Women Poets: a Critical Reader.*

Connor, Steven. '"Speaking Likenesses": Language and Repetition in Christina Rossetti's *Goblin Market*'. *Victorian Poetry* 22 (1984) 439–48.

Cowie, Elizabeth. 'Woman as Sign'. *m/f* 1.1 (1978) 49–63.

Cox, Nick. 'Specters of Greenblatt'. Paper delivered to the Northern Renaissance Seminar Group at Sheffield Hallam University, 9 November 1996.

D'Amico, Diane. 'Christina Rossetti's "From Sunset to Star Rise": A New Reading'. *Victorian Poetry* 27 (1989) 95–100.

D'Amico, Diane. 'Eve, Mary, and Mary Magdalen: Christina Rossetti's Feminine Triptych'. In Kent, *The Achievement of Christina Rossetti.*

D'Amico, Diane. 'Saintly Singer or Tanagra Figurine? Christina Rossetti Through the Eyes of Katharine Tynan and Sara Teasdale'. *Victorian Poetry* 32 (1994) 387–407.

Davies, Lloyd. (Ed.) *Virginal Sexuality and Textuality in Victorian Literature*. New York: State University of New York Press, 1993.

Day, Paula. 'Nature and Gender in Victorian Women's Writing: Emily Brontë, Charlotte Brontë, Elizabeth Barrett Browning, Christina Rossetti'. PhD, The University of Lancaster, 1990.

DeLaura, David J. 'Newman and the Victorian Cult of Style'. *Victorian Newsletter* 51 (Spring 1977) 6–10.

Denman, Kamilla, and Sarah Smith. 'Christina Rossetti's Copy of C.B. Cayley's *Divine Comedy*'. *Victorian Poetry* 32 (1994) 315–38.

Derrida, Jacques. 'The Law of Genre'. In Derrick Attridge (ed.), *Acts of Literature*. New York: Routledge, 1992.

Derrida, Jacques. 'Signature Event Context'. Trans. Alan Bass. In Peggy Kamuf (ed.), *A Derrida Reader: Between the Blinds*. New York: Harvester Wheatsheaf, 1991.

Dickinson, Emily. *Emily Dickinson: the Complete Works*. Ed. by Thomas H. Johnson. London: Faber, 1970; repr. 1975.

Doan, Laura L. 'Narrative and Transformative Iconography in D.G. Rossetti's Earliest Paintings'. *Soundings* 17.4 (1988) 471–83.

Docherty, Thomas. *Alterities: Criticism, History, Representation*. Oxford: Clarendon Press, 1996.

Dolar, Mladen. 'The Object Voice'. In Salecl, *Gaze and Voice*.

Epstein, William H. '(Post) Modern Lives: Abducting the Biographical Subject'. In Epstein, *Contesting the Subject*.

Epstein, William H. (Ed.) *Contesting the Subject: Essays in the Postmodern Theory and Practice of Biography and Biographical Criticism*. West Lafayette: Purdue University Press, 1991.

Erickson, Lee. *The Economy of Literary Form: English Literature and the Industrialization of Publishing, 1800–1850*. Baltimore: The Johns Hopkins University Press, 1996.

Felman, Shoshana. 'Turning the Screw of Interpretation'. *Yale French Studies* 55–6: 94–207.

Fineman, Joel. 'The History of the Anecdote: Fiction and Fiction'. In Veeser, *The New Historicism*.

Fletcher, John, and Andrew Benjamin. (Eds) *Abjection, Melancholia and Love: the Work of Julia Kristeva*. London: Routledge, 1990

Ford, Colin. (Ed.) *The Cameron Collection: an Album of Photographs by Julia Margaret Cameron Presented to Sir John Herschel*. London: Van Nostrand Reinhold in association with The National Portrait Gallery, 1975.

Fraser, Hilary. *The Victorians and Renaissance Italy*. Oxford: Blackwell, 1992.

Freud, Sigmund. *Standard Edition of the Complete Psychological Works of Sigmund Freud*. Ed. and trans. by James Strachey. 24 vols. London: Hogarth Press, 1953.

Freud, Sigmund. 'Fetishism' (1927). *SE* 21: 157.

Freud, Sigmund. 'Three Essays on the Theory of Sexuality' (1905). *SE* 7: 123–245.

Freud, Sigmund. 'The Uncanny' (1919). *SE* 17: 217–56.

Fuss, Diana. *Essentially Speaking: Feminism, Nature and Difference*. London: Routledge, 1989.

Gallagher, Catherine. 'George Eliot and *Daniel Deronda*: The Prostitute and the Jewish Question.' In Yeazell, *Sex, Politics, and Science*.

Gallagher, Catherine. *Nobody's Story: the Vanishing Acts of Women Writers in the Marketplace, 1670–1820*. Oxford: Clarendon Press, 1994.

Gallop, Jane. *Thinking Through the Body*. New York: Columbia University Press, 1988.

Garber, Marjorie. *Shakespeare's Ghost Writers: Literature as Uncanny Causality*. New York: Methuen, 1987.

Garlick, Barbara. 'The Frozen Fountain: Christina Rossetti, the Virgin Model, and Youthful Pre-Raphaelitism'. In Davies, *Virginal Sexuality*.

Gilbert, Sandra M. 'From *Patria* to *Matria*: Elizabeth Barrett Browning's *Risorgimento*'. *PMLA* 99 (1984) 194–209.

Gilbert, Sandra, and Susan Gubar. *The Madwoman in the Attic: the Woman Writer and the Nineteenth-Century Literary Imagination*. New Haven: Yale University Press, 1979.

Gilmore, Leigh. *Autobiographics: a Feminist Theory of Women's Self-Representation*. Ithaca: Cornell University Press, 1994.

Goldberg, Gail Lynn. 'Dante Gabriel Rossetti's "Revising Hand": His Illustrations for Christina Rossetti's Poems'. *Victorian Poetry* 20 (1982) 145–59.

Golden, Catherine. 'Dante Gabriel Rossetti's Two-Sided Art'. *Victorian Poetry* 26 (1988) 395–402.

Golub, Ellen. 'Untying Goblin Apron Strings: A Psychoanalytic Reading of "Goblin Market"'. *Literature and Psychology* 25 (1975) 158–65.

Gombrich, E.H. *Art and Illusion: a Study in the Psychology of Pictorial Representation*. Oxford: Phaidon 1960; repr. 1986.

Gorham, Deborah. *The Victorian Girl and the Feminine Ideal*. London: Croom Hill, 1982.

Gosse, Edmund. *Critical Kit-Kats*. London: Heinemann, 1896.

Gray, Janet. 'The Sewing Contest: Christina Rossetti and the Other Women'. *a/b: Auto/Biographical Studies* 8.2 (1993) 233–57.

Greenblatt, Stephen. *Renaissance Self-Fashioning: From More to Shakespeare*. Chicago: University of Chicago Press, 1980.

Greenblatt, Stephen. *Shakespearean Negotiations: The Circulation of Social Energy in Renaissance England*. Oxford: Clarendon Press, 1988.

Green-Lewis, Jennifer. 'Lanscape, Loss, and Sexuality: Three Recent Books on Victorian Photography'. *Victorian Studies* 39.3 (Spring 1996) 391–404.

Grosz, Elizabeth. 'The Body of Signification'. In Fletcher, *Abjection, Melancholia and Love*.

Handy, Ellen. (Ed.) *Pictorial Effect/Naturalistic Vision: The Photographs and Theories of Henry Peach Robinson and Peter Henry Emerson*. Norfolk, VA: The Chrysler Museum, 1994.

Hanft, Lila. 'The Politics of Maternal Ambivalence in Christina Rossetti's *Sing-Song*'. *Victorian Literature and Culture* 19 (1991) 213–32.

Harrison, Antony H. *Christina Rossetti in Context*. Brighton: The Harvester Press, 1988.

Harrison, Antony H. *Victorian Poets and the Politics of Culture: Discourse and Ideology*. Charlottesville: University Press of Virginia, 1998.

Harrison, Antony H. *Victorian Poets and Romantic Poems*. Charlottesville: University Press of Virginia, 1990.

Harvey, Elizabeth. *Ventriloquized Voices: Feminist Theory and English Renaissance Texts*. London: Routledge, 1992.

Hassett, Constance W. 'Elizabeth Siddal's Poetry: A Problem and Some Suggestions'. *Victorian Poetry* 35 (1997): 443–70.

Hatton, Gwynneth. 'An Edition of the Unpublished Poems of Christina Rossetti, with a critical introduction and interpretative notes to all the posthumous poems'. St Hilda's College, Oxford, BLitt thesis, 1955.

Hawthorn, Jeremy. *Cunning Passages: New Historicism, Cultural Materialism and Marxism in the Contemporary Literary Debate*. London: Arnold, 1996.

Heath, Stephen. 'Difference'. *Screen* 19.3 (Autumn 1978) 53.

Heath, Stephen. 'Female Tones and Timbres'. *Women: a Cultural Review*. 7.3 (Winter 1996) 309–16.

Hedges, Elaine, and Shelley Fisher Fishkin. (Eds) *Listening to Silences: New Essays in Feminist Criticism*. Oxford: Oxford University Press, 1994.

Heffernan, James A.W. (Ed.) *Space, Time, Image, Sign*. New York: Peter Lang, 1987.

Helsinger, Elizabeth K. 'Consumer Power and the Utopia of Desire: Christina Rossetti's "Goblin Market"'. *ELH* 58.4 (Winter 1991) 903–33.

Hilton Timothy. *The Pre-Raphaelites*. London: Thames and Hudson, 1970; repr. 1987.

Holt, Terence. '"Men sell not such in any town": Exchange in *Goblin Market*'. *Victorian Poetry* 28 (1990) 51–67.

Homans, Margaret. *Bearing the Word: Language and Female Experience in Nineteenth-Century Women's Writing*. Chicago: The University of Chicago Press, 1986.

Hunt, William Holman. *Pre-Raphaelitism and the Pre-Raphaelite Brotherhood*. 2 vols. London: Macmillan, 1905.

Irigaray, Luce. 'And the one doesn't stir without the other'. *Signs* 7.1 (1981) 60–7.

Irigaray, Luce. *An Ethics of Sexual Difference*. Trans. Carolyn Burke and Gillian C. Gill. London: The Athlone Press, 1993.

Irigaray, Luce. *Speculum of the Other Woman*. Trans. Gillian C. Gill. Ithaca: Cornell University Press, 1985.

Johnson, Barbara. *A World of Difference*. Baltimore: The Johns Hopkins University Press, 1987.

Jones, Kathleen. *Learning Not to be First: the Life of Christina Rossetti*. Oxford: Oxford University Press, 1992.

Jurlaro, Felicita. *Christina Georgina Rossetti: the True Story*. London: Excalibur, 1991.

van de Kamp, Peter. 'Wrapped in a Dream: Katharine Tynan and Christina Rossetti'. In Liebregts, *Beauty and the Beast*.

Kaplan, Cora. *Sea Changes: Essays on Culture and Feminism*. London: Verso, 1986.

Kent, David A. (Ed.) *The Achievement of Christina Rossetti*. Ithaca and London: Cornell University Press, 1987.

Kent, David A. 'Christina Rossetti's Dying'. *Journal of Pre-Raphaelite Studies* 5 (Fall 1996) 83–97.

Knight, Diana. 'Roland Barthes, or The Woman Without a Shadow'. In Rabaté, *Writing the Image*.

Knoepflmacher, U.C. *Ventures into Childhood: Victorians, Fairy Tales, and Femininity*. Chicago: University of Chicago Press, 1998.

Kohl, James A. 'A Medical Comment on Christina Rossetti'. *Notes and Queries* 213 (Nov. 1968) 423–4.

Kooistra, Lorraine Janzen, 'Modern Markets for *Goblin Market*'. *Victorian Poetry* 32 (1994) 249–77.

Kooistra, Lorraine Janzen. 'The Representation of Violence/The Violence of Representation: Housman's Illustrations to Rossetti's *Goblin Market*.' *English Studies in Canada* 19.3 (September 1993) 305–28.

Kooistra, Lorraine Janzen. 'Visualising the Fantastic Subject: *Goblin Market* and the Gaze'. In Arseneau *et al.*, *The Culture of Christina Rossetti*.

Kristeva, Julia. *The Kristeva Reader*. Ed. Toril Moi. Oxford: Basil Blackwell, 1986.

Kristeva, Julia. *Powers of Horror: an Essay on Abjection*. Trans. Leon S. Roudiez. New York: Columbia University Press, 1982.

Kristeva, Julia. *Revolution in Poetic Language*. Trans. Margaret Waller. New York: Columbia University Press, 1984.

Kristeva, Julia. *Strangers to Ourselves*. Trans. Leon Roudiez. New York: Columbia University Press, 1991.

Kristeva, Julia. 'Stabat Mater'. In Moi, *The Kristeva Reader*.

Lacan, Jacques. *The Four Fundamental Concepts of Psycho-Analysis*. Trans. Alan Sheridan, ed. Jacques-Alain Miller. Harmondsworth: Penguin, 1979.

Lacan, Jacques. 'Seminar on "The Purloined Letter"'. Trans. J. Mehlman. *Yale French Studies* 48: 38–72.

Leighton, Angela '"Because men made the laws": The Fallen Woman and the Woman Poet"'. In Leighton, *Victorian Women Poets: a Critical Reader*.

Leighton, Angela, and Margaret Reynolds. (Eds) *Victorian Women Poets: an Anthology*. Oxford: Blackwell, 1995.

Leighton, Angela. (Ed.) *Victorian Women Poets: a Critical Reader*. Oxford: Blackwell, 1996.

Leighton, Angela. *Victorian Women Poets: Writing Against the Heart*. Hemel Hempstead: Harvester Wheatsheaf, 1992.

Leighton, Angela. '"When I am dead, my dearest": The Secret of Christina Rossetti'. *Modern Philology* 87 (1989) 373–88.

Lentricchia, Frank. 'Foucault's Legacy: A New Historicism?' In Veeser, *The New Historicism*.

Lewis, Roger C., and Mark Samuels Lasner (Eds), *Poems and Drawings of Elizabeth Siddal*. Wolfville, NS: Wombat Press, 1978.

Liebregts, Peter, and Wim Tigges. (Eds) *Beauty and the Beast: Christina Rossetti, Walter Pater, R.L. Stevenson and their Contemporaries*. Amsterdam: Rodopi, 1996.

Linley, Margaret. 'Dying to Be A Poetess: The Conundrum of Christina Rossetti'. In Arseneau *et al.*, *The Culture of Christina Rossetti.*

Lootens, Tricia. *Lost Saints: Silence, Gender, and Victorian Literary Canonization.* Charlottesville: University Press of Virginia, 1996.

Marsh, Jan. *Christina Rossetti: a Literary Biography.* London: Jonathan Cape, 1994.

Marsh, Jan. 'Christina Rossetti's Poetic Vocation: The Importance of *Goblin Market*'. *Victorian Poetry* 32 (1994) 233–48.

Marsh, Jan. *Elizabeth Siddal 1829–1862: Pre-Raphaelite Artist.* Sheffield: The Ruskin Gallery, 1991.

Marsh, Jan. *The Legend of Elizabeth Siddal.* London: Quartet, 1989.

Marsh, Jan. *Pre-Raphaelite Women: Images of Femininity in Pre-Raphaelite Art.* London: Weidenfield and Nicolson, 1987.

Marshall, Linda. '"Transfigured to His Likeness": Sensible Transcendentalism in Christina Rossetti's "Goblin Market"'. *University of Toronto Quarterly* 63.3 (Spring 1994) 429–50.

Marshall, Linda. 'What the Dead Are Doing Underground: Hades and Heaven in the Writings of Christina Rossetti'. *Victorian Newsletter* (Fall 1987) 55–60.

Martínez, Tomás Eloy. *Santa Evita.* Trans. Helen Lane. London: Anchor, 1997.

Matus, Jill L. *Unstable Bodies: Victorian Representations of Sexuality and Maternity.* Manchester: Manchester University Press, 1995.

Maxwell, Catherine. 'Tasting the "Fruit Forbidden": Gender, Intertextuality, and Christina Rossetti's *Goblin Market*'. In Arseneau, *The Culture of Christina Rossetti.*

Mavor, Carol. *Pleasures Taken: Performances of Sexuality and Loss in Victorian Photographs.* Durham: Duke University Press, 1995.

Mayberry, Kathleen. *Christina Rossetti and the Poetry of Discovery.* Baton Rouge: Louisiana State University Press, 1989.

McGann, Jerome J. *The Beauty of Inflections: Literary Investigations in Historical Method and Theory.* Oxford: Clarendon Press, 1985.

McGann, Jerome J. *A Critique of Modern Textual Criticism.* Chicago: Chicago University Press, 1983.

McGann, Jerome. (Ed.) *Historical Studies and Literary Criticism.* Madison, Wisconsin: University of Wisconsin Press, 1985.

Menke Richard. 'The Political Economy of Fruit: *Goblin Market*'. In Arseneau *et al.*, *The Culture of Christina Rossetti.*

Mermin, Dorothy. 'Heroic Sisterhood in *Goblin Market*'. *Victorian Poetry* 21 (1983) 107–18.

Meynell, Alice. 'Christina Rossetti'. *New Review* (12 February 1895) 201–6.

Michie, Elsie B. *Outside the Pale: Cultural Exclusion, Gender Difference, and the Victorian Woman Writer.* Ithaca: Cornell University Press, 1993.

Michie, Helena. '"There Is No Friend Like a Sister": Sisterhood as Sexual Difference'. *ELH* 56.2 (Summer 1989) 401–21.

Miller, J. Hillis. 'The Critic as Host'. In Bloom *et al.*, *Deconstruction and Criticism.*

Miller, J. Hillis. 'The Mirror's Secret: Dante Gabriel Rossetti's Double Work of Art'. *Victorian Poetry* 29 (1991) 333–65.

Moi, Toril. *Sexual/Textual Politics: Feminist Literary Theory.* London: Routledge, 1988.

More, Paul Elmer. 'Christina Rossetti'. *Atlantic Monthly* 94 (December 1904) 815–21.

Nancy, Jean-Luc. 'Finite History'. In Carroll, *The States of 'Theory.'*

Nead, Lynda. *Myths of Sexuality: Representations of Women in Victorian Britain*. Oxford: Blackwell, 1988.

Nichols, Jr., Stephen J. 'Solomon's Wife: Deceit, Desire, and the Genealogy of Romance'. In Heffernan, *Space, Time, Image, Sign*.

Noble, James Ashcroft. *Impressions and Memories*. London: Dent, 1895.

Nolta, David D. 'Whispering Likenesses: Images of Christina Rossetti, 1847–1853'. *The Journal of Pre-Raphaelite and Aesthetic Studies* 2.1 (Spring 1989) 49–55.

O'Brien, Sharon. 'Feminist Theory and Literary Biography'. In Epstein, *Contesting the Subject*.

Oliver, Kelly. *Reading Kristeva: Unraveling the Double-bind*. Bloomington: Indiana University Press, 1993.

Olsen, Tilly. *Silences*. London: Virago, 1980.

Onslow, Barbara. 'Deceiving Images, Revealing Images: The Portrait in Victorian Women's Writing'. *Victorian Poetry* 33 (1995) 450–75.

Ovenden, Graham. *Pre-Raphaelite Photography*. London: Academy Press, 1972.

Packer, Lona Mosk. *Christina Rossetti*. Berkeley: University of California Press, 1963.

Packer, Lona Mosk. (Ed.) *The Rossetti–Macmillan Letters*. Berkeley: University of California Press, 1963.

Palazzo, Lynda. 'Christina Rossetti's "Goblin Market": The Sensual Imagination'. *Unisa English Studies* 26.2 (September 1988) 15–20.

Pearce, Lynne. *Woman/Image/Text: Readings in Pre-Raphaelite Art and Literature*. Hemel Hempstead: Harvester Wheatsheaf, 1991.

Pechter Edward. 'The New Historicism and Its Discontents: Politicising Renaissance Drama'. *PMLA* 102.3 (May 1987): 292–303.

Penkill Foundation. *The Order of the Owl* 3.1 (1987).

Peterson, Linda H. '"Restoring the Book": The Typological Hermeneutics of Christina Rossetti and the Pre-Raphaelite Brotherhood'. *Victorian Poetry* 32 (1994) 209–32.

Pollock, Griselda. *Vision and Difference: Femininity, Feminism and Histories of Art*. London: Routledge, 1988.

Poovey, Mary. *Uneven Developments: the Ideological Work of Gender in Mid-Victorian England*. Chicago: The University of Chicago Press, 1988.

Porter, Carolyn. 'Are We Being Historical Yet?' In Carroll, *The States of 'Theory.'*

Prins, Yopi. *Victorian Sappho*. Princeton, New Jersey: Princeton University Press, 1999.

Proctor, Ellen A. *A Brief Memoir of Christina G. Rossetti*. London: SPCK, 1895; repr. 1978.

Psomiades, Kathy Alexis. *Beauty's Body: Femininity and Representation in British Aestheticism*. Stanford, California: Stanford University Press, 1997.

Psomiades, Kathy Alexis. '"Material Witness": Feminism and Nineteenth-Century Studies'. *Nineteenth-Century Contexts* 31.1 (1989) 13–18.

Rabaté, Jean-Michel. (Ed.) *Writing the Image After Roland Barthes*. Philadelphia: University of Pennsylvania Press, 1997.

Richards, Thomas. *The Commodity Culture of Victorian England: Advertising and Spectacle, 1851–1914*. Stanford, CA: Stanford University Press, 1990.

Riede, David G. 'Erasing the Art-Catholic: Rossetti's *Poems, 1870*'. *Journal of Pre-Raphaelite Studies* 1.2 (1987) 50–70.

Rose, Jacqueline. 'George Eliot and the Spectacle of the Woman'. In *Sexuality in the Field of Vision*. London: Verso, [1986] 1996.

Rose, Jacqueline. *The Haunting of Sylvia Plath*. London: Virago, 1991.

Rosenblum, Dolores. *Christina Rossetti: the Poetry of Endurance*. Carbondale: Southern Illinois University Press, 1986.

Ross, Valerie. 'Too Close to Home: Repressing Biography, Instituting Authority.' In Epstein, *Contesting the Subject*.

Rossetti, Christina. *Christina Rossetti: Poems and Prose*. Ed. Jan Marsh. London: Everyman, 1994.

Rossetti, Christina. *The Complete Poems of Christina Rossetti*. Ed. R.W. Crump. 3 vols. Baton Rouge: Louisiana University Press, 1979–1990.

Rossetti, Christina. *The Complete Poetical Works of Christina Georgina Rossetti*. Ed. William Michael Rossetti. London: Macmillan, 1904; repr. 1906.

Rossetti, Christina. 'Dante. The Poet Illustrated out of the Poem'. *The Century* (February 1884) 566–73.

Rossetti, Christina. *The Face of the Deep: a Devotional Commentary on the Apocalypse*. London: SPCK, 1892.

Rossetti, Christina. *The Family Letters of Christina Georgina Rossetti*. Ed. William Michael Rossetti. London: Brown, Langham, 1908.

Rossetti, Christina. *Goblin Market and Other Poems*. London: Macmillan, 1862.

Rossetti, Christina. *Goblin Market, The Prince's Progress and Other Poems*. London: Macmillan, 1875.

Rossetti, Christina. *The Letters of Christina Rossetti*. Ed. Antony H. Harrison. Charlottesville: The University Press of Virginia, 1997–.

Rossetti, Christina. *New Poems*. Ed. W.M. Rossetti. London: Macmillan, 1896.

Rossetti, Christina. *The Prince's Progress and Other Poems*. London: Macmillan, 1866.

Rossetti, Christina. *Selected Prose of Christina Rossetti*. Eds David A. Kent and P.G. Stanwood. New York: St. Martin's Press, 1998.

Rossetti, Christina. *Time Flies: a Reading Diary*. London: SPCK, 1885.

Rossetti, Dante Gabriel. *The Collected Works of Dante Gabriel Rossetti*. Ed. William Michael Rossetti. 2 vols. London: Ellis and Scrutton, 1886.

Rossetti, Dante Gabriel. *Dante Gabriel Rossetti: His Family Letters*. Ed. William Michael Rossetti. 2 vols. London: Ellis and Elvey, 1895.

Rossetti, Dante Gabriel. *The Letters of Dante Gabriel Rossetti*. Eds Oswald Doughty and John Robert Wahl. 5 vols. Oxford: Clarendon Press, 1967.

Rossetti, Dante Gabriel. *The Paintings and Drawings of Dante Gabriel Rossetti (1828–1882): a Catalogue Raisonné*. Ed. Virginia Surtees. 2 vols. Oxford: Clarendon Press, 1971.

Rossetti, William Michael. (Ed.) *Pre-Raphaelite Diaries and Letters*. London: Hurst and Blackett, 1900.

Rossetti, William Michael. *The P.R.B. Journal: William Michael Rossetti's Diary of the Pre-Raphaelite Brotherhood 1849–1853: Together With Other Pre-Raphaelite Documents*. Ed. William E. Fredeman. Oxford: Clarendon Press, 1975.

Rossetti, William Michael. (Ed.) *Rossetti Papers 1862 to 1870*. London: Sands, 1903.

Rossetti, William Michael. (Ed.) *Ruskin: Rossetti: Pre-Raphaelitism: Papers 1854 to 1862*. London: George Allen, 1899.

Rowland Jr., William G. *Literature and the Marketplace: Romantic Writers and Their Audiences in Great Britain and the United States*. Lincoln: University of Nebraska Press, 1996.

Ruskin, John. 'The Three Colours of pre-Raphaelitism' (1878). *The Works of John Ruskin* vol. 34 (1908).

Ruskin, John. *The Works of John Ruskin*. Eds E.T. Cook and Alexander Wedderburn. 39 vols. London: George Allen, 1903–1912.

Russ, Joanna. *How to Suppress Women's Writing*. Austin: University of Texas Press, 1983.

Ryan, Kiernan. *New Historicism and Cultural Materialism: a Reader*. London: Arnold, 1996.

Salecl, Renata, and Slavoj Žižek. (Eds) *Gaze and Voice as Love Objects*. Durham: Duke University Press, 1996.

Saville, Julia. '"The Lady of Shalott": a Lacanian Romance'. *Word & Image* 8.1 (1992) 71–87.

Schad, John. (Ed.) *Dickens Refigured: Bodies, Desires, and Other Histories*. Manchester: Manchester University Press, 1998.

Schad, John. *Victorians in Theory: From Derrida to Browning*. Manchester: Manchester University Press, 1999.

Schor, Esther. *Bearing the Dead: the British Culture of Mourning from the Enlightenment to Victoria*. Princeton, New Jersey: Princeton University Press, 1994.

Schor, Naomi. 'This Essentialism Which Is Not One: Coming to Grips with Irigaray'. In Burke *et al.*, *Engaging With Irigaray*.

Sellers, Susan. *Hélène Cixous*. London: Routledge, 1996.

Shalkhauser, Marion. 'The Feminine Christ'. *Victorian Newsletter* 10 (1956) 19–20.

Sharp, William. 'Some Reminiscences of Christina Rossetti'. *Atlantic Monthly* LXXV (June 1895) 736–49.

Shaw, W. David. *Victorians and Mystery: Crises of Representation*. Ithaca: Cornell University Press, 1990.

Shefer, Elaine. 'The Woman at the Window in Victorian Art and Christina Rossetti as the Subject of Millais's *Mariana*'. *Journal of Pre-Raphaelite and Aesthetic Studies* 4.1 (1983) 14–25.

Shell, Marc. *The Economy of Literature*. Baltimore: The Johns Hopkins University Press, 1978.

Shell, Marc. *Money, Language, and Thought: Literary and Philosophical Economies from the Medieval to the Modern Era*. Berkeley: University of California Press, 1982.

Shires, Linda M. 'The Author as Spectacle and Commodity: Elizabeth Barrett Browning and Thomas Hardy'. In Christ, *Victorian Literature and the Victorian Visual Imagination*.

Shires, Linda M. 'Literary Careers, Death, and the Body Politics of David Copperfield'. In Schad, *Dickens Refigured*.

Showalter, Elaine. *The Female Malady: Women, Madness, and English Culture, 1830–1980*. London: Virago, 1987.

Smith, Anna. *Julia Kristeva: Readings of Exile and Estrangement*. Basingstoke: Macmillan, 1996.

Smith, Lindsay. 'The Politics of Focus: Feminism and Photographic Theory'. In Armstrong, *New Feminist Discourses*.

Smith, Lindsay. *The Politics of Focus: Women, Children and Nineteenth-Century Photography*. Manchester: Manchester University Press, 1998.

Smulders, Sharon. 'Christina Rossetti: Response and Responsibility'. DPhil, University of Sussex, 1987.

Smulders, Sharon M. 'Women's Enfranchisement in Christina Rossetti's Poetry'. *Texas Studies in Literature and Language* 34.4 (Winter 1992) 568–88.

Stephenson, Glennis. 'Letitia Elizabeth Landon and the Victorian Improvisatrice: the Construction of L.E.L.' *Victorian Poetry* 30 (1992) 1–17.

Still, Judith. *Feminine Economies: Thinking Against the Market in the Enlightenment and the Late Twentieth Century*. Manchester: Manchester University Press, 1997.

Stone, Marjorie. 'Sisters in Art: Christina Rossetti and Elizabeth Barrett Browning'. *Victorian Poetry* 32 (1994) 339–64.

Stuart, Dorothy Margaret. *Christina Rossetti*. London: Macmillan, 1930.

Tate Gallery Catalogue. *The Pre-Raphaelites*. London: Tate Gallery and Alan Lane, 1984.

Taylor, John. *A Dream of England: Landscape, Photography and the Tourist's Imagination*. Manchester: Manchester University Press, 1994.

Thomas, Brook. *New Historicism and Other Old-Fashioned Topics*. Princeton, New Jersey: Princeton University Press, 1991.

Thomas, Frances. *Christina Rossetti: a Biography*. Self Publishing Association, 1992; repr. London: Virago, 1994.

Thompson, Deborah Ann. 'Anorexia as a Lived Trope: Christina Rossetti's "Goblin Market"'. *Mosaic: a Journal for the Interdisciplinary Study of Literature* 24 (1991) 89–106.

Thompson, Nicola Diane. (Ed.) *Victorian Women Novelists and the Woman Question*. Cambridge: Cambridge University Press, 1999.

Tigges, Wim. (Ed.) *Moments of Moment: Aspects of the Literary Epiphany*. Amsterdam: Rodopi, 1999.

Troxell, Janet Camp. (Ed.) *The Three Rossettis: Unpublished Papers to and from Dante Gabriel, Christina and William*. Cambridge, Mass.: Harvard University Press, 1939.

Tynan Hinkson, Katharine. 'Santa Christina'. *The Bookman* (London) LXLI (Jan. 1912) 185–90.

Vaughan, Henry. *Henry Vaughan: the Complete Poems*. Ed. by Alan Rudrum. Harmondsworth: Penguin, 1976; repr. 1983.

Vicinus, Martha. *Independent Women: Work and Community for Single Women 1850–1920*. London: Virago, 1985.

Veeser, H. Aram. (Ed.) *The New Historicism* . New York: Routledge, 1989.

Walkowitz, Judith. *Prostitution and Victorian Society: Women, Class and the State*. Cambridge: Cambridge University Press, 1980.

Warner, Marina. *Alone of All Her Sex: the Myth and the Cult of the Virgin Mary*. London: Weidenfield, 1976.

Warner, Marina. *Monuments and Maidens: the Allegory of the Female Form*. London: Picador, 1987.

Weathers, Winston. 'Christina Rossetti: The Sisterhood of Self'. *Victorian Poetry* 3 (1965) 81–9.

Weissberg, Liliane. 'Circulating Images: Notes on the Photographic Exchange'. In Rabaté, *Writing the Image*.

Whitman, Walt. *Poems by Walt Whitman*. Ed. W.M. Rossetti. London: Chatto and Windus, 1895.

Wiesenthal, C.S. 'Anti-Bodies of Disease and Defense: Spirit-Body relations in Nineteenth-Century Culture and Fiction'. *Victorian Literature and Culture* 22 (1994) 187–220.

Williams, Linda. 'Happy Families? Feminist Reproduction and Matrilineal Thought'. In Armstrong, *New Feminist Discourses*.

Woolf, Virginia. *The Common Reader: Second Series*. London: The Hogarth Press, 1932.

Wordsworth, William. *Poems*. Ed. John O. Hayden. 2 vols. Harmondsworth: Penguin, 1977.

Wright, Elizabeth. (Ed.) *Feminism and Psychoanalysis. a Critical Dictionary*. Oxford: Blackwell, 1992.

Yeazell, Ruth Bernard. (Ed.) *Sex, Politics, and Science in the Nineteenth-Century Novel*. Baltimore: Johns Hopkins University Press, 1986.

Žižek, Slavoj. '"I Hear You with My Eyes"; or, The Invisible Master'. In Salecl, *Gaze and Voice*.

Index